WHOSE NORTH?

The Northwest Territories is a distinct region constituting one-third of Canada's land mass. More than just a vast storehouse for resources, the territories are home to a diverse people, the majority of them Natives, who possess deep-seated cultures that have endured despite the harsh climate and pervasive influence of the dominant culture to the south.

Residents of the Northwest Territories today face a number of difficult political issues: land claims, division of the territories, constitutional development, self-government, resources, and the establishment of their place within the Canadian federation. *Whose North?* provides the context for a better understanding of these issues, and it traces the evolution of an innovative, increasingly indigenous, governmental process.

Mark Dickerson points out that within the NWT there is no unanimity on the nature of the system of government. He addresses the political tension between those advocating the continuation of a centralized government and those preferring a more decentralized form, particularly self-government, whch many northerners view as the only way of preserving their culture. Dickerson's depiction of the development of the territorial government and his discussion of the tension surrounding the choice of government will provide Canadians with an opportunity to begin to understand just what is at stake in this critical process.

MARK O. DICKERSON is a professor in the Department of Political Science at the University of Calgary and a research associate of the Arctic Institute of North America. He is the author of a number of books on Canadian politics and on political change and development.

D1069364

The Arctic Institute of North America is a multidisciplinary research institute of the University of Calgary. Its mandate is to advance the study of the circumpolar North through the natural and social sciences, the arts and humanities; and to acquire, preserve, and disseminate information on physical and social conditions in the North.

Mark O. Dickerson

Whose North?
Political Change, Political Development, and Self-Government in the Northwest Territories

A JOINT PUBLICATION OF UBC PRESS AND
THE ARCTIC INSTITUTE OF NORTH AMERICA

UBCPress

VANCOUVER

ISBN 0-7748-0414-9 (hardcover)
ISBN 0-7748-0418-1 (paperback)

Canadian Cataloguing in Publication Data

Dickerson, M.O., 1934-
Whose North?

Includes bibliographical references and index.
ISBN 0-7748-0414-9 (bound). – ISBN
0-7748-0418-1 (pbk.)

1. Northwest Territories – Politics and government–
1951- *2. Native peoples – Northwest
Territories – Government relations.* 3. Native
peoples – Northwest Territories – Legal status,
laws, etc.* I. Arctic Institute
of North America. II. Title

FC4173.2.D53 1992   971.9'03   C92-091252-4
F1060.92.D53 1992

Publication of this book was made possible
by ongoing support from The Canada Council,
the Province of British Columbia Cultural Services
Branch, and the Department of Communications
of the Government of Canada.

UBC Press
University of British Columbia
6344 Memorial Rd
Vancouver, BC V6T 1Z2
(604) 822-3259
Fax: (604) 822-6083

Printed in Canada

For Barbara

18.7.92

Dear Dad;

We were going to get you a
"Get Well" card, but decided
this would keep you a little more
entertained while you're laid up.

Love Theresa
&
Dave

Contents

Maps, Figures, and Tables

TABLES

Preface

This book is about the development of an innovative governmental process in the Northwest Territories (NWT). It is not concerned primarily with Native cultures, land claims, division of the territory, education systems, non-renewable resource revenues, or economic development. Rather, it is about the evolution of a system of government that must deal with each of these issues – and deal with them in a way that reflects the interests of the people of the territories.

The type of governmental process that emerges in the NWT is critical. It is critical because of the Aboriginal peoples. While the territories comprise a third of the land mass of Canada, it is home to only about 54,000 people, approximately the same number that can watch a Blue Jays game in the SkyDome. What the people do not have in numbers they make up in diversity. The Dene, Métis, Inuit, and Inuvialuit constitute slightly more than 58 per cent of the population – a majority of the voting population. Descendants of the Indians and the Inuit have survived centuries in one of the harshest climates in the world. The environmental challenge has nurtured deep-seated cultures which today are threatened by industrialized Canadian culture. The threat poses a tough dilemma for Native people of the region. As the dominant southern culture becomes more pervasive in northern communities, it becomes more difficult for Native people to preserve anything of their traditional culture. Today these people are facing a cultural challenge that is every bit as difficult, perhaps even more difficult, than the environmental challenges they have faced for hundreds of years. The nature of the governmental process that evolves is crucial, because the government of the Northwest Territories (GNWT) is now, and will be, responsible for public decisions influencing the preservation of Native cultural values in the region.

The Northwest Territories is far more than a vast storehouse of resources for the South. Between the Mackenzie Valley and Baffin Island, between the provincial borders and the Arctic Archipelago, lies one of the most intriguing regions of the world. Baffin Island's Auyuittuq National Park rivals the scenery in any of our national parks. The wildlife, rivers, and lakes of the Barren Lands in the Central Arctic form a remarkable ecosystem. The Mackenzie River, one of the world's great water systems, is surrounded by a vast subarctic forest. One can grow almost any crop in the upper Mackenzie and south Great Slave Lake region and see beluga whales beyond the river delta on the coast of the Arctic Ocean. It would seem that no one could survive the severe climate of the Arctic Archipelago. Yet people at Grise Fiord (Canada's northernmost permanent settlement) have done so since the early 1950s, when the Canadian government was establishing posts in the region to preserve Canadian sovereignty. Most Canadians think little about the region until someone runs a ship through the Archipelago, testing the right of 'innocent passage.'

The Native people who occupy these vast lands should be able to choose whether they wish to live a traditional lifestyle, a modern lifestyle, or a mix of the two. The right to choose should be theirs, but they need some form of self-government in order to exercise that choice. Constitutional development in the NWT has taken on a dynamic of its own. Much of the politics of the region now involves tension over a choice of two models of political development. The first model is rooted in history, going back to the Northwest Territories Act (1875). The prevailing assumption by most southerners involved in the process was that territorial government would follow the pattern of development experienced in Alberta and Saskatchewan prior to 1905. Structurally this was the case. Between 1920 and 1991, the commissioner-council system was transformed into a cabinet system of government.

This transformation has embodied a number of strategic developments. In the mid-1950s, the federal government's interventionist policies were designed to develop non-renewable resources in the region and to prepare Native people for assimilation into the dominant Canadian culture. For almost two decades there was little challenge to federal authority and control in the region.

In 1967, the seat of government for the NWT was moved to Yellowknife, and the rapid growth of the GNWT as a de facto power enabled it to challenge federal dominance in the region. In fact, the territorial government has evolved as a province-like system of government. With two important exceptions, its powers are almost identical to those of the provinces.

The GNWT, however, has taken on an indigenous character of its own. Its leaders, and many northerners, have rejected partisan politics. At present, the legislative process is based on 'consensus.' The process has created its own dynamic between the government leader, ministers of the Crown, and 'ordinary' members of the legislature.

Government in the territories evolved as a highly centralized system. As powers were wrested from Ottawa, they became concentrated in Yellowknife. For many Native people living in the sixty-odd small, isolated communities across the region, the Yellowknife administration is very similar to that of the federal government – centralized and paternalistic. Many Native people believe that local and regional governments should have powers governing education, economic development, health care, housing, policing, and social services. In short, they desire a more decentralized territorial government. The Native people are now a force in the region. Since the early 1970s, the Dene, Métis, Inuvialuit, and Inuit have organized political groups which are challenging the dominant position of the GNWT.

In the NWT, tensions over the centralization-decentralization issue are high – on occasion pitting Natives against Natives or Natives against non-Natives. Often it is difficult to discern the battle lines because they become obscured when involved with other important political issues facing residents of the region: land claims, division of the territories, economic development, the Energy Accord, and self-government.

Self-government is closely linked with constitutional development. Many Native people equate self-government with some form of decentralized government. In fact, they see self-government as critical to their ability to control cultural choices and economic development. Whether Native people in the NWT will be able to survive a life in two cultures may be one of the most important social questions in Canada in the twenty-first century.

Residents of the NWT are facing crucial social, economic, and political changes. In this book, I have traced the development of a government that will be responding to these issues. I am also initiating a discussion of the tension surrounding the choice of a model for political development in the region. The ensuing discourse should enable Canadians to understand what is at stake in this important process.

Acknowledgments

My interest in the Northwest Territories was first aroused when Stu Hodgeson invited me on his final trip across the region in 1979. We stopped in approximately twenty communities from Inuvik to Cape Dorset, and I was very grateful for the chance to see something of this intriguing part of Canada.

A few years later I began to link the evolution of government and politics in the NWT to my ongoing interest in political change and development. At that time Morris Zaslow was visiting the University of Calgary, and I attended his extremely interesting course, 'The Development of the Canadian North.' Then I began to talk to a number of individuals who lived in the region, many of whom had been or were involved in government. Once I realized there was no comprehensive work on how government evolved in the NWT, I knew in what direction my research would take me.

I do appreciate the many individuals who gave willingly of their time as I tried to piece together the story on development of government in the territories. These people include Jim Antoine, Louie Audette, Clair Barnabe, Jim Bourque, Fred Carrothers, Henry Cook, Ewan Cotterill, Mariana Devine, C.M. (Bud) Drury, Don Ellis, René Fumoleau, Scotty Gall, Michael Gardener, Jean Guertin, Larry Hagen, Betty Harnum, Paul Idlout, Bob Janes, Steve Kawfki, Hugh Keenlyside, Don Kindt, S.K. Lal, L.A. Learmouth, Charles McGee, Margaret McGee, Simon McInnes, Iola Metuq, Mike Moore, Ron Mongeau, Bob MacQuarrie, Dan Murphy, Bob Pilot, Carol Roberts, Gordon Robertson, Basil Robinson, James Ross, Graham Rowley, Penny Shafto, Ben Sivertz, Jack Sperry, Mike Stilwell, Gary Vanderhaden, Jack and Rosa Van Camp, James Wah-Shee, Norman Williams, and the people of Fort Good Hope, who, in the summer of 1986, hosted one of René Fumoleau's seminars on the North and introduced me to their cul-

Acknowledgments

ture. I am also grateful to that small group of colleagues who work on things northern and were willing to share ideas – Fran Abele, Ken Coates, Gurston Dacks, Peter Clancy, Ned Franks, Shelagh Grant, Gerry Nixon, Geoff Weller, Doug West, and Mike Whittington. I would like to thank the students who assisted with the research: Tracy Smith, Leonard Clampitt, Cara Stelmack, Gauri Sreenivasan, and Mai Rempel. And I had excellent co-operation from individuals in the Northern Heritage Centre in Yellowknife, the Public Archives of Canada, the GNWT's Bureau of Statistics, and the Legislative Assembly's Research Services. John Leslie in the Treaties and Historical Research Centre, DIAND, was particularly helpful on many occasions.

I am especially indebted to Keith Crowe, John Parker, Mike Robinson, and an anonymous reader who carefully read and made suggestions on earlier drafts of the manuscript. Lloyd Binder and Jim Cunningham also read and commented on selected chapters.

The Institute of Public Administration of Canada provided a grant as seed money for the project. Mike Robinson and the people at the Arctic Institute of North America provided invaluable support while I was on sabbatical leave in 1988-9. Nova Corporation of Alberta and Foothills Pipe Lines assisted financially with the leave, which made it possible for me to travel to the Eastern and Western Arctic.

Working with Peter Milroy and Jean Wilson at UBC Press has been a pleasure, and Paul Norton and Joanne Richardson were very helpful in smoothing out the ragged prose. Holly Keller-Brohman was very effective in steering me and the manuscript along the fast track to production. Also, Judi Powell suffered through many drafts in getting to the final disk. And special thanks to my wife Barbara for her constant support and assistance. Needless to say, none of these people are responsible for any shortcomings in my arguments.

WHOSE NORTH?

Twenty-five years of change in the Northwest Territories: (*top*) 1966
Territorial Council; (*bottom*) Twelfth Legislative Assembly, elected in
October 1991 (photographs courtesy Ben Sivertz and the GNWT)

CHAPTER ONE

Political Change, Political Development, and the Crisis of Legitimacy

The Northwest Territories (NWT) is the largest political jurisdiction in Canada. The federal government, in 1875, enacted the Northwest Territories Act, providing for the administration of this sparsely populated region, also known as Rupert's Land. After the Prairies were settled and Alberta and Saskatchewan became provinces (1905), the remainder of the NWT (approximately one-third of Canada) retained territorial status within Canadian Confederation.

By definition, a territorial government is a government in transition. Originally, the federal government administered the NWT from Ottawa to maintain order and preserve sovereignty. Today, the Government of the Northwest Territories (GNWT), by convention, has acquired constitutional powers almost equivalent to those of the provinces. Two important exceptions exist. The federal government has retained control of Crown lands and non-renewable resources, and neither the NWT nor the Yukon has any formal part in the process of amending our constitution.

Some fundamental questions grow out of this evolutionary process. Will the territorial government follow the pattern that occurred in the South prior to 1905 and become a carbon copy of provincial governments? Or will it deviate from the pattern and take on a character of its own? Are there conditions, circumstances, and political forces nuturing a GNWT with an indigenous character?

Answers to these questions are not obvious. In fact, the GNWT has emerged as a complex organization. The basic form used in establishing it followed conventional, province-like structures. At the same time, this government has taken on an indigenous character of its own by adopting a non-partisan, 'consensus' style of governing. This dualism reflects two schools of thought regarding how the constitutional process should evolve in the NWT.

There are individuals in the region and in the government itself who envision a province-like system similar to jurisdictions in the South. These people argue that a conventional, centralized government model will best serve residents of the territories. This model satisfied requirements for representative and responsible government in the South, and they feel that it can also satisfy the needs of northerners. Indeed, in their minds the evolution of an autonomous, province-like government *is* self-government.

At the same time, many Native people, particularly those in small communities, envision a different model of government. They argue that a strong local and regional government is needed in the area. They accept a territorial jurisdiction but feel that power should reside with local governments. In effect, they call for a decentralized form of government. The current proposals for a 'division' of the NWT into at least two territories is a manifestation of the desire to decentralize the existing GNWT. For those with this viewpoint, self-government has an entirely different meaning.

The struggle between advocates for a centralized model and those who favour a decentralized model of government are shaping the evolution of the constitutional process in the NWT. The tension between these groups shapes much of the political dynamic in the region. Although the jury is still out on the precise nature of the process, it is clear that the system of government has, and will retain, a distinct character. It is not clear, however, whether the constitutional balance will tip toward a more centralized or a more decentralized form of government.

In tracing the evolution of the GNWT, one object of this book is to document the changes that have occurred in the governmental process since 1920 and to explain why these changes have occurred. The study is descriptive in that it documents the structural changes occurring, and it is analytical in that it examines the factors causing these changes. Causal factors include changing political forces that emerge in the NWT – forces that constitute an integral part of the 'context' of the region. That particular context is crucial and is very different from that of the rest of Canada. The book is also prescriptive, arguing that the territories not only has its indigenous context but that that context seems to require a particular governing apparatus: the NWT is a distinct region of Canada, and that distinctiveness dictates a more decentralized than centralized government.

POLITICAL CHANGE AND POLITICAL DEVELOPMENT:
TWO DIFFERENT PROCESSES

Focussing on political change and political development in the NWT poses a number of analytical problems.[1] Political change, for example, is a relatively straightforward phenomenon. It involves changing institutions and processes which form the basis of government and politics. In forty years, government in the territories has evolved into an almost province-like apparatus with most of the latter's powers. The constitutional basis for the system remains the Northwest Territories Act (1875), under which a commissioner had ultimate de jure power. De facto power now resides with the elected Legislative Assembly and the Executive Council of that assembly. As well, since 1967 an extensive territorial bureaucracy has emerged, administering powers devolved from the federal government. This bureaucracy now carries out responsibilities similar to those in provinces: education, health care, housing, public works, municipal affairs, finance, renewable resources, and personnel. Political changes also involve developing the participatory process by which residents of the region elect members of the assembly. In 1991, for instance, twenty-four Legislative Assembly representatives were chosen from constituencies throughout the NWT. It is not difficult to document the political changes that have occurred, but do these changes constitute political development?

In the NWT there are those who argue that these political changes *do* constitute political development. But the problem involves how residents of the territories perceive the changes. In other words, as political changes occur, are these changes leading to the creation of a political system that residents prefer? Are the changes leading to the type of governmental process that individuals envision as appropriate for the territories? The evidence suggests that indeed there is a discrepancy between what many individuals of the region would prefer and the nature of the process that is evolving. Political change and political development may not be synonymous; in fact, they constitute two processes. A critical first step in the analysis is to sort out a more precise meaning of political development.

Political development is a very problematic concept – a complex and contentious phenomenon. Explicit definitions of the term are not easy to find. Many of those addressing the subject write around the concept, avoiding a concise definition. One of the best working definitions of political development is offered by Morton Gorden: 'In the contemporary world, nations are faced with developing political systems that can facilitate economic growth while managing the conflict created by increased interaction among peoples. The process of growing to meet these demands is often referred to as political development ... The word development is not meant to imply an orderly direction of change. It is used here to denote a growth of capacity to manage conflict in the political system.'[2]

Political development, then, involves constructing a political process capable of managing conflict in a society. But this rather simple definition becomes terribly complicated because so much is implied in its use. One problem in using the term 'political development' is that often it is seen to be synonymous with the Westernization of political institutions.[3] Political changes in Western nation-states follow a familiar pattern; a number of writers have traced the emergence of political parties, interest groups, free and fair competitive elections, representative institutions, a strong executive, and functioning bureaucracies. These institutional changes are said to be a response to a desire for greater participation in the political process. Consequently, in developing nations, once these institutions are established, the assumption is that the society has achieved political development. This, of course, is a big assumption – that is, that the Western system of government and politics can provide harmony and political stability regardless of a society's political culture.

Such an assumption may not stand up universally, and nowhere is the evidence for this stronger than in the experiences of emerging nations in the post-colonial era. One problem is that the Western assumption about political development ignores the significant role of political culture.[4] Western ethnocentrism tends to overlook the fact that there must be an accord between the nature of the political institutional structure of a society and the political culture or cultures of that society. In effect, attitudes, beliefs, values, and expectations that individuals hold regarding their government and politics must be in tune with the governmental system.

This problem of cultural accord is obvious in the new states in Africa, Asia, Latin America, and the Middle East. A strong village orientation, a powerful sense of collectivism rather than individualism, deference, spirituality permeating most aspects of one's life, fatalism, strong personal loyalties and clientelism, and a non-industrial economic base are characteristics often associated with more 'traditional' peoples. Grafting modern Western political structures onto societies with different values and traditions has been a common practice, but often the graft does not seem to take. For example, the high incidence of coups and counter-coups as a way of dealing with the problem of political succession indicates a lack of accord between values and traditions and institutionalized procedures. Political development, then, involves more than creating institutions and procedures. It involves creating institutions and procedures that are in accord with the prevalent beliefs and values that individuals hold regarding their governing process.

In the past few decades, the most productive work on the concept of political development has been accomplished by those who challenge the inevitability of political development. In fact, one group of writers has taken a giant step by encouraging a more fruitful analysis of the concept: S.N. Eisenstadt, Samuel P. Huntington, and Mancur Olson have challenged the notion that political change inevitably leads to political development.[5] They suggest that rapid and pervasive changes occurring in societies can result in political breakdowns, political decay, or political instability. Political change can lead to turmoil rather than to order and stability. Huntington makes this clear when he separates the processes of political change and political development. He notes that political change is manifested in the mobilizing and politicizing of individuals in a society, but increased participation does not automatically lead to the development of a system of government capable of managing conflict.

This argument represents a landmark in the analysis of the process of political development. Huntington and others suggest that the process of political change is not deterministic – that it is not a unilinear but a multilinear process. Political change may lead to political development, but it also may lead to political decay. The two different modes of analysis can be expressed as follows:

unilinear analysis: → political change   → political development

                                              ╱ political development
multilinear analysis: → political change
                                              ╲ political decay

Because political changes may or may not lead to political development, a multilinear analysis is more accurate than is unilinear analysis with respect to the real world of politics in developing nations.

The question surrounding the issue of political development is: What causes the difference? What is the factor, or factors, which result in political development in one society and political decay in another? If one agrees that multilinear analysis is more realistic than unilinear analysis, then the analytical objective is to locate those factors (or variables) which determine political development.

POLITICAL DEVELOPMENT AND POLITICAL LEGITIMACY

One factor instrumental in engendering political development is political legitimacy. While the term has often been used in an abstract way, current analysts are moving toward a more concise and measured definition. Seymour Martin Lipset, for example, suggests that political legitimacy 'involves the capacity of the system to engender and maintain the belief that the political institutions are the most appropriate ones for the society.'[6] John H. Schaar elaborates on this definition: 'The new definitions all dissolve legitimacy into belief or opinion. If a people hold the belief that existing institutions are "appropriate" or "morally proper," then those institutions are legitimate. That's all there is to it. By a surgical procedure, the older concept has been trimmed of its cumbersome "normative" and "philosophical" parts, leaving the term leaner, no doubt, but now fit for scientific duty.'[7] Political legitimacy, then, depends upon the perceptions and sentiments that individuals hold concerning their political system. What is the origin of these perceptions or sentiments? On what basis do members of a society perceive whether their political system is legitimate or illegitimate? Herbert Spiro has suggested that one of the foundations on which political legitimacy rests is 'procedural factors.'[8] Procedures in this case refer to the institutionalized procedures which are a part of the political apparatus. In modern societies they represent those procedures which enable individuals to elect and to oppose or to support governors. These procedures can include elections, letter writing, and interest group activity such as lobbying or the process of declaring oneself a candidate and running for public office. Individuals or groups of individuals then see the system as legitimate because, through these procedures, they may be able to change public policy or oust a government. Institutionalized procedures which facilitate involvement in the political process underlie the perceptions one holds about the legitimacy of a political system.

Another way of conceptualizing what political legitimacy means goes back about 300 years to John Locke's idea of political consent. In constructing a political system with 'power' over individuals in a community, 'this power has its original only from compact and agreement, and the mutual *consent* of those who make up the community' (italics added).[9] Locke's idea of consent and what Lipset and Schaar mean by political legitimacy go hand in glove. If individuals perceive the political system as right or appropriate for their society, then they will consent to the laws and policies of that system. Engendering this sense of legitimacy is also an integral part of the process of political development.[10]

Thus, there are two dimensions to the concept of political development – a structural dimension and an attitudinal dimension. The structural dimension involves establishing institutions and procedures capable of managing conflict in society. The attitudinal dimension involves engendering within the citizens of a polity the sense that the system of government is right for their society. Building structures and procedures may be an easier task than engendering within the minds of individuals the sense that those structures and procedures are legitimate. But the institutions and processes, and attitudes toward them, should evolve simultaneously in order for political development to occur.

THE CRISIS OF LEGITIMACY IN THE NWT

This is precisely the problem of political development in the NWT. To date, many of the structural characteristics of the institutional arrangement follow the southern model of a conventional, provincial government, with the two exceptions mentioned above: residents of the territories are denied control of land and resources, except for those lands within land claim settlements, and they do not have equivalent provincial status at first ministers conferences and in the process of amending the constitution. A Westminster parliamentary apparatus provides the structural framework for the system of government, but the GNWT has devised its own version of responsible government. Political parties are not part of the process; 'consensus' is used as the basis of decisionmaking in the Legislative Assembly.

Nevertheless, this rather conventional, southern structure of government is not accepted as legitimate by certain Native groups in the NWT. On a number of occasions, Dene Nation president Billy Erasmus has challenged the legitimacy of the territorial government. For example, Erasmus has said that the existing Legislative Assembly is an interim government, and the GNWT is 'by no means a legitimate government. The NWT does not even have a constitution and so it has no mandate from the people.'[11] For many of the Dene, the land claims settlement and the realization of self-government will give their people an opportunity to create a form of government different from the existing territorial government – and one to which they can consent.

The Inuit of the Central and Eastern Arctic do not just call the existing GNWT illegitimate; their interest is to create a new territory, Nunavut, and a new territorial government. Paul Quassa, former president of the Tungavik Federation of Nunavut (TFN), the body negotiating land claims for the Inuit of the Central and Eastern Arctic after the signing of an agreement in principle (AIP) with the federal government on 30 April 1990, said:

> I want to talk a little today about the future of our land, our culture and
> ourselves as a people; and about the AIP we are signing, and the final
> agreement to create Nunavut – the Inuit homeland ...

> We want to be full citizens in our home and country, our native land.
> Settlement of the land claim and creation of a Nunavut Territory will
> bind us closer to Canada and to all Canadians and promote a more
> productive relationship between Inuit and the federal government.[12]

For the Inuit, developing political legitimacy requires creating
Nunavut, the proposed new territory and governmental system for
the Central and Eastern Arctic. Presumably, some form of self-
government for the Dene Métis, and Inuvialuit, and a new territory
for the Inuit would engender consent and, thus, represent a more
legitimate political process than the one which now exists. Different
perceptions about the nature of the governmental process create a crisis
of legitimacy for the GNWT.

If, in the process of political development in the North, legitimacy
of the existing government is questioned, why is this the case? Why
are people in the NWT challenging the present course of political
development and suggesting new alternatives for the region? In order
to better understand the different perceptions of political legitimacy
one must have an appreciation of the context of the NWT. Subsequent
chapters will deal with the geography, demography, and cultures of
the region, with the historical experiences that residents of the region
have had with political evolution, and with the emerging political
forces in the region today.

CHAPTER TWO

Geography, Demography, Economy, and Cultures

The Northwest Territories today constitutes about 34 per cent of the area of Canada, or 3,376,698 square kilometres (1,304,903 square miles). It is almost twice the size of Mexico and is larger than either Europe or the subcontinent of India. Within Canada, the distance from Aklavik to Iqaluit is approximately 2,800 kilometres – the same distance from Calgary to Ottawa. And from the territorial border, 60°N latitude, to the top of Ellesmere Island, above 80°N, it is approximately 2,000 kilometres.

In contrast to its physical size, the population of the NWT is minuscule. Approximately 54,300 people (1991) reside there – a total slightly larger than the populations of Medicine Hat, Alberta, or Trois-Rivières, Quebec. The NWT is one of the least densely populated regions of the world. At the same time, this region is not just part of the Canadian mosaic, it is a mosaic in itself. This diversity is an integral part of the context within which political change occurs in the NWT, and it is reflected in the terrain and climate, the people and cultures, and the economy.

LAND AND CLIMATE

What is called the Northwest Territories today is the result of numerous additions and deletions of territory. Part of it at one time was Rupert's Land, administered by the Hudson's Bay Company. These lands were transferred to the Dominion government in 1870 and became the North-Western Territory – lands west and north of central Canada. This vast area began to be carved up immediately with the creation of the province of Manitoba (1870). In 1880, more area was added to that province, and, in 1898, the Yukon was made a federal territory. Alberta and Saskatchewan became provinces in 1905, and in 1912 additional areas of the NWT were added to Manitoba, Ontario, and Quebec. The Arctic Archipelago was added to the region in 1880, when the British government transferred its jurisdiction to Canada.

Geographically, the NWT is an extremely diverse region (Map 1). The heart of the area is the Precambrian Shield, which lies north of Alberta, Saskatchewan, and Manitoba.[1] These Barren Lands represent the tundra, containing thousands of lakes and muskeg. The tree-line divides the region along an imaginary line from Churchill, Manitoba, northwest to the Mackenzie Delta. The tree-line, in the past, separated the Inuit to the north from Aboriginal people to the south. Much of this area encompasses the Keewatin region, one of five administrative regions in the territories.

The western flank of the territories is formed by part of the Rocky Mountain chain, including the Mackenzie and Richardson mountains. In these mountains there are elevations of over 2,500 metres, forming the western side of the Mackenzie River Valley. The Franklin Mountains, with elevations to 1,700 metres, form the eastern side of the valley.

The Mackenzie River is one of the great fresh water systems of the world. The total length of the river from the head of the Finlay River in British Columbia to the Beaufort Sea is 4,241 kilometres. The main river, from Great Slave Lake to its delta, is 1,800 kilometres long – equal to the distance from Toronto to the mouth of the St. Lawrence River. For explorers and trappers, the river system was the primary mode of transportation from Alberta and southern Canada to the Western Arctic. Soon after the turn of this century, Edmonton was the gateway for travel down the Mackenzie. A rail line was built, terminating just south of what is now Fort McMurray. From there one could take a boat down the Athabasca to Fort Chipewyan on Lake Athabasca – one of the oldest communities in Alberta. The Slave River was then used for about 125 kilometres to Fort Fitzgerald. At this point it was necessary to portage almost twenty-six kilometres around four sets of rapids and to enter the river again at Fort Smith. From there it was a relatively easy trip into Great Slave Lake and down the Mackenzie (after a channel was blasted through one set of rapids on the Mackenzie). This was the main source of transport until the 1960s, when a rail line was built to Hay River on Great Slave Lake. The rail line, barge, and air transport are the major conveyors of goods to the region today, bypassing the historic river route via Fort Smith. An early account of travelling this historic route is found in a Department of the Interior publication, 'Local Conditions in the Mackenzie District, 1922.'[2] The area around the upper Mackenzie and to the south of Great Slave Lake is wooded, and the Liard Valley has great potential for produc-

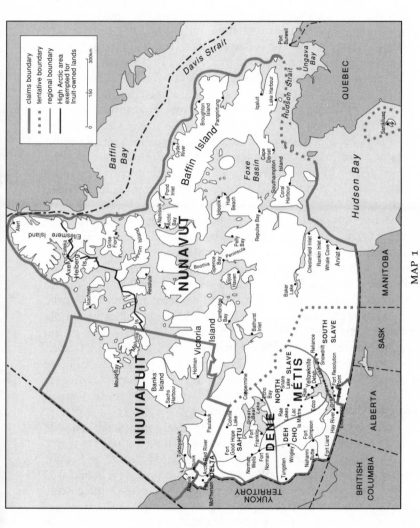

MAP 1

The Northwest Territories

ing forest products.

The Franklin Mountains taper to the western edge of the shield. Here, Great Slave and Great Bear lakes, along with Lake Athabasca, are remnants of a major drainage system that existed approximately 10,000 years ago. Water over much of this area formed Lake McConnell, bounded on the west by the Franklin Mountains and to the east by glaciers covering the centre of the continent.[3]

The eastern flank of the NWT is Baffin Island, an area of 507,453 square kilometres – the fifth largest island in the world. The eastern part of the island is mountainous, with elevations of up to 2,100 metres. At the end of the many bays and fiords around the island, one can see the terminus of glaciers which wind their way down the mountain valleys. While Baffin is approximately twice the size of Great Britain, there are only about 10,000 people living in small communities around the coastline. Baffin also constitutes one of the administrative regions of the NWT. The Inuit of Baffin have an identity and loyalty often associated with life on an island – not unlike Newfoundland or Prince Edward Island.

The Arctic Archipelago constitutes the fourth area of the NWT. The geography of the south-central and western islands, for example, Victoria and Banks islands, is more like the shield country above the tree-line, whereas the eastern and northern islands up from Baffin are more mountainous. Barbeau Peak on Ellesmere Island, for instance, is 2,616 metres high. There are only a handful of settlements on the islands, Grise Fiord (on the south end of Ellesmere) being the northernmost permanent settlement in Canada. This archipelago has been at the heart of an ongoing sovereignty dispute with the United States (which will be discussed in Chapter 3). The United States claims right of innocent passage through waters around the islands, whereas Canada's claim to sovereignty includes control of these waters. Sovereignty over the land is not disputed.[4]

The climate is one reason the NWT is sparsely populated. In 1988 the coldest temperature recorded in the Mackenzie Basin was –55.6°C and the warmest was 34.4°C. In Yellowknife, from November to March, the average temperature is –22°C, and at Iqaluit on Baffin Island it is –21°C. Summer temperatures average 21°C along the Mackenzie River and 10°C on the Arctic Archipelago. The area north of the tree-line is almost a northern desert in terms of rainfall. Precipitation averages fifteen to forty centimetres per year – one of the lowest averages in Canada.

Geographically, the cordillera along the Mackenzie River Valley constitutes the Western Arctic, the Barren Lands make up the huge Central Arctic, the Arctic Archipelago the far north, and Baffin Island the

Eastern Arctic. Each of the regions has been home for Native groups for centuries, and each group has a distinctive culture.

RESOURCES AND ECONOMY

Much of the interest in Canada's North stems from southerners' interest in its natural resources. Although Alberta and Saskatchewan became provinces in 1905, the federal government retained control of resources until 1930, and the Department of the Interior was responsible for the remainder of the Northwest Territories. As had been the case with the Prairies before the turn of the century, this new 'northern frontier' and its resources were promoted by the federal government. It was anticipated that the new Northwest Territories would be the object of great development and settlement. A departmental booklet entitled 'The Unexploited West' (1914) reflects this optimism.

> While the trend of immigration is turning northward, the eyes of the capitalist are attracted in the same direction. Information concerning the resources of the country once ignored is now sought for. Facts about the climate, the soil, the timber, the rivers, the lakes, the minerals, the fish, the game obtained at the risk of life and limb by fur trader, explorer, missionary, geologist and sportsman, even those facts regarded not so long ago as merely interesting, have now a practical value ...
>
> By connecting with the three thousand miles of almost uninterrupted steamboat communication on Athabaska, Peace, Slave and Mackenzie rivers, and Athabaska and Great Slave lakes, the railway being pushed into the Athabaska country will place the whole of Mackenzie basin within easy reach of the prospector, the explorer, the sportsman and the tourist.[5]

While there has been considerable interest in the resources of the region, it has never captured the imagination of Canadians or foreigners as did the Yukon in 1898. The NWT has never experienced the bonanza to fuel a great and rapid migration into the region. Nevertheless, non-renewable resource development has been a driving force in creating a very dynamic territorial economy. In 1987, the territorial GDP was $1,794 million and grew to $1,824 million in 1989.[6] At the same time, this economy has failed to touch the lives of many Native people in small communities, leaving them in a very difficult economic situation. This fact remains one of the dilemmas of northern development.[7]

Furs were the resource attracting most early explorers and trappers. The area below the tree-line provided caribou, moose, bear, beaver, fox, lynx, muskrat, marten, mink, and otter. The Arctic coastline above the tree-line was a source of whales, walrus, seals, and polar bear. The Hudson's Bay Company and the North West Company began to assess the potential of the region in the latter part of the eighteenth century. Samuel Hearne made a number of trips into the interior of the region for the Hudson's Bay Company between 1769 and 1772. In 1778, Peter Pond was sent into the Lake Athabasca region by Montreal fur merchants, who formed the North West Company in 1784. He was replaced by Alexander Mackenzie in 1787, and, in 1789, Mackenzie began his exploration of the river which would bear his name. Aboriginal people in the valley called the river Dehcho. After a fierce rivalry, the two fur trading companies amalgamated in 1821, with the Hudson's Bay Company interest prevailing.

By 1827, the Mackenzie River District of the Hudson's Bay Company was a major producer of furs. In that year, furs shipped were worth almost £13,000 and included 4,800 beaver, 6,700 marten, and 33,700 muskrat.[8] Over the next century, the Hudson's Bay Company established a number of permanent trading posts not only in the Mackenzie Valley but also around the Arctic coastline and on Baffin Island. For example, posts were established at Fort Smith and the present site of Fort Good Hope in 1822 and 1836, respectively, and at Pangnirtung and Coppermine in 1921 and 1927, respectively.

The fur trade has been an important part of the economy of the NWT. In 1987-8 the value of fur production was between $5.6 and $6.1 million, including beaver, fox, muskrat, and lynx.[9] Trapping in the region poses an interesting paradox. Introduction of the fur trade in order to meet foreign demand provided Native people with some cash income. At the same time, a cash economy created dependence on volatile prices and fluctuating outside markets. From an historical, economical, and cultural perspective, life in the region was never the same after the introduction of trapping.

Trapping has provided a way for many Native people to earn sufficient income to overcome some of the very real hardships which were part of their traditional way of life. The tragic fact is that today animal rights groups have destroyed a significant portion of the fur industry, thereby undercutting one source of independent income earned by Native people. This development undermines their opportunity to benefit from living off the land.[10]

Whales were another resource of the region exploited by outsiders, and that exploitation also changed the lives of Native people. In the 1800s, whale oil and baleen (whalebone) were in commercial demand.

Whalers from Great Britain (many of them from Scotland) came into the Eastern Arctic in the early 1800s. By 1851, they were wintering on Baffin Island, with stations established in Cumberland Sound, Frobisher Bay, and Pond Inlet. While the British initiated most of the early whaling, by the 1860s firms from Connecticut and Massachusetts also had ships in the Eastern Arctic. Blacklead and Kekerken islands in Cumberland Sound were thriving stations. Inuit often gathered at the stations, crewing on the whaleboats and working at the station. They also supplied the ships' crews with meat and clothing and, in turn, obtained rifles, boats, knives, and other manufactured items. By the latter part of the nineteenth century, American whalers from the Pacific coast began to visit the Beaufort Sea. Herschel and Baillie islands became their bases. They, too, established trade with and employed local Natives.[11]

The intrusion of foreign ships, crews, and trade posed a problem for the government. In 1894-5, for example, fifteen ships and 600 men were wintering on Herschel Island.[12] Not only was there no control of the resources taken from Canadian waters, but the presence of the ships posed a question of sovereignty in the region. Furthermore, a number of social problems developed as a result of the contact between Native people and the whalers – not the least of which was disease. To cope with these problems, the government established a Royal North-West Mounted Police post on Herschel Island in 1903. The two constables reported to Sergeant F.J. Fitzgerald of Fort McPherson.[13] The purpose was to establish some control over trade and to protect the Inuit from exploitation. The action was too late, however, because the whale population was diminished significantly, and, within five or six years, substitutes for baleen and whale oil (e.g., plastics and kerosene) were found and the market collapsed. Nevertheless, Native contact with whalers and fur traders left its mark on their way of life. It was the beginning of a process of rapid change for Native people.

Developing the mineral resources of the NWT has been and remains, for the most part, a responsibility of the federal government. In the past, this responsibility was the primary focus of federal departments which preceded the Department of Indian Affairs and Northern Development (DIAND), created in 1966. In the departments of the Interior (until 1936), Mines and Resources (1937-49), Resources and Development (1950-3), and Northern Affairs and Natural Resources (1954-65), the flagship of each was the branch responsible for non-renewable resource development.

In the 1950s and 1960s, the departments also began to focus on the welfare of Native people. Many officials believed non-renewable resource development would provide the vehicle for economic development for all residents of the region. In effect, this model of economic development was thought to be the 'cure-all' for social and economic problems. If Native people could just become a part of the wage economy, this would be the first step in integrating them into the mainstream of Canadian culture. And it was assumed that once they became acculturated, social and economic problems associated with their traditional culture would disappear.

Interest in the territory's minerals and mining goes back to the turn of the century. Gold fever spilled over into the NWT from the Yukon. By the 1920s, gold mining companies were working areas around Great Slave Lake.[14] By the 1930s interest had centred on the area which is now Yellowknife. The Consolidated Mining and Smelting Company of Canada was producing gold by 1938, and by 1940 Yellowknife had the first municipal government in the region. Interest waned because gold was not a high priority during the Second World War, but by 1944-5 it again began to flourish. In 1953 the first mayor of Yellowknife was elected.

The mining of radium and uranium was also an important part of the industry's development in the region. Eldorado Gold Mines set up operation at Port Radium on Great Bear Lake in 1931, and a healthy market for radium kept the mine going until 1940. The Second World War disrupted the market but generated a need for uranium. By 1942, Eldorado reopened to supply the material for use in atomic weapons. In 1944, production was taken over by the Crown corporation Eldorado Mining and Refining, and production continued until 1960.

Currently, there are six operating mines in the NWT producing gold, silver, lead, and zinc. In 1987, the value of non-fuel minerals shipped was $810 million, and about 2,000 people were employed in the industry (10 per cent of those employed in the territorial work force).[15] Territorial mining accounts for about 7 per cent of Canada's total mineral production.

At the same time, a number of mining operations in the NWT have had to close due to economic conditions or because the supply of minerals was exhausted. The lead and zinc operation at Pine Point closed in 1988, as had the nickel mine at Rankin Inlet in 1962. These closures caused hardships in their respective regions. Rankin Inlet today, however, remains a viable community – a government centre with some entrepreneurial activity. But the town of Pine Point no longer exists.

Perhaps the most important direct benefit from mining operations for the people of the NWT was the accompanying infrastructure. For example, mining activities provided the stimulus for the construction of roads and a railway line into the territories, justified the construction of hydroelectric generating facilities, spawned the creation of numerous communities, and have been the incentive for the development of innovative technologies creating thousands of direct and indirect jobs.[16] By the same token, mining has rarely provided a great source of employment for Native people. With the exception, for a short time, of Rankin Inlet, it has never provided a means for integrating the economy of small Native communities into the modern mining sector.

Oil and gas also figure prominently in the development of non-renewable resources in the NWT. The first successful oil well was drilled by an affiliate of Imperial Oil in the Mackenzie Valley in 1920. The discovery of oil at Norman Wells jolted the Department of the Interior into action and was the reason the government negotiated Treaty 11 with Natives in the region. Members of the department anticipated a boom similar to the gold rush in the Yukon and took steps to move the requisite personnel into the region. Fort Smith became the administrative centre for the department's northern operations.

A lack of interest and the Great Depression dampened expectations, but interest was rejuvenated during the Second World War. The United States government saw Norman Wells oil as a possible safe fuel supply for any troop build-up in Alaska, anticipating that the area might provide a springboard for an invasion of Japan. The Canol pipeline was constructed from the Mackenzie Valley to Whitehorse – quite a logistical accomplishment in 1942, given the weather and terrain. As the war progressed, interest in the strategic importance of Alaska waned and, with it, interest in the Norman Wells field. By the 1960s, however, oil and gas exploration expanded down the Mackenzie to the Beaufort Sea and into the Arctic Archipelago.

The oil and gas potential for the NWT is significant. Oil and gas shipped in 1988 was valued at $140 million. At the same time, the Mackenzie Valley, Beaufort Sea, and Arctic Archipelago contain approximately 50 per cent of Canada's potential oil resources and 67 per cent of its potential gas reserves.[17]

Discussions concerning a pipeline down the Mackenzie Valley to transport oil and gas became serious in the early 1970s, at the height of the oil crisis. The Trudeau government appointed Mr. Justice Thomas Berger to conduct an inquiry into the consequences of constructing a pipeline in the Mackenzie Valley. Commissioner Berger, recognizing the intense feelings of the Native people of the region, recommended a ten-year moratorium on the project. Discussions on a pipeline are now being revived, with a number of proposals from Gulf Canada, Shell Canada, Polar Gas, and Esso Petroleum.[18]

In spite of large investments by industry in mining and in gas and oil explorations and operations, most analysts today would agree that trying to build the region's economy on non-renewable resources alone is folly. These projects can be very beneficial, especially in the short run, but, as K.J. Rea pointed out years ago, usually they cannot provide the principal engine for sustainable economic development.[19] Other means have to be considered in trying to extend the benefits of a wage economy.[20]

Renewable resources, such as forests, fish, and wildlife, may, in time, be important elements in the development of the economy of the NWT. While investments and financial returns from these commodities are now small compared to what is generated from non-renewable resources, nevertheless, they could contribute to the local economy almost indefinitely if managed properly.

Small sawmills, for example, have been in operation south of Great Slave Lake since the turn of the century. Missionaries, miners, trappers, and government officials used the lumber in constructing their dwellings. Indeed, the government of Canada used a small mill in supplying part of the materials required for constructing facilities after 1920. But there has never been a successful commercialized operation that could supply wood products across the entire NWT. Most construction materials are imported from the South.

The resource is there. In the Liard Valley alone there is potential for cutting '20 million board-feet, which could service most of the Western Arctic's estimated softwood demand of 22 million board feet annually.'[21] In 1987, for example, production in the NWT was about four million board feet, far below the allowable cut of twenty-five million board feet, which would enable a sustained yield of timber in the territories.[22] There may be ways to better utilize this existing resource in order to minimize imports from the South and to create jobs for residents of the region. In effect, the North is competing with southern operations in which economies of scale are working.

Fishing is also a potentially valuable resource. Since the 1930s, there have been attempts at commercializing a fishing operation on Great Slave Lake, principally at Hay River. The problem, however, has been the marketing of freshwater fish outside the territories, which, by federal law, is required to go through a marketing board in Winnipeg. The overcoming of interprovincial hurdles should enable an increase in revenue from fishing, which in 1987 was $2.1 million.[23]

Another side to the economy of the NWT is that involving small Native communities. Figures from this sector reveal the disparity that exists in the region. Based on 1988 tax returns, the NWT had the highest average personal income ($23,610) when compared with other jurisdictions in Canada (Ontario $22,802, the Yukon $23,029).[24] But territorial figures are deceptive. For example, in Norman Wells (the site of Esso's refinery) in 1984 the average annual income was $27,412, whereas in Rae-Edso, about 100 kilometres to the northwest of Yellowknife, the average annual income was $10,882. And in the Baffin region, in the mining town of Nanisivik, the average annual income was $32,974, while in Cape Dorset it was $9,425.[25]

Employment figures also illustrate disparities in the territorial economy. In the '1989 NWT Labour Force Survey,' the reported work force (fifteen years and older) was 34,650. Of this figure, 20,328 individuals were classified as employed and 3,922 as unemployed. Therefore, the official unemployment rate in the NWT was 16 per cent compared to a national average of 8 per cent (6 per cent in Ontario and 16 per cent in Newfoundland and PEI).[26] A graphic breakdown of the unemployment rates in Native and non-Native categories further illuminates disparities in the economy:[27]

Non-Native	5%
Native	30%
Dene	35%
Inuit	31%
Inuvialuit	27%
Métis	19%

There are at least two economies in the NWT: the non-renewable resource economy and the renewable resource economy of the region's scattered, small communities. The consequences of this dualism will be discussed in Chapter 6, but a demographic picture of the region helps one realize the gravity of the economic problem.

DEMOGRAPHICS

Two characteristics of the NWT's population are extremely important because they affect the process of economic integration. First, the territories has the fastest growing population of any jurisdiction in Canada, and this growth is not from migration into the region. Second, because the population is dispersed in small, isolated communities, it is difficult to operate on the principle of economies of scale. This dispersion of communities is a major economic problem, and it facilitates the continuation of hunting, fishing, and trapping in the region. Population figures for the NWT over the past eighty years are:[28]

1911	6,507
1931	9,316
1951	16,004

1961	22,998
1971	34,804
1981	45,700
1991	54,300

The interesting fact about current figures is that the annual rate of growth in the population today is 3 per cent per year – almost three times the average for Canada.[29] More important, this growth is from a population explosion *within* the territories. Since 1985, out-migration in the region has exceeded in-migration; for example, in 1988, 4,026 individuals left the territories and 3,631 moved in.[30]

The second important demographic fact is related to the nature of the sixty-plus communities in which the people live. In spite of the small number of communities, there is variety in terms of size, culture, and economic base. Jack Van Camp has provided an excellent description of these communities.

At least five categories of communities can be recognized. Yellowknife is a large (approximately 12,000), modern government and mining centre. No other community in the NWT comes close to Yellowknife with respect to population size, affluence, economic activity or prevalence of non-aboriginal people (about 82 per cent) and culture. A second category of communities is the medium-sized (1000-3500), ethnically integrated (35-60 per cent aboriginal), regional centres of Inuvik, Hay River, Iqaluit, Fort Smith and Fort Simpson. These communities have small but resilient business and service sectors and moderate levels of infrastructure development. A third category of NWT communities is the large (500-1500) aboriginal (75-95 per cent) centres (such as Rae-Edzo, Coppermine, Baker Lake and Pangnirtung). These are the communities with high growth rates, low levels of infrastructure development, low income levels, high unemployment, and poorly developed business and service sectors. In many ways these communities are caught in transition between traditional, land-based economies and wage-oriented mixed economies of the larger regional centres. A fourth category of communities is the small (50-500) aboriginal settlements (such as Whale Cove, Colville Lake, Clyde River and Snare Lake) which have economies that remain primarily land-oriented, informal and traditional. A fifth category of communities is the ephemeral, resource extraction-based mining [and petroleum] towns like Nansivik and Norman Wells. Pine Point and Tungsten would also have fit this category. These communities are largely self-sustaining and externally oriented.[31]

Even though the communities are small by southern standards, they vary in many ways. In Yellowknife, for example, non-Natives have brought with them most of their cultural baggage, from bars to bowling alleys, fitness centres to restaurants. In the smaller, more isolated communities, one finds many features of traditional Native cultures, including language, hunting and fishing, the making of clothing, and close family ties. And one must remember that most of these communities are almost inaccessible. Only about ten are served by all-weather roads; others are reached by plane, barge, or vessel when the water is open.

A rapidly increasing population and the wide distribution of that population are problematic. The growth rate means that many northern communities are full of young people looking for jobs. The NWT will have to generate jobs at a rate three times that required in the South. At the same time, it is in the small communities that unemployment rates are highest.

This problem again highlights the dual nature of the NWT economy. In the region, the viable resource industry has flourished. Alongside this success, however, are the small, isolated Native communities where incomes are low and unemployment is high. When demographies and economies are combined, conditions in the territories do not appear very encouraging. These conditions are further complicated by extreme cultural diversity.

CULTURAL DIVISIONS IN THE NWT

The NWT is as diverse culturally as it is geographically and economically. The Native population constitutes 57.9 per cent of the total population, and the non-Native population constitutes 42.1 per cent. The Native population is divided between Dene Métis (22.4 per cent) and Inuit (35.5 per cent) and is, therefore, not homogeneous.[32]

The cultural differences between aboriginal peoples are significant. Except for the Cree, Indian residents of the NWT are the Dene ('the people'). Their ancestors are believed to have migrated into the region approximately ten to twelve thousand years ago, locating in and around the Mackenzie corridor. Linguistically, the majority are Athapaskan, but five different regional languages have evolved.[33] The peoples of the lower Mackenzie Valley, northern Yukon, and eastern Alaska speak Gwich'in; the people of Alaska speak western Gwich'in; and the people of the Mackenzie area speak eastern Gwich'in. They live in the communities of Fort McPherson, Arctic Red River, and, to some extent, Inuvik and Aklavik (Map 2).

Along the Mackenzie River southward, three different aboriginal peoples speak North Slavey: the Hare, Bearlake, and Mountain. They

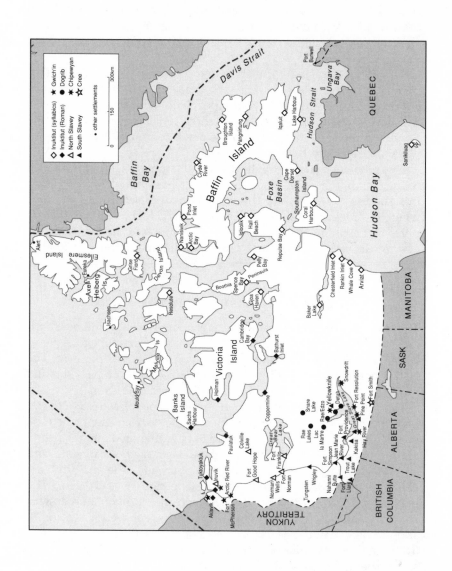

Legend:

◇ Inuktitut (syllabics)   ★ Gwich'in
◆ Inuktitut (Roman)   ● Dogrib
△ North Slavey   ✱ Chipewyan
▲ South Slavey   ☆ Cree

• other settlements

0   150   300km

MAP 2

Northwest Territories communities. The following is a list of place-names with local Native-language equivalents:

Community	Native	Community	Native	Community	Native
Aklavik		Fort Providence	Zhahti Koe	Pangnirtung	Panniqtuuq
Arctic Bay	Ikpiarjuk	Fort Resolution	Deninu Kue	Paulatuk	Paulatuuq
Arctic Red River	Tsiigehtshik	Fort Simpson	Liidli Koe	Pelly Bay	Arviligjuat
Baker Lake	Qamanittuaq	Fort Smith	Tthebacha	Pine Point	
Bathurst Inlet		Gjoa Haven	Uqsuqtuq	Pond Inlet	Mittimatalik
Broughton Island	Qikiqtarjuaq	Grise Fiord	Aujuittuq	Rae	Behcho Ko
Cambridge Bay	Ikaluktutiak	Hall Beach	Sanirajak	Rae Lakes	Gameti
Cape Dorset	Kingnait	Hay River	Xatt'o Dehe	Rankin Inlet	Kangiqtiniq
Chesterfield Inlet	Igluligaarjuk	Holman	Uluqsaqtuuq	Repulse Bay	Naujat
Clyde River	Kangiqtugaapik	Igloolik	Iglulik	Resolute	Qausuittuq
Colville Lake	K'ahba Mj Tuwe	Inuvik	Inuuvik	Sachs Harbour	Ikaahuk
Coppermine	Kugluktuk	Iqaluit		Sanikiluaq	
Coral Harbour	Salliq	Jean Marie River	Tthedzehk'edeli	Snare Lakes	Wekweti
Detah	Tezehda	Kakisa	K'agee	Snowdrift	Lutselk'e
Edzo	Edzoo	Lac La Martre	Tsoti	Spence Bay	Talurjuat
Enterprise		Lake Harbour	Kimmirut	Trout Lake	Saamba K'e
Eskimo Point	Arviat	Nahanni Butte	Tthe nago	Tuktoyaktuk	Tuktuujaartuq
Fort Franklin	Deline	Nanisivik		Umingmaktok	
Fort Good Hope	Radili Ko	Norman Wells	Legohli	Whale Cove	Tikirarjuaq
Fort Liard	Echaot'j Koe			Wrigley	Thedzeh Koe
Fort MacPherson	Teet'it Zheh			Yellowknife	Sombak'e
Fort Norman	Tulit'a				

SOURCE: Frances Abele, *Gathering Strength* (Calgary: Arctic Institute of North America 1989), xxv

live in Colville Lake, Fort Good Hope, Fort Franklin, Fort Norman, and Norman Wells. South Slavey is spoken by people residing in the southwestern corner of the territories, living in communities from Wrigley to Fort Providence, Hay River, and Enterprise. A fourth language is Dogrib, spoken by people living east of the Mackenzie, for example, in Rae, Edzo, Lac la Martre, Rae Lakes, Snare Lakes, and Detah. Chipewyan is spoken by people on the edge of the Barren Lands and below the tree-line, living in Fort Resolution, Snowdrift, and Fort Smith. A sixth language, Cree (an Algonquian language), is used by some people on the southern boundary of the NWT. These people moved north as explorers or marauders, extending their control of the fur trade.[34]

Métis are found in most Dene communities along the Mackenzie River. Often cultural lines between the two groups are indistinguishable, but in some cases they are separate. There are approximately 4,000 Métis in the NWT.

The second large Native population in the territories is the Inuit. They live above the tree-line in the Eastern, Central, and Western Arctic. The Inuit may constitute a more homogeneous population than do 'Indians', but they, too, have regional dialects. Inuit cultural roots go back approximately 4,000 years to the pre-Dorset migration. The Dorset culture evolved in the region approximately 2,500 years ago. Over time, these people were integrated with another migration, the Thule people from Alaska, approximately 1,000 years ago.[35] The Thule were the dominant culture and ancestors of most of today's Inuit.

There are five groups of Inuit in the NWT today. The Mackenzie Delta Inuit, the Inuvialuit, live in the area around the mouth of the Mackenzie River. The interior Inuit include the Copper Inuit, who live at the northern fringe of the Barren Lands along the shore of the Arctic Ocean, and the Caribou Inuit, who live on the Barren Lands to the southwest of Hudson Bay. The remaining Inuit live in and around Baffin Island and in Sanikiluaq in the Belcher Islands. Culturally, the latter are linked to the Quebec Inuit. Four distinct dialects have emerged among the Inuit in the territories, and, while they are distinct, Inuit from the different regions can, with effort, understand each other.

Another part of the cultural mosaic of the NWT is, of course, the non-Natives. They are a substantial part of the population and live principally in the MacKenzie Valley and south of Great Slave Lake. In a number of Western Arctic communities, the non-Native population is larger than the Native population, for example, Fort Smith, 54 per cent; Hay River, 71 per cent; and Inuvik, 58 per cent. In the Eastern Arctic, the Inuit usually constitute from 80 to 90 per cent of community residents.[36]

Three basic categories of non-Natives can be identified: permanent residents who go north to earn their livelihood, civil servants who go north for the job but frequently retire somewhere in southern Canada, and the skilled resource industry personnel who usually reside in resource communities. In the case of the latter, these communities are becoming few and far between as resource companies fly employees in for shift work, perhaps two weeks on, two weeks off. These workers may live in Calgary or Edmonton and commute on company planes or commercial flights. Often they live in compounds and usually do not become residents of the NWT.

Different and conflicting interests are extensive in the North. Differences are ameliorated to some extent by the number of Native and non-Native marriages in the region. Nonetheless, one must appreciate the northern mosaic in order to understand the politics of the region. These differences are not just between those who live above or below the tree-line or Native and non-Natives. Very deep economic and cultural divisions do exist among Natives, between Natives and non-Natives, and even among non-Natives. These divisions, along with geographic, social, and economic problems, form an integral part of the context of the NWT, and this context significantly influences the nature of political change and political development in the region.

The problem of cultural change for Native peoples has been, and remains today, one of the most difficult issues in the North. Cultural change began with European colonization. Change was accelerated by the impact of the fur trade, whaling, the introduction of Christianity and a formal education system, the availability of Western health care, the Second World War, the Cold War, the construction of permanent communities, and improved communications and transportation systems. For Native people, these changes created, and continue to create, a difficult cultural dilemma. On the one hand, they want and need a great deal from the culture of non-Natives. Much of what modern, Western culture has to offer makes life easier for them. On the other hand, too much modernity undermines their traditional ways. Modern values and beliefs are rarely compatible with traditional values and beliefs. The challenge is to strike a balance. Indeed, one of the most difficult problems Native people are facing today is how to live under the influence of two powerful cultures.[37]

CHAPTER THREE

Formulating Process and Policies: The Historical Dimension, 1920-50

Political development in the Northwest Territories today is impossible to understand without knowledge of the history of federal policies in the region. The evolution of the governing apparatus and the experiences of individuals within that apparatus is an integral part of that history. Federal administration of the new NWT began in 1905, after Alberta and Saskatchewan became provinces. Until 1921, however, there was no established policymaking process. For thirty years after 1921, a handful of civil servants in Ottawa ran the region as if it was their own bureaucratic feifdom.

THE GOVERNING APPARATUS, 1920-50

The constitutional basis for government in the territories consists of two federal statutory acts, the Indian Act (1873) and the NWT Act (1875). These acts provided for a dual system of government. The latter was amended in 1905 to accommodate new territorial boundaries, to make the chief executive officer a commissioner rather than a lieutenant-governor, and to establish a four-person, appointed Territorial Council to assist the commissioner.[1] Thus, the act provided for executive and legislative authority in the region: the 'commissioner-in-council' could legislate ordinances and administer the provisions of those ordinances. Designated responsibilities under the act included mainly matters of a local nature (e.g., licensing, public health, municipal taxing, protection of game, police, and roads). After 1920, the commissioner and council became an integral part of the Department of the Interior, answering to the minister of the Interior. As was the case in the provinces, the governor-in-council could disallow within one year territorial ordinances passed by the commissioner-in-council.

The Constitution Act (1867) was the basis for the federal government's responsibility for all Indians, including Indians in the NWT. The federal Parliament enacted the Indian Act, and the Department of Indian Affairs was created to administer it. In the field, Indian agents were the administrative representatives of the department. Under the Indian Act, the Department of Indian Affairs was responsible for all 'Indians' in the NWT.[2] The Department of the Interior was responsible for the Inuit and the Métis. In a court decision in 1939, the Inuit were declared to have the same Aboriginal status as 'Indians', and in the Constitution Act, 1982, Métis received the same status.

In 1905 Lieutenant-Colonel Fred White, comptroller of the Royal Northwest Mounted Police, was named commissioner of the NWT, but no council members were appointed. White's responsibilities were not that onerous. The primary federal presence in the territories was the police, and problems with order were minimal. In terms of governing, one of White's principal tasks was to make quarterly payments to seven schools operating in the south Great Slave region, Fort McPherson, and Herschel Island. Residential schools received $400 per year, day schools $200.[3]

By 1920, in the Mackenzie region, there were six RCMP posts, two Indian agents, twenty trading posts, and sixteen church missions.[4] The budget for the Government of the Northwest Territories was $7,000, of which $3,000 went to schools.[5] In fact, there was very little formal governmental machinery to cope with problems in the region.

White died in 1918, and in 1919, W.M. Cory, the deputy minister of the Department of the Interior, was appointed commissioner of the NWT. This began a tradition of combining, in one individual, the deputy minister of the department and the chief executive officer of the NWT. The precedent lasted until 1963. Thus, the executive, legislative, and administrative roles of government in the region were performed by the commissioner, the council, and the departmental administration.

In 1920, one event began to change expectations about the North. A successful oil well was drilled in August 1920, approximately 80 kilometres north of Fort Norman on the MacKenzie River. This event galvanized the officials responsible for the region. Their sense of anticipation is conveyed in a statement by the minister of the Interior in the *Annual Report* of 1922: 'All indications pointed to an oil stampede into the Mackenzie district on the opening of navigation in 1921, and it was deemed advisable to establish the Northwest Territories Branch in Ottawa for the purpose of administering the natural resources and transacting departmental business pertaining to those territories.'[6] Imperial Oil's successful drilling program in the Mackenzie Valley began to foster the perception by many Canadians that the

North was a great storehouse of exploitable resources.

By 1921, the first order of business in the Department of the Interior was to organize for increased activity in the region. It was necessary to put in place a governing mechanism which could handle resource development demands and to establish the rules, regulations, and policies for maintaining order in the region.

In April 1921, the initial move was to appoint four Territorial Council members to assist Commissioner Cory. At the first council meeting on 28 April, members recommended that the minister have the NWT Act amended to expand membership of the council to six and to designate a deputy commissioner who would preside at meetings when the commissioner was absent. With only four members, it was feared a quorum would be difficult to muster during summer months. The proposal was passed by order-in-council and the expanded council met in June 1921.[7]

The membership of the first Territorial Council is important, for it established the character of that body until 1947. Membership consisted of high ranking civil servants whose responsibilities involved administration in the NWT. In addition to the commissioner (also deputy minister of the Department of the Interior), the assistant deputy minister was made deputy commissioner, in this case, Roy A. Gibson. Other members included J.W. Greenway, Commissioner of Dominion Lands in the Department of the Interior; Colonel A.B. Perry, Commissioner of the RCMP; Charles Camsell, Deputy Minister of Mines; H.H. Rowatt, Superintendent, Mining Lands and Yukon Branch, Department of the Interior; and O.S. Finnie, Chief Mining Engineer, Department of the Interior.

In 1929, after the death of Greenway, Duncan Campbell Scott, Deputy Superintendent General of Indian Affairs, was appointed to council. The minister of the Interior was also the superintendent general of the Department of Indian Affairs. Theoretically, by having the deputy minister of the Interior and deputy superintendent of Indian Affairs on the council, the workings of the two departments could be integrated. The representative from Indian Affairs at the administrative level was important, because a great deal of what the council did (e.g., in game laws) involved the welfare of Aboriginal peoples. The functions of the council have been described as follows: 'As the Council was composed entirely of the senior officials of the various federal departments involved in northern administration, it acted as something much more than a legislative body. It became, through the years, an interdepartmental committee of consultation and co-ordination, a general advisory body on all northern administration.'[8]

In addition to the commissioner and council, in 1921 the Northwest Territories Branch (after 1922, called the Northwest Territories and Yukon Branch) was established as a part of the Department of the Interior. In the summer a crew of approximately thirty people was dispatched to Fort Smith to construct departmental offices. A district agent was the officer in charge, who also served as mining recorder and Dominion lands and Crown timber agent for the Mackenzie District. This move did create an administrative presence in the region, again designed primarily to facilitate resource development.[9] The NWT and Yukon Branch functioned within the department as one of five divisions: Dominion Lands, Forestry, Canadian National Parks and Water Power, and Reclamation. A sixth division, the Surveys Bureau, was added later.

By 1930 the NWT and Yukon Branch had a relatively high profile in the department, with its emphasis on science and exploration (Figure 1). From 1921 to 1931 Director Oscar Finnie took a hands on approach to managing affairs of the North, travelling to the region on a number of occasions. He sought opportunities to get qualified people into the field, encouraged scientific expeditions to work in the region, and worked to improve health care and the supply of wildlife for Native people.

FIGURE 1
Administrative organization of the Northwest Territories
and Yukon Branch, 1930

Head Office: Northwest Territories and Yukon Branch, Department of the Interior, Ottawa
Director: O.S. Finnie
Arctic exploration and development officer: G.P. Mackenzie
Chief inspector: J.F. Moran
Chief investigator: L.T. Burwash, ME
Investigators: W.H.B. Hoare, J. Dewey Soper
Special investigators (Reindeer): A.E. Porsild, R.T. Porsild
Medical officers:
    L.D. Livingstone, MD, Chief medical officer
    J.A. Urquhart, MD, Aklavik, NWT
    R.D. Martin, MD, Coppermine, NWT
    A.L. Macdonald, MD, Fort Smith, NWT
    C. Bourget, MD, Resolution, NWT
    W.A.M. Truesdell, MD, Simpson, NWT
    H.A. Stuart, MD, Pangnirtung, NWT
    (Vacant), Chesterfield, NWT

District agent (Mackenzie District): J.A. McDougal, Fort Smith, NWT
Agent of mining recorder (Mackenzie District): T.W. Harris, Fort Simpson, NWT
Superintendent Wood Buffalo Park: J.A. McDougal, Fort Smith, NWT
Stipendiary magistrate: Hon. Lucien Dubuc, Edmonton, Alberta
Sheriff: Col. Cortlandt Starnes, Ottawa
Registrar of lands titles: K.R. Daly, Ottawa
Legal adviser: W.M. Cory, Ottawa
Public administrators:
   Mackenzie District, H. Milton Martin, Edmonton, Alberta
   Keewatin District, vacant
   Franklin District, W.M. Cory, Ottawa

SOURCE: Department of the Interior, *The Northwest Territories*, 1930 (Ottawa, 1930), 3

After 1931, however, many of Finnie's initiatives were lost. The NWT and Yukon Branch became a victim of personality differences and budget cuts under the new Conservative government in 1930. Finnie and many of his staff were retired or transferred as the branch was dismantled. This move was criticized by individuals such as Diamond Jenness and Richard Finnie, both of whom had considerable experience in the North.[10]

In 1936, northern administration suffered another blow. The Department of the Interior was abolished, and its functions were absorbed into the newly created Department of Mines and Resources (Figure 2). Responsibilities for administering the NWT fell to the Bureau of Northwest Territories and Yukon Affairs, a part of the Lands, Parks, and Forests Branch of the department. That branch operated alongside the Mines and Geology, Surveys and Engineering, Indian Affairs, and Immigration branches. Even within the Lands, Parks and Forestry Branch, NWT affairs were competing with National Parks and the Dominion Forest Service (Figures 3 and 4). This structure remained essentially unchanged until a government reorganization in 1950.

After the restructuring in 1931, however, the administration of the NWT did not command a very high priority within the Department of the Interior or the Department of Mines and Resources. Budget figures are an indication of priorities. Table 1 lists the expenditures of the three departments responsible for most administration in the North.

By the late 1940s, the administration of the NWT began to regain some of its previous status and with this status came financial resources. The branch's spending between 1945 and 1949 increased from $413,673.95 to $2,477,904.70, approximately a sixfold increase. In 1938-9, northern administration made up approximately 16 per cent of the Department of Mines and Resources budget and, by 1948-9, it made up about 58 per cent. This change partly reflected a change of attitude in the old guard, which had dominated northern affairs policymaking since 1931.

FIGURE 2
Government departments responsible for
Native Affairs and Northern Development

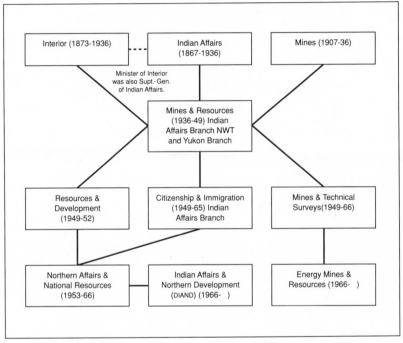

SOURCE: *Annual Reports,* appropriate years for appropriate departments

TABLE 1
Expenditures of departments responsible
for northern administration

Department	1932-3	1938-9	1948-9
NWT administration (depts. of interior & mines and resources)	$206,224.48	$283,776.11	$2,477,904.70
Indian Affairs	210,438.62	196,699.16	962,243.21
RCMP	182,668.85	176,025.60	378,225.92

SOURCE: PAC, R.G. 85, vol. 33, file 120-1-2

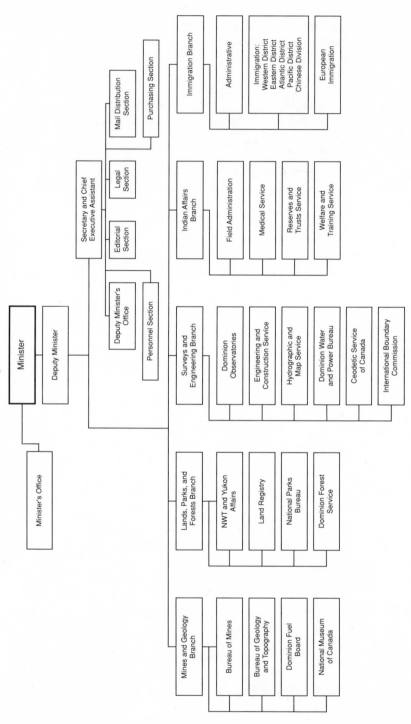

FIGURE 3: Organizational chart, Department of Mines and Resources, 1937

SOURCE: Department of Mines and Resources, *Annual Report*, 1937

FIGURE 4: Organizational chart, Lands, Parks, and Forests Branch, Department of Mines and Resources, 1937

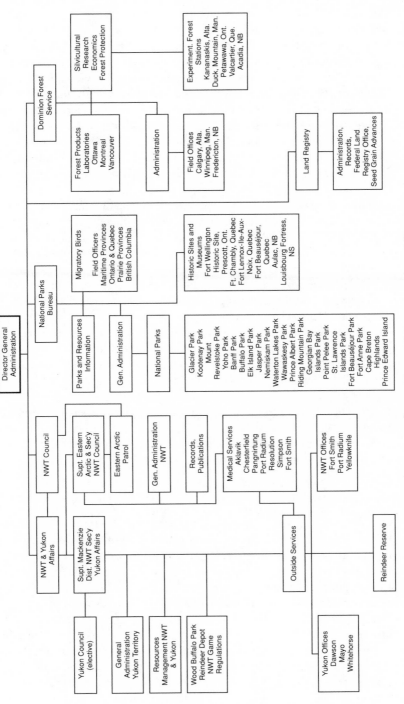

SOURCE: Department of Mines and Resources, *Annual Report*, 1937

Charles Camsell, commissioner and deputy minister of Mines and Resources since 1936, retired in December 1946. Camsell had also served on the council since June 1921. In January 1947 Hugh Keenleyside became deputy ministry of Mines and Resources and commissioner of the NWT. Keenleyside was an outsider in the sense that he came from the Department of External Affairs, although he had served as a member of the Territorial Council from 1941 to 1945. Part of the budget increases reflected his emphasis on education in the North.[11]

Another factor influencing expenditure increases after 1945 was expressed by R.A. Gibson, deputy commissioner and director of the Lands, Parks and Forests Branch. In the 1947 *Annual Report*, he wrote:

> During the past year, Government expenditures in the Northwest Territories provided substantial evidence of faith in the potentialities of the mining areas of the Mackenzie District, particularly in the field which centres on Yellowknife. Some of the more important projects on which outlays were made included the Grimshaw-Great Slave Lake road; the hydro-electric power development on the Snake River and the transmission line to Yellowknife; the improvement of the Yellowknife airport which now provides facilities for the larger type of transport and passenger aircraft; the improvement of roads, the installation of water and sewer services and assistance in the construction of a modern public school and Red Cross hospital in Yellowknife, and the construction of adequate administration buildings at Yellowknife, Fort Smith, and elsewhere.[12]

In spite of expenditure increases in the late 1940s, criticism of departmental philosophy and policies continued. The foundation for this criticism will be more evident with an understanding of the nature of northern public policies in the 1921-50 period.

PRINCIPAL PUBLIC POLICIES IN THE NWT

Initially it was thought that the Department of the Interior's primary responsibility would involve matters associated with resource development in the NWT. Resource development would be followed by a migration of miners, speculators, developers, and settlers from the South. In fact, gold and other minerals were discovered, but no phenomenal rush occurred to pose insurmountable problems. As a consequence, the Territorial Council faced the responsibility of formulating policies and regulations for running the everyday business of government on a frontier: granting liquor licenses and consequent regulations, placing departmental staff in the field, keeping vital statistics, overseeing transport facilities such as navigational aids and roads, apportioning land to be distributed into lots, and creating municipalities. In addition to 'housekeeping' chores, policies were required which involved the lives of residents of the region: education, health care, welfare, and wildlife harvesting regulations. In these four areas, because of a lack of interest in the North by most Canadians and most elected officials in government, the will of the commissioner and the council was law.

Education Policies

Providing basic education for people in the North represented a fusion of church and state. In the nineteenth century, missionaries had followed trappers into the region, often building schools as an integral part of their work. The government assisted by providing grants to the churches to operate day and residential schools. Churches, in effect, hired the teachers and set the curriculum.

This modus operandi worked until the late 1940s, by which time the educational system was becoming more complex. The Anglican and Roman Catholic churches maintained their schools, the Northwest Territories had started schools in Fort Smith and Yellowknife, the Department of Indian Affairs operated four schools, and an independent school board was being organized in Yellowknife. Problems with the school system were starting to become evident. R.A.J. Phillips describes the circumstances very well:

> Eight different authorities operated schools in the North. The Department of Northern Affairs provided only three classrooms. Though it paid grants to other agencies to run classes, the classroom standards were uneven. Some schools operated only four hours a day, four days a week. One teacher in three held no teaching certificate of any kind. Only 117 of all the Eskimos got full-time schooling. There was no vocational education of any kind, no adult education, and no teaching for the growing ranks of hospital patients.[13]

The fundamental problem with education during the 1930s and 1940s, however, lay with the philosophy of members of the council. Their view was that Native people would continue to live a traditional, subsistence lifestyle. This way of thinking was convenient in many respects. Education did not need to be as elaborate as in the South, and costs for programs such as health and welfare could be held to a minimum. Nowhere was this philosophy expressed more clearly than in a report submitted by J.A. Urquhart to the council in October 1934. Although Urquhart was a physician in Aklavik, physicians employed by the department were expected to do a variety of administrative chores. Because of his experience in the region, his views on education were important and were shared by members of the council. A section of the report was included in the council minutes.

Training
From a purely academic standpoint, this should be limited very much to the original Three R's, and manual training, carried out as much as possible with the idea of making the schools more industrial than they are at the present moment.

Graduation Age
I consider that no boys should be kept in school after the age of twelve. These children are not going to be absorbed into industry, and must return to a life of trapping and hunting. The ideal time, or the receptive age for boys, is between twelve and fifteen, and throughout this period, the boys should be back home with their fathers, and learning to trap by travelling with them on the trapping line and actually, under the father's supervision, setting their own traps. This is their natural native custom.

With regard to the girls, the age of graduation should be later, approximately fifteen, as in that same period, between twelve and fifteen, they learn to sew, cook and to perform the ordinary duties of a housewife.

Future Prospects
These children, whether boys or girls, are going to live out their lives in the country. It is, therefore, necessary that everything possible should be done to avoid having the boys over-educated in a scholastic way, particularly if this is to be at the expense of their ability to make a living off hunting, trapping and fishing.[14]

Policymakers assumed that the only option for Native people was a traditional, subsistence way of life. In the minds of these government officials, the existing church and state school system was adequate, providing basic skills in reading and writing. By 1940, the two departments responsible for education were spending slightly over $70,000 in the NWT (Tables 2 and 3).

Perhaps more significant than the amount spent on education were the results. Almost no Native children went beyond grades five or six (Table 4). Obviously, these individuals, once adults, would be limited in job opportunities because of their educational deficiencies. This school system came under heavy criticism, nowhere more vividly than in the work of Diamond Jenness. His statements regarding the 'Eskimo' apply to all Native people in the NWT.

Each year it was becoming more and more impossible for the Eskimos to gain even a bare subsistence, because, quite apart from the fluctuations in the supply of fish and game, their incomes, which hinged directly in the prices of furs, were diminishing rather than increasing, while their needs – or what they had come to consider their needs – were growing both in price and in number. Unless then they could find some source or sources of income additional to the trap-line, or in place of it, they would continue to lean on the government more and more heavily until they became permanent dependants on a dole, victims of all the evils such dependence brings. If that happened, their dead weight, like the badly adjusted brake of a wagon, would slow up the wheel of northern development that seemed already on the point of moving forward. They possessed the necessary intelligence to contribute to that development;

TABLE 2

Education/school expenditures, NWT, 1923-50 (Northern Affairs)

Fiscal year ended 31 March	Expenditure recorded
1923	$ 3,000.00
1924	3,000.00
1926	3,200.00*
1928	3,460.00
1930	12,787.50
1932	11,676.76
1934	15,660.31
1936	19,828.34
1938	23,109.91
1940	25,992.31
1942	24,695.50
1944	21,585.49
1946	30,190.17
1948	55,928.94
1950	83,840.19†

SOURCES: Department of the Interior, Report of the Director, *Annual Report*, fiscal years ended 31 March 1923-36; Department of Mines and Resources, Bureau of Northwest Territories and Yukon Affairs, *Annual Report*, fiscal years ended March, 1938-48; Department of Resources and Development, Northern Administrations, *Annual Report*, 1950

* includes grants to destitute children
† includes $2,000 grant to Yellowknife School District

TABLE 3

Statement of education expenditure, NWT, 1920–50 (Indian Affairs)

Fiscal year ended 31 March	Day schools	Residential schools	Miscellaneous	Total
1920	$ 1,425.59	$30,131.72	$ 157.04	$ 31,714.35
1922	904.11	17,969.43	270.00	19,143.54
1924	1,434.78	26,138.74	488.51	28,062.03
1926	1,162.90	29,085.92	716.45	30,965.27
1928	1,022.00	31,919.85	1,398.23	34,340.06
1930	2,245.25	52,103.98	486.10	54,835.33
1932	1,520.96	40,707.84	1,017.61	43,246.41
1934	1,729.72	30,979.51	899.18	33,008.41
1936	1,650.00	34,783.48	1,261.18	37,694.66
1938	1,378.07	37,466.51	—	38,844.58
1940	1,375.59	45,242.68	—	46,618.27
1942	1,420.80	37,987.10	—	39,407.90
1944	1,621.00	35,945.78	—	37,566.78
1946	1,464.71	46,483.68	—	47,948.39
1948	54,273.28	71,203.99	—	125,477.27
1950	217,637.89	94,251.41	—	311,889.30

SOURCES: Department of Indian Affairs, *Annual Report*, fiscal years ended 31 March 1920-38; Department of Mines and Resources, Indian Affairs, *Annual Report*, fiscal years ended 31 March 1940-48; Department of Citizenship and Immigration, Indian Affairs, *Annual Report*, fiscal year ended 31 March 1950

TABLE 4

Summary of school statements, NWT, 1920-50

Fiscal year ended 31 March	Day school	Residential school	Total on roll	Average attendance	Standard											
					I	II	III	IV	V	VI	VII	VIII	IX	X	XI	XII
1920	5	3	270	206	136	40	56	28	8	2	—	—	—	—	—	—
1922	4	3	201	162	77	42	29	47	6	—	—	—	—	—	—	—
1924	4	3	246	182	137	44	36	13	13	3	—	—	—	—	—	—
1926	5	3	254	196	112	55	40	24	15	8	—	—	—	—	—	—
1928	5	4	312	213	159	55	50	21	19	8	—	—	—	—	—	—
1930	4	4	277	204	167	32	44	24	5	5	—	—	—	—	—	—
1932	2	4	210	189	108	33	25	25	14	5	—	—	—	—	—	—
1934	2	4	223	198	120	44	21	22	13	3	—	—	—	—	—	—
1936	4	4	259	196	141	47	30	23	16	—	—	2	—	—	—	—
1938	3	5	252	199	126	41	35	25	15	10	—	—	—	—	—	—
1940	4	4	272	232	150	38	42	17	20	5	—	—	—	—	—	—
1942	4	4	232	186	133	38	28	13	11	5	1	3	—	—	—	—
1944	3	4	216	182	89	51	27	18	19	6	6	—	—	—	—	—
1946	2	4	272	187	151	37	38	12	14	8	7	5	—	—	—	—
1948	5	4	307	241	144	56	44	27	18	12	2	2	2	2	1	—
1950	8	4	651	548	303	98	81	58	41	42	15	6	3	2	1	1

SOURCES: Department of Indian Affairs, *Annual Report*, fiscal years ended 31 March 1920-38; Department of Mines and Resources, Indian Affairs, *Annual Report*, fiscal years ended 31 March 1940-48; Department of Citizenship and Immigration, Indian Affairs, *Annual Report*, fiscal year ended 31 March 1950

they possessed also certain qualities, for example, mechanical ability, familiarity with the arctic environment, and a capacity greater than the white man's to withstand its cold; but they lacked the necessary education and training. We may observe the same situation today in many other parts of the world, in southeast Asia, in Africa, and in South America, regions which would gladly develop their natural resources and raise the living standards of their populations, but which lack the trained men to initiate and direct that development because they have been unable to give their people the requisite education.

Despite these examples all around us of the necessity to educate and train every citizen, whatever his race or colour, many people in Canada still cling to the outworn doctrine of the Department of the Interior in the 1930s concerning the Eskimos, although the alarming decrease in the herds of wild caribou should give them pause. As late as 1952 a Round Table Conference on Eskimo Affairs, held under official auspices in Ottawa, upheld that discredited policy by affirming 'that Eskimo should be encouraged and helped to live off the land and to follow their traditional way of life. (*Arctic Circular* 1952:41)[15]

Jenness recognized the department's efforts at education. It was not that the government short-changed students in the NWT. In fact, more was spent on a per pupil basis than was the case in Alberta (Table 5). Jenness' point, however, was that the educational program was misguided. It was not preparing Native people to have the *option* of participating in a modern, industrial economy. Education policies did not provide a choice. It was assumed by officials in Ottawa that the Native way of life was best for all Natives. Native people were being denied the opportunity to choose for themselves how to live. Of this omission, Jenness was severely critical, and the validity of his argument is borne out in the territories today. Many Native people still lack the training for job opportunities in large and small businesses, in the resource sector, in the professions, and in the public sector.

The other side of this issue, the cultural problem, poses a dilemma for Native people. This point was made by Keith Crowe, who noted that for Native people to attain full competence in the white man's world would mean a great change in philosophy, culture, and values. Few Natives want to make such a change.[16]

By the late 1940s, another issue arose regarding education policy. Hugh Keenleyside tried to move toward more secularization of the school system. The move encountered strong and entrenched church interests. In the end, Keenleyside did not win totally; a compromise was worked out which would give the territorial administration a greater role in the educational process, yet enable the churches to have a hand in operating the residences where students boarded while attending school.[17]

The problem of the churches was that they were unable to sustain for long the high costs of running, by themselves, an education system that could compete with schools in the South. Therefore, they were willing to accommodate a greater role for the state in the education process. The state, on the other hand, could not afford a frontal assault on entrenched interests. There was strong sentiment for preserving the church's role, particularly the Roman Catholic role, in the training of young people. This sentiment had powerful supporters in the Liberal party and government leadership of the day. Therefore,

TABLE 5

Average cost per pupil based on total enrolment
and average attendance for the NWT (1920-50) and Alberta (1920-51)

Year	Total enrolment	Average attendance	Cost per pupil total enrolment	Cost per pupil av. attendance
NWT*				
1920	270	206	$117.46	$153.95
1924	246	182	114.07	$154.19
1930	277	204	198.00	268.00
1934	223	198	148.02	192.32
1940	272	232	171.39	200.94
1944	216	182	173.92	206.41
1950	651	548	479.09	569.14
Alberta†				
1920	135,750	82,417	$ 58.06	$ 95.63
1924-5	147,796	107,880	59.27	81.20
1930-1	168,730	136,733	65.24	80.58
1934-5	167,954	136,202	54.07	66.59
1939-40	163,892	139,886	60.82	71.28
1944-5	152,532	130,095	85.49	100.23
1950-1	173,969	150,012	166.08	192.60

SOURCES: NWT: Department of Indian Affairs, Annual Report, fiscal years ended 31 March 1920-38; Department of Mines and Resources, Indian Affairs, Annual Report, fiscal years ended 31 March 1940-8; Department of Citizenship and Immigration, Indian Affairs, Annual Report, fiscal year ended 31 March 1950. Alberta: Department of Education, Province of Alberta, Fortieth Annual Report, 1945, Forty-sixth Annual Report, 1951

* average cost per pupil calculated using gross expenditure for education for the fiscal year. The expenditure included payments to residential and day schools as well as miscellaneous expenses
† average cost per pupil calculated using actual cost figure/expenditure

the compromise enabled the churches to keep a hand in the school system, while the government took a more commanding position. As it turned out, the compromise was the beginning of a state-determined education system in the NWT now run by the territorial Department of Education. But for almost three decades, education policy was dominated by churches and a council that made little attempt to prepare young Native people for anything other than a traditional way of life. While the intent was to retain the traditional culture, the educational system itself had an impact. Being absent from their families and acquiring new values and new customs radically affected the lives of Native children.

Health Care Policy

While the Department of the Interior had a part to play in providing health care facilities in the North, the principal role again involved the churches. Initially, hospital facilities were constructed alongside a few of the older missions, for example, in Fort Smith and Fort Simpson and, later, Aklavik and Pangnirtung. These facilities were operated by the Anglican and Roman Catholic churches, but the territorial administration supported them financially by providing a per capita allowance for each patient. This state-supported church policy is spelled out clearly in a letter written by the deputy minister of the Department of the Interior in 1934 to an official of the Consolidated Mining and Smelting Company of Canada.

> Replying to your letter of the 13th ultimo, urging that more adequate medical and hospital services be provided for the Great Bear Lake mining area I may say that the Dominion Government does not build hospitals in the Northwest Territories. Instead assistance is given to the mission hospitals which have been established primarily for the treatment of the native population. The usual grant is 50¢ per patient per day – $2.00 per day in the case of the destitute. In addition Government doctors are usually stationed at the hospitals. On one occasion a cash grant was made to assist in re-establishing a hospital that had been burned. The Department has no funds available to assist in the establishment of hospitals this year and only sufficient funds have been included in the estimates to cover the treatment of natives and the destitute.
>
> It has been expected that as the Cameron Bay District developed either the Roman Catholic or Church of England missions would open a hospital at that point. We understand that the Church authorities are keeping an eye on the situation to see if a hospital is needed. When Dr. T.O. Byrnes went to Cameron Bay he was retained as Medical Health Officer for the

District and in addition is paid a small amount for looking after the Police. He is also furnished with medical supplies to help out in the treatment of Indians and any destitute. The Department expects the mining companies to look after their employees.

If the mining companies decide to put up a hospital for the treatment of their employees at Great Bear Lake the matter of payment for services rendered the native population and any destitute white people who are not the responsibility of the mining community will receive consideration.[18]

This health care policy, at least what existed of it, was one of the more contentious issues facing northern administrators. Criticism was directed at Northern Affairs as well as Indian Affairs administrators for their lack of care for Native people. Native people were affected by diseases for which they had no immunity. Periodically, epidemics would sweep Native communities – epidemics such as smallpox, influenza, or measles. The Department of Indian Affairs admitted that tuberculosis was five times more prevalent in Native people than in the Canadian population as a whole.

The consequences of epidemics, for example, were particularly devastating. In 1927-8, a flu epidemic hit the Mackenzie Valley. In the annual statement by the superintendent general of Indian Affairs, Charles Stewart, the situation was reported as follows:

The outstanding event of the past year was the epidemic of influenza which swept the basin of the MacKenzie River during the month of July. The disease, which was of a very severe type, broke out at Fort Smith, and spread to the Great Slave Lake and down to Aklavik with great rapidity. This vast region is inhabited by scattered bands of Indians whose needs are ministered to by Indian agents and doctors at Fort Smith, Fort Resolution and Fort Simpson, and by missionaries and church establishments at these and other points. At Hay River there is a mission school and at Fort Smith, Fort Simpson and Aklavik are small mission hospitals. The doctor at Fort Smith was out of the country on leave of absence, but was at once replaced by a doctor from Edmonton. The doctor at Fort Resolution and the mission personnel at that point and at Hay River looked after the Indians about the Great Slave Lake. The doctor at Fort Simpson followed the epidemic down the river to Aklavik. All the workers were handicapped by lack of drugs and supplies, owing to the fact that the year's supplies had been burned in a warehouse fire at Edmonton where they were collected for shipment by the first boat of the season. Emergency supplies were sent in. Accounts of the epidemic which have reached the department tell of whole settlements stricken

at once, so that there were not enough well persons to care for the sick
or bury the dead, of mission workers carrying on though suffering from
the disease themselves, and in one or two cases, of isolated families or
small settlements being completely wiped out.[19]

Local accounts from missionaries, from the Hudson's Bay Company
people, and from the RCMP were even more graphic. One estimate
was that the 1928 epidemic wiped out one-sixth of the Dene population.[20] Accounts from the Eastern Arctic were just as graphic. Inspector Wilcox of the RCMP described conditions in Igloolik:

> I found about 20 igloos at this camp, and of their number 15 were ill with
> a form of pneumonia. The conditions were pitiful in the extreme. The
> weather was getting warm, with the result that during the day the in-
> terior surface of the igloos was thawing and then freezing at night. As
> a consequence the interior of the igloos was a mass of icicles. The floors
> were covered with about six inches of slush, and to add to their discom-
> fort they were without oil for their lamps. I found three of the women
> were running temperatures of 105 and 106 and their bodies were covered
> with sores. As can readily be understood their spirits were very low, they
> were thoroughly disheartened and feared the worst.
>
> I immediately made hot tea and gave all a ration of tea and biscuit,
> and treated those that were sick with Dover powders, poulticed their
> chests and gave them a laxative. It was very noticeable how their spirits
> rose after my arrival.[21]

In spite of these problems, no 'roving' doctor was employed to serve
the Indians and the Inuit. The department's response, in conjunction
with the churches, can be seen in Table 6. By 1946, nine of the twelve
hospitals were operated by the Roman Catholic and Anglican
churches, two by mining companies at Yellowknife and Port Radium,
and one by the Indian Affairs Branch. Native people in the vicinity
of these hospitals were cared for, but many lived great distances from
them.

The problem was, in part, ideological. As Richard Diubaldo suggests, in the 1930s government officials did not perceive health care
as a public responsibility: 'For decades the government wished to keep
out of the hospital business.'[22] In fact, there *was* a policy – or half a
policy. The government accepted part of the financial responsibility
for maintaining church or mining company constructed health facilities. In the Central and Eastern Arctic, two hospitals were operating
– one at Chesterfield Inlet and one at Pangnirtung. Two institutions
obviously could not cover health responsibilities for an area larger than

TABLE 6

Hospital and medical service expenditures, NWT, 1923-50 (expenditures excluding 'Indian'-only medical service)

Fiscal year ended 31 March	Number of hospitals	Payments to hospitals	Payments to provincial inst.	Payments to industrial homes	Total expenditure
1923	2	$ 6,925.00	$ —	$ —	$ 6,925.00
1924	2	5,887.50	—	—	5,887.50
1926	3	6,106.50	—	—	6,106.50
1928	5	10,778.58	—	—	10,778.58
1930	5	10,947.50	—	—	10,947.50
1932	5	16,185.00	—	—	16,185.00
1934	6	21,468.00	—	—	21,468.00
1936	7	14,664.50	—	—	14,664.50
1938	NA	18,882.50	2,356.53	1,255.88	22,494.91
1940	8	28,700.00	4,600.31	4,231.11	37,531.42
1942	11	27,134.31	4,466.14	—	31,600.00
1944	12	25,199.19	7,845.51	3,895.67	36,940.37
1946	12	39,368.76	17,431.80	6,012.37	62,812.93
1948	13	24,952.50	18,441.91	7,996.94	51,391.35
1950	NA	38,119.25	—	13,656.04	51,775.29

SOURCES: Department of the Interior, Report of the Director, *Annual Report*, fiscal years ended 31 March 1923-36; Department of Mines and Resources, *Annual Report*, Bureau of the Northwest Territories and Yukon Branch, fiscal years ended 31 March 1938-48; Department of Resources and Development, Northern Administrations, *Annual Report*, fiscal year ended 31 March 1950

NOTE: Number of hospitals does not include provincial or industrial institutions.

Ontario and Quebec.

One attempt to address the problem started in 1923. The Canadian government ship *Arctic* was pressed into service, beginning again what had come to be known as the annual Eastern Arctic Patrol. These expeditions had many functions, not the least of which was to show the flag in the Arctic Archipelago. New RCMP posts were established, old posts supplied, and scientists went along to gather information. For example, J.D. Soper of the Geological Survey (also an artist) was taken to Baffin Island in 1924 to spend a year.

L.D. Livingstone was also part of the complement of the *Arctic* in 1923, beginning a number of years as ship's doctor and even remaining on Baffin Island for a year. His task was to treat any cases he could at their stops. While this was an attempt to do something about medical problems in the area, it was no solution. Livingstone and doctors who accompanied later expeditions spoke of the limited coverage of their services. In the ship's doctor's report of the SS *Ungava* in 1932, it is clear that effort was less than satisfactory. 'It should be understood that none of the native camps or hunting villages of the Eskimos were seen, only the Police and Trading Company posts being visited, so that it cannot be said that a complete study of the Eskimo mode of living was made or can be recorded from personal observation.'[2] In most reports one finds the plea that permanent medical officers at strategic posts be increased or roving doctors periodically visit the remote communities.

In short, health care remained an issue in the North. In November 1945, the health responsibilities of Indian Affairs and northern administration were transferred to the Department of National Health and Welfare. In part, this move was a response to a report by G.J. Wherrett on health services in the NWT. He observed that most Native people lived without the opportunity to consult a nurse or physician and without basic immunization programs.[24] While the move helped focus attention on health problems and increased per capita expenditures (Table 7), it did not remove the issue from controversy. For example, the policy on treatment of tuberculosis patients by sending them to sanitariums in the South led to a heated debate within the department and caused many problems for Indian and Inuit families.[25]

The point is that in health care, as in education policies, the government was covering its responsibilities with a minimum commitment. It was relying heavily upon the Anglican and Roman Catholic churches to provide basic health services and education to the people of the NWT. And with both policies, the churches more than the state determined the nature and extent of the program delivery.

TABLE 7
National health and welfare expenditures, NWT, 1945-50

Year	Expenditure
1945-6	$146,002.29
1946-7	409,009.58
1947-8	476,166.00
1948-9	480,368.78
1949-50	474,064.24

SOURCE: PAC, R.G. 85, vol. 33, file 120-1-2

Relief or Welfare Policy

'Relief,' or welfare, was a nagging problem for the Territorial Council. It was linked to the fact that Native people were moving away from their more traditional way of life. For example, during the first few decades of this century, there were serious depletions of wildlife. With southern whites moving into game harvesting areas, plus bad cycles due to severe weather, it became difficult to survive in the NWT by fishing, hunting, and trapping. Native people frequently faced the possibility of starvation or near starvation. Often the churches or the trading companies would provide minimum rations to tide people over into the spring, when foods were more plentiful. When government officials began to move into the region, public responsibility was assumed for providing minimum food for those facing hard times. Initially, Indian agents carried out this responsibility. After the 1920s, when other government personnel moved into more communities, the RCMP would authorize relief rations. If there was no RCMP official, then a doctor, missionaries, or trading company personnel would sign for dispensing emergency rations.

The funds never amounted to a great deal of money. Indian Affairs, in 1934, dispensed $39,300.63 (Table 8). The Northern Affairs Branch assumed responsibility for this kind of support for all Inuit, Métis, and 'destitute' whites. These figures are not itemized separately in Northern Affairs budgets. Between 1932 and 1934, however, the department spent $2,232.82 on vouchers issued in the Arctic. Typical individual vouchers would be for fifty pounds of flour and tea, costing about $2.75.[26] On the other hand, where trading companies operated without open competition, they assumed the responsibility of relief for Natives. In other words, when the companies had the field to themselves, they 'should look after needy natives.'[27]

The real issue with relief arose from the fundamental position held by the territorial administration from 1921 to the early 1950s, that Native

TABLE 8

Relief and supplies for the destitute, NWT, 1920-36

Fiscal year 31 March	Description	Agency (fort)	Total expenditure
1920	Supplies for the destitute	Simpson	$ 3,653.61
1922	Supplies for the destitute	Simpson	5,516.26
1923	Supplies for the destitute	Simpson	2,144.21
1926	Supplies for the destitute	Simpson, Resolution	24,927.70
1928	Relief	Simpson, Resolution	27,383.72
1930	Relief	Simpson, Resolution	27,846.74
1932	Relief	Simpson, Resolution, Smith, Good Hope	18,186.38
1934	Relief	Simpson, Resolution, Smith, Good Hope	39,300.63

SOURCE: Indian Affairs, details of expenditure and revenue, *Auditor General's Report*, fiscal years ended 31 March 1920-36

people should be encouraged to maintain their traditional way of life. If they did this, schooling and relief payments would be held to a minimum. At the time there were stories coming out of the North about insufficient game to support Native families. This situation placed administrators on the horns of a dilemma. On many occasions at Territorial Council meetings, the arguments were repeated. At the thirty-sixth session, held in September 1932, Gibson noted that the policy of the Hudson's Bay Company is to keep Natives away from the trading posts and to keep down the amount of relief furnished.[28] And in a letter of instruction to doctors in the NWT dated 30 May 1933, the deputy minister stated: 'It is understood that in most of the Provinces those looking after the distribution of relief usually make it rather difficult for anyone to obtain relief, and although the supply of rations, etc., is fairly generous it is sufficiently low so as to not encourage indolence.'[29]

Thus, the administration was very concerned about individuals becoming dependent on the state, more concerned perhaps than with some of the reports coming in about the tough conditions in the region. In spite of adverse reports coming to Ottawa, the administrators clung to their position of maintaining a traditional way of life for Native people in the North.

As critics like Diamond Jenness pointed out, however, the forces of change already touched most communities in the North. The problem was not a question of remaining solely in the traditional culture. Life was changing in the region, and Natives and non-Natives were hit by the changes. Therefore, the government policy emphasizing and maintaining an old culture was unfair to Native people. Rather, critics argued, the government of Canada should provide the opportunity for Native people to go to school, for example, or to train themselves so that they could, *if they chose*, give up their traditional ways or combine the traditional ways with modern ways. Relief itself was not the only contentious issue. Most generally, at issue was the vision that administrative officials in Ottawa had for Native peoples, and it was a very limited vision for almost three decades after 1921.

Wildlife Regulation Policy

Harvesting wildlife was the backbone of the traditional way of life for Native people. Prior to 1800, they depended on rabbits, caribou, moose, fish, polar bear, muskoxen, walrus, seals, and whales. Between the 1780s and 1860s, fur harvesting was introduced in the western NWT; trapping provided furs which could be traded for commodities introduced by southern whites: coffee, tea, sugar, flour, utensils, guns, and ammunition. The boreal forest provided beaver, lynx, marten, and muskrat. Little was done in the region to control the supply of wildlife until 1916.[30] In 1916, an Advisory Board on Wildlife was established in Ottawa. The chairman of the board and administrative support came from the Parks Branch in the Department of the Interior. In 1922, responsibility for wildlife in the territories was transferred to the NWT and Yukon Branch, which, of course, was part of the Department of the Interior.

In effect, a two-track policy emerged as a way of attempting to conserve wildlife. Ordinances were established governing open and closed seasons, licensing, issuing permits for trading posts, and limiting harvests. Other provisions introduced were designed to control the use of poisons, types of traps, and the use of aircraft in the harvest. A second policy introduced game preserves and sanctuaries whereby hunting and trapping was restricted to Native people. By 1927, the following protected areas had been established (Table 9).[31]

TABLE 9
Protected wildlife areas, NWT

	Sq. miles
Slave River Preserve	2,200
Peel River Preserve (portion in NWT)	3,300
Yellowknife Preserve	70,000
Arctic Islands Preserve	332,320
Victoria Island Preserve (effective before this branch assumed control)	26,335
Wood Buffalo Park (area in NWT)	3,625
Thelon Game Sanctuary	15,000
Total	533,230

SOURCE: NWT Council Minutes, 6th Session, 28 December 1927, memorandum from O. Finnie to W.G. Cory

At the end of 1947, the area had increased to 917,194 square miles with additions coming from the Arctic Archipelago and the Mackenzie Mountains Preserve (69,440 sq. miles).[32] The Slave River area was intended to protect muskrats and the Peel River marten. Other areas were established principally to conserve muskox and caribou.

There were cross-cutting issues concerning wildlife in the Mackenzie Valley. On the one hand, Native people were encouraged to maintain their hunting and trapping, which required a constant supply of game. On the other hand, political pressures developed from non-Natives in the region to provide more access to game. Prospectors, for example, pressured for permission to trap and hunt. It appeared impossible for both groups to live off the supply of wildlife. The following is a report to the council from an official in the region: 'The supply of fur bearing animals today is insufficient for the needs of the resident population which necessitates distribution of relief by the Federal Government. Granting licenses to prospectors will greatly increase the privations of the natives and will also increase the Federal Relief Grant for destitute natives.'[33]

Duncan C. Scott of the Department of Indian Affairs, in a letter dated 16 February 1932, quotes one of his inspector's reports:

The hunting Indian of the North has gradually been forced to the wall by the competition of white trappers and their illegal methods of trapping. This was dealt with to some extent in my report for 1928, but I propose to state the case in extenso once more in the hope that some definite results may be achieved. Unless something can be accomplished along these lines there is little use of an Inspector from this department making a long and expensive annual or bi-annual visit.[34]

In addition, the bishops of both the Anglican and Roman Catholic churches were making appeals for more stringent ordinances to protect the wildlife.[34]

Two problems existed. Due to local political pressures from non-Natives, the NWT Council was reluctant to establish game preserves for the Dene in areas around white settlements such as Hay River or Fort Smith. And, with the departmental cutbacks in the early 1930s, there were not enough administrative people in the field to enforce ordinances that were on the books.[36] Further to this, Native people relying on furs to earn a little cash were victims of the price fluctuation on world fur markets (Figure 5). There was also the problem of price received from the Hudson's Bay Company, the principal buyer of furs with a virtual monopoly in the region.

Sovereignty Policy

Government formulation of northern policies on education, health care, relief, and wildlife did not provide the most exciting material for a public forum in Ottawa. However, when sovereignty was challenged in Canada's North, that issue was guaranteed to raise the blood pressure of politicians and the public.

For example, after whalers entered the Beaufort Sea in the late 1890s and early 1900s and began to winter on Herschel Island, the government established a police post (1903). In 1913, Vilhjahmur Stefansson was organizing an Arctic expedition, and once Canadian sponsorship of the expedition became an issue, the government backed his famous five year research and scientific inquiry. And the government supported Captain J.E. Bernier's excursions to Hudson Bay, Baffin Island, and the Arctic Archipelago. As Morris Zaslow puts it:

Thus the years after 1903 saw an increased surveillance being exercised over the activities of Americans and other whites in the Canadian Arctic in response to a growing demand for action on the part of the Canadian public, coupled with the greater capability of the Dominion government and its agencies to mount such operations, in part, using (and paying for) facilities provided by the objects of investigation them-

FIGURE 5
Average raw fur value, Canada, 1919-20 to 1964-5

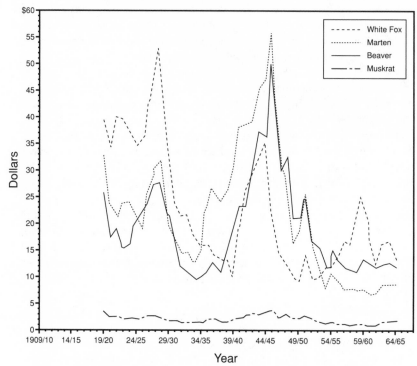

SOURCE: Peter Clancy, 'Game Policy in the Northwest Territories: The Shaping of Economic Position,' paper presented at the annual meeting of the Canadian Political Science Association, Vancouver, 6-8 June 1983

selves. Though their numbers were ridiculously small in view of the vast area they were intended to control, the mere presence of police and fisheries officers sufficed to demonstrate that the territory was under Canadian law, and to establish Canadian standards, even if they were honoured more in the breach than the observance.[37]

In the 1920s, the government began to establish a number of RCMP posts in the Arctic Archipelago in order to assert sovereignty. In 1922, posts were set up at Pond Inlet on Northern Baffin Island and Craig Harbour on Ellesmere Island. By 1930, Bache Peninsula had been established on Ellesmere Island, pushing the flag to approximately 79°N.

Much of this activity was spurred on by Otto Sverdrup's Norwegian expedition on Ellesmere Island from 1898 to 1902. Sverdrup's claim lingered even though the United Kingdom had given the islands to Canada in 1880. Threats also came from intrusions by the United States. In 1909, Robert Peary claimed to have reached the North Pole, and, by the 1920s, Captain Donald B. MacMillan led a number of expeditions to the region. One response was to maintain the Eastern Arctic Patrol in the area, which would establish new posts and supply those already 'showing the flag.' The cost of that patrol, initially, was approximately $100,000.[38]

During the Second World War, a number of projects were undertaken, which, in time, raised Canadian concerns about intrusions by the Americans. The Alaska Highway (1942), the Canol Pipeline Project from Norman Wells on the Mackenzie River to Whitehorse, Yukon (1942), and Project Crimson, building airfields across the North to support ferry operations for fighters and transports, all involved large American investments and deployment of troops and material.[39] The concern during the war was that the Americans often saw Canadian territory in the same way they saw their own, and sovereignty was not always respected.[40] In any event, Canada received the Alaska Highway as a gift, but paid $9,342,208 for its accompanying telephone and tele-type system.[41] There was no effort made by the Canadian government to buy the Canol pipeline, but Imperial Oil purchased the refinery at Whitehorse. The airfields were also purchased, at a cost of $76,811,551, to build up part of an infrastructure which would be useful in future development of the region.[42] These figures diminish greatly the few million dollars the northern administration was spending on the NWT.

After the war, when northern Canadian territory became strategically involved in the Cold War, there were again problems with an American presence in the region. The management of weather stations and operation of the Distant Early Warning (DEW) Line raised serious concerns about Canadian sovereignty. Hugh Keenleyside, deputy minister of Mines and Resources and commissioner of the NWT (1947-50) wanted to strengthen the NWT Council and its role in the region as one way of coping with potential problems.[43]

In January 1948, the Advisory Committee on Northern Development (ACND) was formed, apparently through the effort of Keenleyside and Arnold Heeney, clerk of the Privy Council. Thus, just as Oscar Finnie had done thirty years earlier, when problems reflected sovereignty issues, the base of decisionmakers was broadened.

The ACND was established to advise the government of Canada and to co-ordinate northern policies. Its membership included Keenleyside and Heeney, the deputy minister of transport, the undersecretary of state for External Affairs, chief of the Military General Staff,

chief of Air Staff, Canadian chairman of the Permanent Joint Board
on Defense, and chairman of the Defence Research Board.[44] The committee secretariat was located in the Privy Council Office and Heeney
was the link to Cabinet. The committee met five times up to 1 December 1949 and then remained inactive until its revival in February 1953.[45]
    Policies on sovereignty were handled very differently than were
other northern policies. Due to the high degree of emotion the issues
could generate, decisionmaking often involved more than the small
circle of officials involved in northern administration. Also, on
sovereignty issues there always seemed to be a way to find the necessary resources to deal with the problem.

NORTHERN POLICY AND ADMINISTRATION IN THE NWT

From 1920 to the latter 1940s, most northern policy was formulated
by the commissioner and Territorial Council. These policies were administered by individuals in the Department of the Interior or the
Department of Mines and Resources. Policies on education, health
care, welfare, and wildlife were made with little interference from
elected officials. When sovereignty was concerned, higher-ranking
administrators and politicians usually became involved in the policy
process.
    The Department of the Interior and, later, the Department of Mines
and Resources, provided resources to the churches, trading companies, or the RCMP, who, in turn, conducted most administrative duties.
Schools were provided where church missions existed. Health care
was available in hospitals at mission sites or mining towns. Relief rations were administered, sparingly, if one in need happened to be
close to a mission, trading post, or RCMP detachment. But many Natives in remote areas did get into trouble and frequently were confronted with starvation, even down to the mid-1950s.[46]
    Obviously there is more than one interpretation of the success or
failure of these policies.[47] In reading the annual reports of the departments, there is always a sense of optimism; development is just around
the corner, and conditions for Native people were improving. A clear
manifestation of this view can be seen in Roy Gibson's remarks to the
council just before his retirement in 1950. The minutes of the meeting
record Gibson reflecting on his twenty-nine years on the NWT Council.

    The Government of the Northwest Territories embraces about all the
    activities of a provincial government. No attempt has been made to set
    up various sub-divisions such as the provincial ministries to handle the
    affairs of the Northwest Territories Council as Council preferred to con-

sult existing government agencies which were able to give advice to all features of government. In his long experience he has yet to meet an official who did not willingly put to one side whatever he might have been doing in order to give immediate advice on the problems of the Northwest Territories. Consequently, it has been possible to bring to bear on the government of the Territories the most enlightened thought available of the technical administrative officers of the Government and of scientists who went out to explore or kept abreast of developments elsewhere in the world. While the limitations of the budget and the fact that it was not possible at times to get the type of staff needed, delayed progress of certain features which Council has studied, the fact remains that by wise and enlightened administration which has been reported to the world, the Minister has been able to justify Canada's position as custodian of a vast area which is sparsely inhabited at a time in the world's development when many other areas of the world are terribly overcrowded. It has been possible to tell people about the Territories and the development of mineral wealth of which there is an abundance there. It is probable that Council has not taken sufficient pride in what has been accomplished; now is a good time to think of it. He felt that the members of the Northwest Territories Council who have gathered together to review conditions regularly over the years and to bring to the attention of the ministry those features which required legislative or administrative action on a higher plane, have made a worthwhile contribution to this country's welfare and development and while there may, at times, have been evidence of a certain amount of dissatisfaction which usually accompanies a government at long range, at no time has anyone questioned the desire of the Administration to give to that vast territory the best government that could be given to it. This Council gathered information from every reliable source and gave full credit to those people who made the contribution.[48]

There is a certain amount of self-adulation in these remarks. It is not, however, different from the way a lot of people involved in decision-making at the time viewed their actions: 'we did well with what we had.'[49]

There is another side to the story. The council and administration had their own agenda for the North, and that agenda persisted for a remarkably long period of time. Ottawa administrators ran a third of the landmass of Canada as though it were their own feifdom. While they pushed the development of resources of the region as rapidly as possible, at the same time, they tried to keep Native people essentially living a traditional way of life. It was almost as if they established two worlds – the world of resource development and the world of the Native people – and rarely did these two worlds meet.

Moreover, the administrators fought anything that threatened the process by which they ran their domain. For example, in 1932, there was a petition to the minister of the Interior to change the administration of the region. The suggestion was that the commissioner reside in the territories, that the council be made up of half elected and half appointed members, that the commissioner be chairman of the council, and councillors be paid a nominal fee for their service. The council rejected the suggestion.

> Dr. Camsell expressed the opinion that the seat of Government for the Northwest Territories was more satisfactorily located at Ottawa than would be the case at Fort Smith ...
>
> Mr. Rowatt said that in the Yukon Territory the *appointive system* of Territorial Government had been more satisfactory and economical than the elective method [italics added].[50]

After discussion, the council recommended 'that the present administration, which appears adequate and most economical, be not changed.'[51] Costs and convenience were cited as reasons. There was no discussion of the merits of representation of interests or responsible government.

The thinking of the council is revealed on another occasion. At the forty-second session of the council (1933), it was noted that an RCMP corporal had reported consumption of wood alcohol by some Native people. This report was picked up and made the subject of a story in the *Ottawa Citizen*. It was noted that when 'these extracts got into the hands of a newspaper man they were made more sensational and were not accurately interpreted.' In the end, General MacBrien, commissioner of the RCMP and member of the council, said that he would instruct his men 'that nothing be included in any of their reports that might be construed as a criticism of the administration. Council felt that this would be adequate.'[52]

Other views on Roy Gibson and the council confirm this rather narrow view of administration. Shelagh Grant, in *Sovereignty and Security*, interviewed a number of people who had worked with Gibson. She suggests that Gibson 'was a hardworking, dedicated bureaucrat, but one who resented any interference or criticism from outsiders.'[53] She goes on to say he distrusted anyone who might 'upset his procedures and power.' And at one time he was heard to remark 'we don't want any goddamm scientists in our Arctic.'[54] An employee of northern services is quoted: '[Gibson] was a dictator and an autocrat, the

North was his kingdom and he ruled it.'[55] An Anglican priest in the Mackenzie Valley in the 1930s also used the word 'Tsar' to describe the way many people saw Gibson at the time,[56] and an individual who joined the northern administration in the late 1940s said that at the time morale was low and employees resented not being able to travel to the North to gain knowledge about problems in the region.[57] Thus, there was the council's own view of its efficient administrative process, but there were also perceptions by NWT residents that the territorial government was a heavy-handed, insensitive bureaucratic process.

CONCLUSION

Political development in the present Northwest Territories began in 1905 when the federal government assumed responsibility under an amended NWT Act. Actual administration began in 1921 (after the discovery of oil on the Mackenzie River), and the administrative pattern established then lasted for almost thirty years. Government was administered by a small group of senior administrators in Ottawa, concerned principally with the development of non-renewable resources in the region. Within budgetary guidelines, the administration had a relatively free hand to set the administrative agenda for the territories.

The period from 1921 to 1950 has often been described as the period of 'benign neglect' for the North. While neglect may be one way to characterize the record, doing so misrepresents a great deal of what was going on in the administration of the North. Indeed, there was a dynamic process taking place within the bureaucracy. Officials responsible for northern administration had an agenda and established deliberate policies to further that agenda.

There was controversy over interpretations of the consequences of this agenda. Nevertheless, northern administrators were able to set and stick to it for two reasons. First, there was little pressure for change from individuals in the North. The number of whites were few and most were transient and not vociferous about conditions, and Native people were not yet organized as a political force. Second, the only political forces in the region were the churches and the trading companies, usually the Hudson's Bay Company. Church bishops did occasionally protest to the council about the conditions of Native people or lobby for more support for hospitals and schools. Usually council responded. But the primary work of the churches was saving souls, not radically transforming the school curriculum. The trading companies were satisfied as long as Native people supplied the labour for trapping furs. And they were against any policies which would transform the lives of Native people.

In sum, there was little pressure for the council to do anything to change substantially the way of life of Native peoples. Even though there was no concerted effort to alter the lives of Native people, things like education and health policies did begin to have an impact. In the final analysis, northern administrators could stick to their agenda because there was little pressure from politicians or the southern public to change things in the North. With the exception of sovereignty issues, most Canadians were not stirred by issues in the North. In short, the North was in the backwater of Canadian politics. Administrators could run their bureaucratic feifdom as they chose, adjusting occasionally to the forces of the churches or trading companies. Change, however, did begin to occur in the late 1940s and early 1950s, and that change would end an era in which policies in the North were shaped by the vision of a few administrators in Ottawa.

CHAPTER FOUR

Changing Policies, Not the Process: The Colonial Legacy, 1950-67

The early 1950s marked a turning point for federal government policy in the NWT. One fundamental assumption which dominated the policy process for almost thirty years – that Native people should continue to live a traditional lifestyle – finally gave way under a barrage of criticism. Government policies were altered accordingly. All governments during the 1950s and 1960s made an explicit commitment to development of the North: those of St. Laurent (1948-57), Diefenbaker (1957-63), and Pearson (1963-8). During these years the agenda for the northern affairs program continued to be controlled by the relevant department – Resources and Development (1950-3) or Northern Affairs and National Resources (1953-66).

At the same time, however, political pressures on the department were increasing due to a greater sensitivity to northern issues. Prime ministers, cabinet officials, and party leaders were becoming sensitive not only to the issue of sovereignty but also to the socio-economic conditions of Aboriginal peoples. These issues called for a more extensive policy response.

At least three major reasons explain policy changes in the North.[1] First, during the Second World War and the early years of the Cold War, the Canadian government had little presence in the region. Since the 1930s, little money had been spent by the federal government on research or on training experienced personnel with knowledge about the North to support northern defence projects. Therefore, to have some degree of independence from the overwhelming American influence, and to maintain some degree of sovereignty on Canadian territory, there had to be greater government involvement in the North. Second, criticism of Canadian policy toward Native people had become very sharp. During the war years some United States military officials were critical of government Native policy. Often this criticism was reported in New York and Washington newspapers and returned to embarrass officials in Ottawa. Farley Mowat, writing in the early 1950s, got even wider circulation. Past government policies were claimed to be shameful and comparisons were made with the more enlightened treatment of Native people in Alaska and Greenland.

Third, Canada was beginning to play the middle power broker within United Nations organizations. This role often led to our government's criticism of colonial systems such as those in Africa. It was embarrassing indeed to have foreign critics come back with arguments about the treatment of Native people in Canada, particularly in the North. These reasons provided the rationale for establishing new goals in the North and an array of new policies to achieve the goals.

An ideological change, too, was behind the policy response in the North. Many individuals who came into government service after the Second World War began to dominate the policy scene. Their ideas and experiences were different from those whose experiences had been shaped by the Depression. Many were interventionist, believing in a reformist liberal ideology. This new, interventionist perspective was rooted in both the Depression and the war years. Advocates argued that state intervention could provide solutions to social and economic problems.[2] In effect, this was the beginning of 'colonialism' in the North. If, by colonialism, one means state control through a bureaucratic apparatus on the ground, the 1950s represent the period when it started. Certainly one could hardly call the 1920-50 period 'colonial.' It had been more government by default than government in the sense of running a colony.[3]

Two fundamental goals emerged from the Department of Northern Affairs and National Resources which influenced the nature of new public policies. Economic development took on a new emphasis. Traditionally, economic development of natural resources had been an objective of departments responsible for northern affairs. The new emphasis, however, stressed tying this development of resources to the wage economy as it applied to Native people. This was a significant change, because it recognized that Native people should have an opportunity for a choice of lifestyles. Prior to the 1950s, the traditional way of life was the only choice for most Native people. The wage economy was available only to the few Natives working for the trading companies, the churches, the RCMP, or on special projects like the DEW Line. When Native people *did* obtain jobs for which wages were paid, usually the work involved menial tasks. Most Natives did not have the educational qualifications for equal opportunities in the work force. A second goal was to provide northern residents with government services equivalent to, or nearly equivalent to, those services enjoyed by most Canadians. In sum, northerners began to benefit from the universality of federal social programs: family allowances, old age pensions, health care, and special northern policies in education, housing, and economic development.

The scope of the new policies were outlined in Prime Minister St. Laurent's speech on the floor of the House of Commons on 8 December 1953. He announced that the North had been administered 'in an almost continuing state of absence of mind.'[4] He explained how the North, from now on, would be given priority in terms of government policy. For example: the name Department of Resources and Development would be expanded to Department of Northern Affairs and National Resources (the first time northern affairs had been included in a department title); new and greater 'emphasis and scope to work' would occur in northern policies; care would be taken to maintain sovereignty of the Canadian north; and efforts would be made to improve economic and political development in the NWT. Furthermore, he said that the government should become more active in an area of Canada growing in strategic importance, doing what could be done 'to integrate the Native Eskimo population into the development, and probably the administration also.' The speech indicated that times had changed for government policies in the North. While the fortunes of northerners did not experience a sudden change, after a time policy changes did have an impact on the lives of Native people in the region.

ADMINISTRATIVE CHANGES

From 1953 to the early 1960s, departmental structural changes also occurred. Under government reorganization in 1950, the Indian Affairs Branch was moved to the Department of Citizenship and Immigration, again separating Indian and Northern Affairs. In the organizational chart for the new Department of Northern Affairs and National Resources (1953) the place of northern administration did not change. It remained a part of the Northern Administration and Lands Branch, one of six units in the department (Figure 6). In 1963-4, the Northern Administration Branch gained equal status with National Resources and acquired its own assistant deputy minister (Figure 7). In 1965, Indian Affairs responsibilities were returned to the Department of Northern Affairs and National Resources. In 1966, another major governmental reorganization created the Department of Indian Affairs and Northern Development (DIAND). The new department would be responsible for Indian Affairs across Canada, including the North, and for northern affairs, including economic development.

FIGURE 6: Organizational chart, Department of Northern Affairs and National Resources, 1953-4

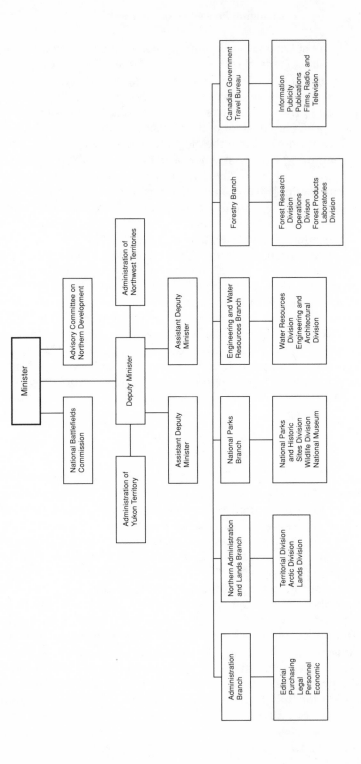

SOURCE: Department of Northern Affairs and National Resources, *Annual Report*, 1953-4

FIGURE 7: Organizational chart, Department of Northern Affairs and National Resources, 1963-4

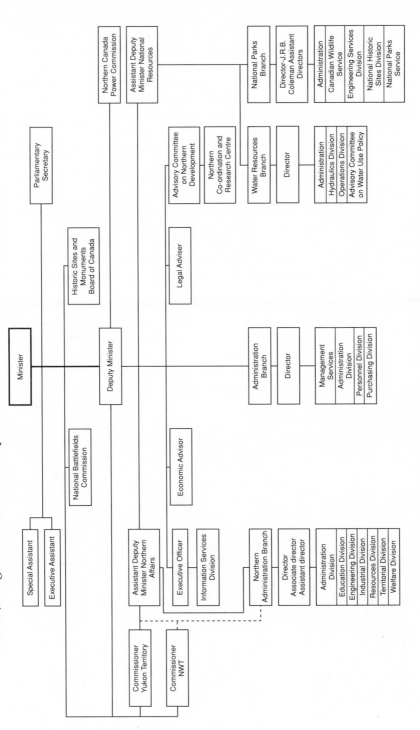

SOURCE: Department of Northern Affairs and National Resources, *Annual Report*, 1963-4

After Indian Affairs was transferred to Citizenship and Immigration, its budget for the NWT was $420,895 in 1953, and, under DIAND, grew to $1,392,132.49 in 1966 – approximately a threefold increase. These figures included costs for Indian agencies, social programs, economic development, community employment, and statutory Indian annunities.

Within the Department of Northern Affairs and National Resources, the Northern Affairs Branch budget grew from $2,837,307.36 in 1953 to $34,296,872.43 in 1966 – almost a twelvefold increase (Table 10). Northern affairs were beginning to get some priority within the department. For example, in 1954, northern administration was spending about 14 per cent of the department's budget. By 1964-5, prior to the transfer of Indian Affairs, it was spending approximately 44 per cent of the department's budget. In 1966, $10 million went to education and $4 million to welfare and maintenance payments for individuals in industrial homes for the aged. Moreover, in 1959, departmental funds were supplemented. For example, under Diefenbaker's government, $1,750,732.77 was expended on 'Roads to Resources.' These funds were used to link the Alberta and territorial road systems. Construction was undertaken from the Alberta border to Yellowknife, Hay River, Fort Simpson, and Fort Smith. This road would be the connecting link for developing Cominco's lead and zinc deposits at the Pine Point mine. Funding was increased to $8,999,995 and $12,000,000, respectively, for 1960 and 1961.

TABLE 10
Administrative expenditures in the NWT, 1953-66

Year	GNWT	Northern Affairs and National Resources/Northern Administration Branch	Citizenship and Immigration/Indian Affairs Branch
1953		$ 2,837,307.36*	$ 420,895.00
1954	$ 607,705.47	2,925,742.57*	358,893.00
1955	1,334,771.48	3,509,964.00*	414,671.00
1956	1,368,053.31	5,966,828.40*	305,873.00
1957	1,797,890.35	8,943,406.72	259,657.00
1958	2,654,792.00	15,756,928.73	284,919.00
1959	2,992,946.00	20,504,150.43	477,505.00
1960	2,746,840.25	23,350,632.92	530,948.25
1961	3,672,078.68	14,048,165.22†	579,217.00
1962	4,535,131.96	23,821,630.00†	695,297.99

(continued on next page)

TABLE 10 (continued)

Year	GNWT	Northern Affairs and National Resources/Northern Administration Branch	Citizenship and Immigration/Indian Affairs Branch
1963	$6,372,420.00	$26,533,975.00†	$ 822,900.55
1964	6,775,128.00	27,862,519.38†	721,126.48
1965	7,486,928.00	28,635,332.91†	847,562.45
1966	10,306,599.79	34,296,872.43†	1,392,132.49‡

SOURCES: *Annual Report*, Department of Citizenship and Immigration, Indian Affairs Branch, 1953-65; *Annual Report*, Department of Northern Affairs and National Resources, Northern Administrative Branch, 1954-66; *Annual Report*, Department of Northern Affairs and National Resources, 'Annual Report of the Commissioner of the Northwest Territories,' 1953-9; *Annual Report of the Commissioner of the Northwest Territories*, 1960-6 (published separately after 1959)

* Northern Administration Division figures include the NWT and the Yukon, 1953-6.
† NWT figures under the Northern Administration Branch include education and welfare and industrial expenditures for the NWT and Yukon.
‡ The Indian Affairs Branch was moved to Northern Affairs and National Resources in 1965, and the 1966 figure is an expenditure listed in that department.

The largest gains in northern expenditures, however, went to the GNWT. Between 1953 and 1966, its budget increased seventeen times. This growth indicated program expansion within the territorial government. The revenue side of the budget also began to increase. By 1965-6, for example, it was $8,235,154.00 (Table 11). Of this amount, 36 per cent was raised in the NWT, most of which came from liquor sales. With greater revenue, public spending could increase, and, of course, this meant the expansion of functions of the GNWT. In fact, as Table 11 indicates, expenditures of the NWT began to look like those of a provincial government.

At the same time, by 1965, there was also a growing sense of alienation and autonomy on the part of the GNWT. In 1963, Gordon Robertson, the deputy minister and commissioner since 1953, became secretary to the Cabinet under the new Liberal government. The minister, Arthur Laing, departed from tradition and, rather than making the deputy minister also the commissioner of the NWT, separated the two posts. Ben G. Sivertz, who had been executive assistant to Hugh Keenleyside, chief of the Arctic Division in the Northern Administration and director of Northern Administration, was named commissioner. E.A. Côté, who had been assistant deputy minister, was made deputy minister of the department. Within three years,

TABLE 11
Operation and capital revenues and expenditures of the GNWT, 1965-6

Million dollars	Source	Million dollars	Application	Million dollars
OPERATING ACCOUNT:				
10	Tax revenues	$1,145,214.41	Legislative costs	$ 65,622.09 — 10
	Services provided	27,534.07	Administration	102,002.78
9	Liquor revenues	2,719,478.02	Health	625,464.57 — 9
	Grants (federal)	2,556,556.00	Hospital services	1,553,158.25
8	Recoveries – shared	1,765,019.32	Education	1,845,746.33 — 8
			Welfare	535,134.30
7	Cost-shared programs		Development services	160,077.48 — 7
	Compensation assessments	21,352.20	Municipal affairs	209,774.95
6	Co-operative development		Liquor costs	1,369,446.68 — 6
			Police and justice	743,285.48
5			Tourist promotion	72,996.09 — 5
			Fitness & amateur sport	65,433.19
4			Library services	7,497.63 — 4
			Game management	70,992.02
3				— 3
2			Administration of workers' comp.	29,778.70 — 2
			Co-operative dev't	93,684.84
1			Others	26,564.88 — 1
	Total	$8,235,154.02	**Total**	$7,576,660.26

CAPITAL ACCOUNT:

Loans from federal government	$2,642,000.00	School construction and facilities	$ 943,150.67	
Recoveries – shared	72,861.00	Hospital and nursing station construction	685,437.98	3
3		Roads, sidewalks, street lights	99,219.18	
Cost-shared projects				
Campsites	13,298.08	Fire protection	43,519.87	2
2 Community centres	13,387.08	Water & sewer systems	84,077.79	
Water and sewer service	—	Grants for community centres	29,085.98	
Fire fighting equipment	—	Loans to municipalities	185,500.00	
Vocational training	—	Winter works	172,731.13	1
1 Winter works	584.50	Hay River water & sewer	406,328.97	
		Other small projects	80,887,.96	
Total	$2,742,130.66	**Total**	$2,729,939.53	

SOURCE: *1965-6 Annual Report of the Commissioner of the Northwest Territories* (Ottawa: Queen's Printer 1966), 22-3

there was a growing rift between departmental administration and the GNWT. The break came in 1967, with the move of the commissioner and his staff to the new seat of government in Yellowknife.

Another factor which may have contributed to a sense of autonomy on the part of the GNWT was the changing nature of the membership of the council of the Northwest Territories. In 1947, for the first time, an individual outside the bureaucracy in Ottawa was appointed to the council. J.G. McNiven, a mine manager in Yellowknife, was appointed one of five members of the Territorial Council. In 1951, the NWT Act was amended to include eight council members, three of whom would be elected. Finally a response was made to long-time objections by non-Native NWT residents that they had been denied a fundamental principle of democracy – representation. Three constituencies were created in the Mackenzie Valley, and, in 1954, the act was amended again to include a fourth elected member (Table 12).

TABLE 12
General elections: council of the NWT 1951-64

Year*	Appointed members	Elected members		Total votes†	Per cent of electors voting	Constituency
1951	5	3		2,816	57.5	(3) Mackenzie Valley
1954	5	4	(1)‡	2,767	63.3	(4) Mackenzie Valley
1957	5	4	(2)	1,513	60.9	(4) Mackenzie Valley
1960	4	4	(2)	1,470	52.7	(4) Mackenzie Valley
1964	4	4		4,522	65.5	(4) Mackenzie Valley

SOURCES: Government of Canada, 'Report of the Chief Electoral Officer on the General Election of Members to The Council of the Northwest Territories,' respective years, Ottawa
* By-elections not included
† Includes rejected ballots
‡ Number of members elected by acclamation

The changes in the nature of the council of the NWT were a step toward representative government, but they were not necessarily democratic changes. The constituencies, for example, were in the Mackenzie Valley, where most non-Natives resided. If this change represented a move toward democracy, it was not a democracy for Aboriginal peoples. Indeed, Indians were barred from voting prior to 1960. In subsequent elections, however, they did become participants in the electoral process. Barriers prohibiting Inuit voting were removed in 1954, but no constituencies existed in the Central or Eastern Arctic, the home of most Inuit. It was not until the 1966 by-elections that the

Inuit gained territorial representation.

After elections for council members, many people anticipated that divisions on the council would take place along elected and non-elected lines. According to Louie C. Audette, this was not the case. He pointed out that in his years on the council (1947-59), members often divided on issues but never did it come to a fight between elected and non-elected members.[5] This phenomenon can probably be explained by the fact that during this period policies did change (at least after 1953), and most non-Natives in the region, who were also the voters, agreed with the initiatives.

Initially at least, elections did not make a great deal of difference in the outcome of legislative policies of the council. But these elections did reinforce the perception by non-Natives in the Mackenzie Valley that they now had a voice in Ottawa. The gradual transition to an elected assembly was a first step toward representative and responsible government for the GNWT.

POLICY CHANGES

The fundamental change in goals by the northern administration affected a number of northern policies. People in the administration began to talk of the 'broader needs' of Native people – immediate needs such as 'health, education, and a social economy.' These needs were not to be considered separate problems: 'Each is related to the other. It is not enough to cure disease, the cause of disease must be removed; this is largely a matter of education, and the improvement of economic conditions. Education must be provided, but this depends on good health and the needs and opportunities of the economy.'[6] Thus, officials in the department changed the northern agenda to include an inter-related set of social policies that would transform life in the NWT.

Education

Once the commitment was made to help Native people participate in a wage economy, much more emphasis was placed on the nature of the school system in the NWT. As previously mentioned, Commissioner Keenleyside initiated a policy of greater departmental influence in the education system. After 1953, education policies became the flagship for the department and the government of the Northwest Territories. By 1955, the federal government had launched an 'extensive program' of school and hostel construction: 'In reaching this decision the Federal Government had taken into account the steady increase in the Indian and Eskimo population of the North and the general decline in fur prices which has made it increasingly difficult for the native population to continue to rely entirely on the wildlife resources of the country. Other employment and sources of income must be found and this has made the need for education more important than ever.[7] By the end of Ben Sivertz's term as commissioner in 1967, he was comparing school facilities in the North with the best of those in the South.[8] Also, the target was to make schools available to all northern children by 1970.[9]

Achieving that goal would be no easy task. In 1954, for example, responsibility for education in the NWT remained fragmented. The Department of Citizenship and Immigration's Indian Affairs Branch was responsible for educating Indian children. Inuit, Métis, and other children were the responsibility of the Northern Administration and Lands Branch and the GNWT. At the same time, the churches were delivering part of the program through their mission schools.

Consolidation of school systems began in 1955. Responsibility for the education of 'Indian' children was transferred to the Northern Administration and Lands Branch of the DNANR. Government policy emerged with two objectives: school construction and vocational training. Extensive construction was necessary to be able to provide schooling in all northern communities. Vocational training was necessary to provide the skills necessary for wage employment.

The construction phase, initiated in 1955, originally was to focus on the Mackenzie Valley and was to take six years to complete.[10] Eventually, it included Arctic communities and the target was extended to 1970. Between 1955 and 1965, the number of federal schools in communities increased from ten to fifty-one at a cost of $30 million. Enrolments increased from 2,018 to 6,033.[11] In the same period, vocational schools were created in Sir John Franklin School in Yellowknife and in the Churchill Vocational Centre. Included were programs such as motor vehicle repairs, heavy duty equipment operator, or hairdressing. By 1966, a total of 759 Native people had been or were participating in vocational training.[12]

While many of these figures were positive, there remained a fundamental problem. Most Native students were not getting past the fifth or sixth grade. As illustrated in Figure 8, very few Native students graduated from secondary schools. This posed a particular problem, because it often limited their ability to participate in training programs requiring a high school diploma.

While the number of schools constructed was impressive, the school record for Native children was dismal. In fairness to the department, it was recognized that curriculum changes had to be made. The

FIGURE 8

Distribution of pupils by grade and ethnic origin, NWT schools,
January 1965 (vocational pupils not included)

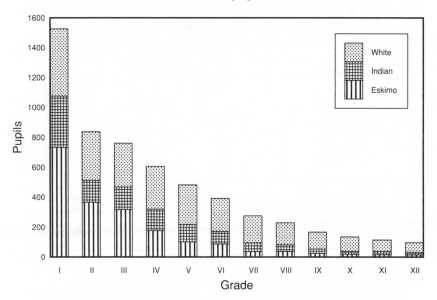

SOURCE: Department of Northern Affairs and National Resources, 'The Northwest Territories Today,' reference paper for the Advisory Commission on the Development of Government in the Northwest Territories, 1965, 70

curriculum adopted in the North was similar to the curriculum used in the province of Alberta. Obviously, it had to be modified for northern schools. Work was started in 1954.[13] By 1963, it was admitted that 'development and implementation of a unique curriculum for northern schools is necessarily a slow and painstaking process.'[14]

There were many views on the reasons for such a poor record with respect to Native children completing the school program. This was a more difficult problem than school construction, and, even after the transfer of education responsibilities to the new GNWT in 1969-70, causes for the problems were still being debated. And, as indicated in Chapter 6, they are still being debated.

Housing, Health Care, and Community Development

Policy changes were initiated in the areas of housing, health care, and community development. These changes ultimately led to the development of small northern communities as they exist today – communities of a few hundred to a few thousand residents. But small communities in the early 1950s were very different; they included a trading post, a church mission, perhaps an RCMP post, and, occasionally, a school, nursing station, or wireless station. There were a few frame houses for employees. Most Native people at the time were seasonally nomadic, usually camping around the communities to trade. A few Native employees were permanent residents of the communities, often living in sub-standard housing. With the development of schools and other services, a change in living patterns began to occur. There was a 'drift from the land to the towns but the social consequences of this movement are much more sharply defined in the small northern communities. In many communities neither housing nor employment is available for these newcomers, who usually have limited education and few employable skills. These circumstances make government assistance in providing housing, sanitary services, training and employment essential.'[15]

Native people began to move into communities for a variety of reasons but, primarily, to provide education for their children. Often they constructed shelters from any materials that could be scrounged, and living conditions were often wretched. Circumstances in Coppermine in 1963 were described as follows:

During the winter of 1963 there were 52 houses in Coppermine, of which 48 were occupied. These 48 houses were occupied by a total of 59 families comprising 261 individuals. The 52 houses are broken down in the following manner:

Frame	9
Wood	4
Scrap	39

Four of the frame houses are Government owned and occupied by Government employees, two are Government welfare houses, the remainder are houses supplied by private agencies within the settlement, for their employees.

Three of the houses are constructed of plywood, and the other of boards and shingles. These are homemade houses and do not have any insulation.

The scrap houses are constructed of a wood frame, generally of wood from packing cases, with canvas on the outside (the outside covering varies from canvas to sheet metal, cardboard or skins). The insides of these houses are generally floored, although in several cases they are not, and the material most generally used is the lumber from surplus packing cases. Insulation is generally lacking, although in one or two cases cardboard or moss is being used.

None of the wood and scrap houses have chemical toilets or electricity.

The sanitation problems caused by this are only accentuated by the fantastic overcrowding that exists ...

[T]he average number of square feet per person in the frame houses, is 87.0; in the homemade houses the average is only 23.3 square feet per person ...

Due to the limitations of the building material, used walls must be frequently patched and buttressed, and even when banked with snow during the winter cannot keep out the wind and extreme cold. In the spring the melting snow turns the canvas and cardboard outer walls into a soggy sodden mass, and the interiors become damp and inordinately cold. The size of the houses alone precludes any effort to maintain a minimum standard of cleanliness and the lack of sanitary facilities add to create an environment that by any standard must be intolerable.[16]

Conditions in Eskimo Point in 1963 were no better.

In the course of a recent medical survey, the responsible medical officer described living conditions at Eskimo Point as 'probably the worst in Canada' ...

During the medical survey, a detailed examination was made of the 64 Eskimo houses in the community. Of this number, 24 were condemned outright and another 20 described as 'hopeless,' i.e., presently unsuitable and beyond repair. The present urgent housing requirements are thus 44 homes.[17]

In report after report by the Northern Health Services of the Department of National Health and Welfare, living conditions were directly related to health conditions, especially respiratory diseases. In a memo, Dr. P.E. Moore, director of Medical Services, to the director of the Northern Administration Branch in April 1964, wrote:

During the preparation of our 1963 Annual Report for the Council of the Northwest Territories, the following facts emerged –

The Eskimo birth rate is 57 per 1000 population which is more than twice the national rate, and the natural increase among Eskimos is 4% per annum.

The Eskimo infant mortality rate is 155 or 6 times the national rate – this is the lowest recorded in recent years.

Over 50% of diagnosed Eskimo infant deaths are due to pneumonia. No doubt many infant deaths recorded as 'unknown causes' are also due to this disease.

Respiratory disease accounted for 44% of all diseases treated at nursing stations and for 27% of all hospital days. Separate figures are not available for the Eskimo population, but it is estimated that over 50% of Eskimo hospitalization is due to respiratory disease.

The incidence of tuberculosis among Eskimos has been increasing steadily over the last four years and in 1963 2.1% of the Eskimo population were evacuated as new active cases.

Most of the diseases causing high mortality and morbidity rates in the Territories are due to a great extent to the unsatisfactory living conditions of the people, especially inadequate housing, and poor sanitation. There has always been a very close association between the incidence of tuberculosis, infant mortality rates and housing standards, and a decrease in the incidence of tuberculosis has usually followed improved housing standards rather than improved treatment facilities. A decrease in mortality may be expected following improved treatment and the attached graph shows that the Inuit mortality from this disease is decreasing even though the incidence is rising.[18]

The problem was real, but the response was slow and inadequate. In 1958, approximately 100 houses were being built each year. But as Health and Welfare Canada pointed out, the slowness of the program was not good economics. For example, in an outbreak of tuberculosis in Eskimo Point in 1962, about ninety men, women, and children were evacuated to Manitoba. The cost of maintaining this type of program was used as a rationale for expanding the housing program.

Northern Health Services has estimated that it will cost about $500,000 to provide hospital treatment alone for the 90 or more T.B. patients recently evacuated from that community. If one were to add to this loss of income and the very heavy welfare expenditures of caring for dependents now and convalescents later, the total costs would indeed be formidable. This takes no account of the immeasurable cost in terms of human suffering. What is of even greater concern is the defensible suggestion by Health and Welfare that the situation might have been avoided altogether had only a portion of this money been diverted to housing at an earlier date.[19]

The average price of northern houses at the time was $2,400 FOB Montreal. Therefore, for less than half the hospital costs, ninety houses could have been purchased for Eskimo Point. Clearly, medical costs to the government were a factor in developing a housing policy.

By 1959, some semblance of a housing program within the department was under way for Inuit families. The Indian Affairs Branch of

Citizenship and Immigration was responsible for 'Indian' housing. Loans were available under the National Housing Act, administered through the Central Mortgage and Housing Corporation. These loans could be supplemented by second mortgages made available through the GNWT. Most northerners, however, could not afford the loan payments. By 1965, about seven loans had been administered.[20]

Many northerners who benefitted from government housing participated in the low cost houses provided by the department. Initially, a basic house, 288 square feet, was supplied for about $7,000. By 1965, the basic house was increased to 384 square feet. The government provided a $1,000 subsidy and the balance could be paid by labour of the buyer, a loan, or cash. By 1965, about 800 of these houses had been constructed, but an additional 1,500 were needed.[21]

For many families it remained very difficult to purchase houses. Therefore, in 1965 a Northern Rental Housing Program was developed. By 1971, 1,378 houses had been built under this program.[22] In 1965, for example, 230 low cost, rental houses were delivered for 1966 construction – 30 one-bedroom, 30 three-bedroom, and 170 one-room houses.[23]

The housing program was a significant development for northerners. Not only did it provide better permanent shelter, but it also meant the establishment of permanent residence in communities. And with permanent communities, greater services could be provided. With improvements in health services and housing, health conditions did begin to improve. As can be seen in Figures 9 and 10, infant mortality showed a decline, as did the number of new cases of tuberculosis. It seems ironic that as health problems began to decline with the construction of permanent communities, a host of social problems were encountered.

ECONOMIC DEVELOPMENT POLICIES

The new emphasis on economic development was initiated to broaden the base of the economy for Native people. It grew out of a realization of the economic dilemma they faced. The following statement about the conditions experienced by the Inuit illustrates the point.

[The Native] population has been growing, increasing the pressure on decreasing or stationary resources of game and fur-bearing animals. Hunting, trapping and fishing still continue to provide the means of livelihood for the greater number of the native people. Of these occupations, only trapping provides them with cash income. Fur trapping during the past few years has been a depressed industry because world prices have fallen seriously. Catches of some animals have gone down, and this has aggravated the difficulties of the native people.[24]

Whose North?

FIGURE 9

Infant mortality rate, NWT, 1955-67

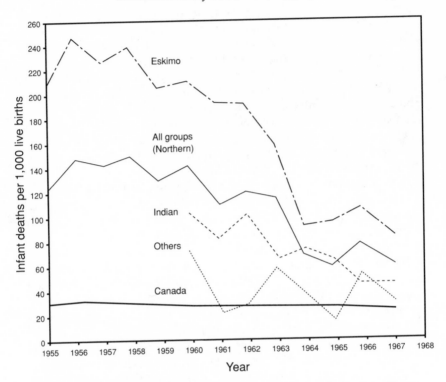

SOURCE: Department of National Health and Welfare, Northern Health Services, 'Report on Health Conditions in the Northwest Territories, 1967,' 15

With declining fur prices and wildlife numbers and increasing costs for Native people, new policies were called for – all designed to get Native people into the wage economy.

As the opportunities for employment in the industries of the north and in defence establishments become more widespread and as educated and trained young people become available, those Eskimos and Indians who wish to enter wage employment should be able to do so in skilled and semi-skilled trades. It will not be good enough for them to remain as untrained and largely uneducated labour engaged in the more menial tasks. These native Canadians will with training be able to develop their abilities and to make their full contribution to the nation's growth and

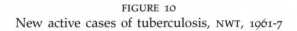

FIGURE 10
New active cases of tuberculosis, NWT, 1961-7

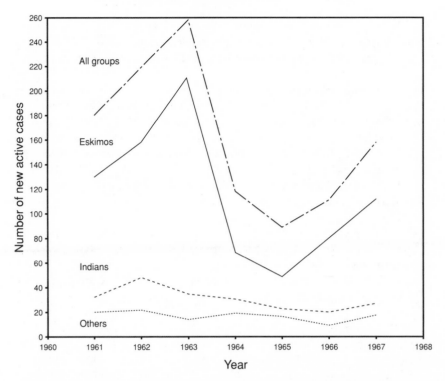

SOURCE: Department of Northern Health and Welfare, Northern Health Services, 'Report on Health Conditions in the Northwest Territories, 1967,' 17

to their own welfare. *Integration* into the national life and activities will follow progressively [italics added].[25]

Generally, in reference to Indians, 'as the opportunities for employment in mining, construction, lumbering and agriculture increase in the District of Mackenzie and in the Yukon, each succeeding generation will see more Indians fully *integrated* into our industrial economy and our national life [italics added].'[26]

Three assumptions underlie these statements. First, it was imperative to make wage employment available to Native people; they could not be expected to live by hunting, fishing, and trapping alone. Second, it would require a lot of new and different training within the education system in order to prepare these people for new job opportunities. Third, it was assumed that the end result would be the integration of Native people into the industrial economy and our national life. In other words, if wage employment could be achieved, most problems associated with the Aboriginal way of life would disappear.

New policies and programs were either in the mill or would be developed. In the old Department of Resources and Development, an Arctic Services section had been established, designed

> for administration of the Canadian Arctic and Eskimo affairs, except education and health; making patrols and inspections of centres of population in the Arctic; studying the Eskimo economy, the health and rehabilitation problems of the Natives, and administering family allowances on behalf of the Department of National Health and Welfare; administering old age assistance, old age security, and blind pensions to Eskimos; and maintaining the vital statistics record for the Northwest Territories and similar records of all Eskimos in Canada.[27]

Gradually, greater emphasis was placed on economic development, and that fact became even more important when the Arctic Services section was made into an Arctic Division (1953-4). Ben Sivertz was its director and a number of programs were launched to help provide a wage economy for the Inuit. One of the more significant contributions coming out of the division was its effort to improve the handicraft industry. Sivertz endorsed Jim Houston's idea that a representative be sent to Japan in the late 1950s to study various art forms the Inuit could develop and market. This provided the impetus for establishing the Cape Dorset Co-operative in 1961, its purpose being to develop and market all forms of Inuit art.[28] By 1966, there were nineteen co-operatives operating in the NWT.[29]

In addition, by 1955-6 eight Northern Service Officers (NSO) were posted in communities 'scattered from Frobisher Bay in the east to Tuktoyaktuk at the mouth of the Mackenzie River in the West.'[30] These individuals were to be the point persons in communities, doing everything from helping Native people fill out necessary forms for government benefits to developing community projects which would provide wage employment.

An interesting story was related by Bob Pilot, who transferred from the RCMP to the Northern Administration Branch to become an NSO.[31] During the early 1950s, establishing Canadian sovereignty in the Arctic was considered a priority, and a number of posts and communities were settled to shore up the claim in the region. Ironically, when the recruiting posters were first printed, advertising jobs for Northern Service Officers, the posters actually read 'Foreign Service Officers.' This was an ironic slip for a department working to secure Canadian sovereignty in the High Arctic.

Other experiments included boat building in the Eastern and Western Arctic as well as tanning sealskins and eiderdown collecting.[32] Attempts were made to encourage the Inuit to seek employment in mining, transportation, administration, and defence installations.[33] In 1957-8, it was estimated that approximately 10 to 15 per cent of the Native population in the territories was in wage employment.

By the mid-1960s, applications for oil and gas permits and leases increased significantly in the NWT (Figure 11). Wells had been drilled in the Arctic Archipelago and it was anticipated that an oil or gas boom could be used as a vehicle on which increased Native employment might be based.

Two glaring problems remained, however. First, megaprojects were

FIGURE 11

Acreage held under oil and gas permit, Canada lands, 1950-66

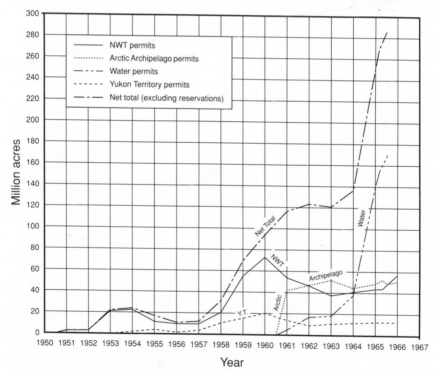

SOURCE: Department of Northern Affairs and National Resources, *Annual Report*, 1965-6, 107

not good sources for Native employment. On the DEW Line operation, about 1,000 individuals were employed in 1964, approximately
600 of which were full-time. In that year, sixty Inuit were employed
on the operation, but few of these people worked in any skilled capacity. The problem with Native employment was the same in the
oil industry. In 1961, sixty-seven people were employed in refineries
and almost none of them were Native people. In 1963, only 16 per cent
of the Indian and Inuit potential labour force were wage earners, while
the figure for whites was 65 per cent.[34]

Second, the average income per capita for Natives remained far
below that of whites, Native people earned approximately six times
less than whites in the NWT (Table 13). Thus, with very low average
annual incomes and few opportunities for wage employment,
economic prospects for Native people were not good.

TABLE 13
Per capita personal cash income for the NWT
and selected provinces, 1963

Northwest Territories	$1,439
Indian	510
Eskimo	426
White	2,922
Newfoundland	1,029
British Columbia	1,967
Canada (average)	1,734

SOURCE: Department of Northern Affairs and National Resources, 'The Northwest Territories Today,' reference paper for the Advisory Commission on the Development
of Government in the Northwest Territories, 1965, 123

By the late 1960s, Native people were settling into a changed way
of life in permanent communities. One rationale for the change was
that public services could then be provided – services that were available to all Canadians. Indeed, housing was provided in most communities, but there was never enough housing and the houses were
not always suitable to the environment. The health of Native people
did begin to improve, but solutions to health problems were devised
in Ottawa and were not always in accord with Native values. More
education became available, but many Natives did not take advantage of existing programs. And increased wage employment for the
most part remained an illusion. One problem was that administrators were dealing with people whose culture was different from their

own. Administrators were, in effect, involved in a process of social engineering for people with a different value system. And there was little, if any, consultation with Native people in order to devise policies compatible with their value system. One way of overcoming the problem was to build local government organizations through which individuals in communities could not only voice their views but could also shape their own policies.

LOCAL GOVERNMENT

Under the NWT Act, the commissioner in council was empowered to establish municipal councils in the territories. In 1939, with the growing activity and congestion in Yellowknife, it was decided that the Territorial Council would exercise that authority, forming a local council with the power to tax and legislate local by-laws.[35]

An administrative district was created and a local trustee board established, with three elected and three appointed members. The commissioner made the GNWT appointments. Tax revenues meant that communities could begin local improvements, usually with financial assistance from the government in Ottawa. The composition of the trustee board was changed in 1948, with the election of five of a total of nine members. Appointed members were reduced to three in 1950. In 1953, legislation provided for the formation of a council with a mayor and eight elected councillors.[36]

In 1949, Hay River had also become an administrative district. In 1953, designations for local government were altered and Yellowknife became a municipal district. In practice, Yellowknife was referred to as a 'town.' Fort Simpson and Fort Smith, in 1954, became local improvement districts (that designation replacing the administrative district), with councils of five elected and three appointed members. In 1963 Hay River became a town. Also in 1963, the municipal ordinance was again altered, establishing five categories in the evolution of municipal governments:[37] (1) unorganized communities with advisory committees (by 1965, about forty of these); (2) development areas with advisory committees (Inuvik, Frobisher Bay, Enterprise, and Norman Wells); (3) local improvement districts (Fort Simpson); (4) villages (Fort Smith); and (5) towns (Yellowknife and Hay River). By the mid-1960s, many communities in the Mackenzie Valley and the Eastern Arctic were moving toward some form of municipal status. In the Carrothers Commission *Report* (1966), members of that commission saw the development of local governments in the NWT as a vital step in the political development of the region.

The Carrothers Commission was appointed in 1965 by the minister

of Northern Affairs and National Resources, Arthur Laing. This
Advisory Commission on the Development of Government in the
Northwest Territories was established for two reasons. First, unsuccessful and contentious proposals had been made to divide the NWT
into two territories (to be discussed below), and Laing wanted a
recommendation from the commission to the government on this
issue. Second, the commission was to advise the government on the
nature of the governmental process to be developed in the region.

The chairman of the commission was A.W.R. Carrothers, then dean
of the Faculty of Law at the university of Western Ontario. The other
members were Jean Beetz and John Parker, mayor of Yellowknife. Their
recommendations included the necessity of establishing strong local
government organizations.

> In most settlements of the north there is not yet established a form of
> local government in any sense in which the term is used in the south.
>   We consider that a continuing and intensified program for the develop-
> ment of local government, in which all residents can be offered the
> opportunity of a meaningful role which they can understand, is crucial
> to the economic, social and political development of the north. In a
> sparsely populated country where the population is polarized into many
> small communities between which communication is not easy – what
> has been described earlier as pinpoint development – decentralization
> of government is of first importance. Local problems handled locally run
> the best chance of being solved expeditiously and appropriately. In terms
> of education, too, local government (including, where feasible, a local
> school authority) has an important role to play in the north at this time.
> It is a means by which people can perceive a relationship between
> problems and their solutions; and for people who have been obliged
> to rely on welfare and other unearned income – who view 'government'
> as 'people who look after others,' and to whom 'if' means 'when' – par-
> ticipation in local government may be a most significant means to respon-
> sible citizenship. Experience in public affairs at the local level provides
> a means to a greater interest in broader public issues and offices at the
> territorial and federal levels.[38]

The above statement is extremely important for political development
in the NWT. The Carrothers Commission, in 1965-6, travelled to
fifty-one communities in the region. In these visits, members of the
commission detected a very strong community orientation. This
orientation was manifested in a strong desire for some degree of local
control of public decisions. Therefore, one significant recommendation by the commission was the creation of viable local government

organizations in the NWT. Members of the commission felt that municipal organization would enable individuals in the communities (many of whom already relied heavily upon welfare) to begin to use local government to handle local problems. Also, members of the commission saw involvement in local government as an integral part of developing a sense of citizenship in a democracy.

Almost fourteen years later, C.M. Drury, in his *Report on Constitutional Development in the NWT*, was impressed by the same strong sense of local orientation. Creating a territorial government did not suddenly create a strong sense of identity and loyalty to that government. Travelling to NWT communities today, one is struck by the same strong sense of local identity and loyalty. The establishment of *effective* local government organizations was a problem in 1966, and, even today, it remains one of the most contentious political issues in the territories.

THE GNWT IN TRANSITION: DIVISION, THE CARROTHERS COMMISSION, AND YELLOWKNIFE

By the mid-1960s, a rift had developed between the Department of Northern Affairs and National Resources and the GNWT. A number of incidents had taken place which indicated a growing sense of the need for autonomy for the territorial government.

The first was the protracted issue of dividing the NWT into two territories.[39] A bill was introduced in Parliament in 1962 to create a western portion (to be called the Mackenzie Territory) and an eastern portion (to be called Nunatsiaq). The 105th meridian (west of the Saskatchewan-Manitoba border) would constitute the boundary. Division was pushed by non-Natives in the Western Arctic because they thought it would be easier to attain provincehood if the Eastern Arctic, which they saw as less advanced politically, was removed.

Because of the federal election of 1963, the bill never passed Parliament. Interest in division persisted, however, and a similar bill was introduced by the Liberals in 1964. Northerners were not of one mind on the issue, and a few Quebec MP's wanted to redraw the NWT/Quebec border before division. Liberals were not able to get the bill through the House in 1964, and Commissioner Ben Sivertz and the Territorial Council posed an alternative which removed some of the pressure on the government.

After being appointed commissioner in 1963, Sivertz noticed that governmental changes had occurred in Greenland that were well received by Greenlanders. The changes were brought about as a result of a Royal Commission appointed in Denmark in 1958. Therefore, Sivertz and the council recommended to Laing that a Royal Commission be appointed to investigate the development of government in the NWT.[40]

The government of Canada did not appoint a Royal Commission, but it did establish the Carrothers Commission. With regard to division of the territories, the commission's recommendation was: 'To retain the Territories as a political unit, to locate the government of the Territories within the Territories, to decentralize its operations as far as practicable, to transfer administrative functions from the central to the territorial government in order that the latter may be accountable on site for the administration of the public business, and to concentrate on economic development and opportunity for the residents of the north.'[41]

Essentially, the recommendations were a call for a more autonomous GNWT – a GNWT which would be out from under the wing of the department. The commissioner would remain responsible to the minister, but he or she would have deputy minister status. After 1967, this report served as the blueprint for officials of the new government in Yellowknife, who were attempting to develop representative and responsible government.

Ben Sivertz and the council supported the recommendations of the Carrothers Commission, but this was not necessarily the case with all department officials. In a weekly letter to his staff in October 1966, Sivertz said of the report: 'Speaking generally, the senior men in the Department of Indian Affairs and Northern Development are not enthusiastic. I believe attempts will be made to shelve it.'[42]

This was just one issue on which the officials of the GNWT and of the department differed. Other bureaucratic battles had raged since 1964. In a December 1966 letter to his staff, Sivertz recalled: 'A thing was proposed two years ago with the idea of hamstringing me. It was to isolate me.'[43] He went on to explain that departmental officials had proposed that the commissioner be transferred to Fort Smith, with the intent of putting the government closer to the people. At the same time, no support staff would be transferred from Ottawa, and all communication would have to go through the department's deputy minister. The proposed arrangement, of course, was unacceptable to Sivertz and his staff. But the efforts of Sivertz, with the aid of the Carrothers recommendations, were significant factors in establishing a more autonomous GNWT in Yellowknife in 1967.

CONCLUSION

The 1950s and 1960s brought significant policy changes to the NWT. Prior to 1950, federal government policy was designed to keep Native people living a traditional way of life. After the early 1950s, government policy was designed to enable Native people to participate in the wage economy. To facilitate this policy, the federal government in Ottawa launched a number of programs which changed the lives of most residents of the region. Education, health care, and housing policies had a significant impact and sharpened the cultural dilemma for Native people. More and more modern culture made it more and more difficult to retain traditional values and beliefs. Creating the balance between cultures was a difficult task in 1967, and it is an even more difficult task today. For Native people, the task would be made easier if they had greater influence or control over the policies that affected their lives. Native people were not necessarily opposed to the policies but felt that often they were enacted with little sensitivity to Native cultural values. They thought that if they could gain greater influence or control of the public policy process, they might make public policies more compatible with their cultural norms. Such influence or control was almost non-existent until 1967.

While the policy changes were impressive in many ways, they were initiated by Ottawa. In few, if any, cases was there consultation with the beneficiaries of the policies. Thus, after almost fifty years, government in the NWT remained an administrative government. The Northern Affairs Branch of the Department of Northern Affairs and National Resources still controlled the public agenda for the territories.

But change was beginning in the region. Four of the eight Territorial Council members were elected, representing for the most part non-Native voters in the Mackenzie Valley. The GNWT in Ottawa also began to distance itself from the department, and, in 1967, the seat of government was moved to Yellowknife. Native people, when the opportunity arose, expressed discontent with the nature of policies in areas such as health care and housing. And when the Carrothers Commission travelled to communities in the North, strong local governments were perceived to be one way Native people could become involved in the governmental process. In short, political development was beginning to evolve, and, by moving the GNWT to the territories, an entirely different political situation was created. Armed with the Carrothers Report as a blueprint for action, the territorial government began almost immediately to build an administrative power base from which it could dominate the political agenda of the region.

CHAPTER FIVE

Changing the Political Process of the Northwest Territories, 1967-79

After 1967, politics in the Northwest Territories changed considerably from the days when the federal government dominated the political agenda. The territorial government was moved to Yellowknife and immediately began working to free itself of Ottawa's domination. At the same time, Native people in the region were politicized, organizing into effective interest groups. This new process was analogous to a triangle, one corner being the federal government and DIAND, one the GNWT, and the third the Native organizations. The interaction of these three forces created a new political dynamic in the policy process of the NWT.

Moving the government of the Northwest Territories to Yellowknife in September 1967 was, first of all, a symbolic act. It signified a new beginning for government in the region, government which in the past had not been perceived to be responsive to the needs of the people. It also signified a growing autonomy from the Department of Indian Affairs and Northern Development and an opportunity to initiate policies free of Ottawa's influence. This new beginning was marked by a great deal of optimism on the part of officials of the GNWT. Stuart M. Hodgson, appointed commissioner in March 1967, conveyed the sense of a fresh start in his opening remarks to the Territorial Council on 13 November 1967:

> I take great pleasure in being able to stand before you in our new capital today, on what is indeed a historic occasion, to officially open the Thirty-fifth Session of the Council of the Northwest Territories.
>
> I have always believed that people with their needs and aspirations must be the most important consideration that any government has if it is to function democratically as the servant of those it purports to govern.

It is for this reason that I am so very happy to address you from this seat of government in Yellowknife – because I can say to you that the Government of the Northwest Territories has moved so much closer to our people. We are among them now, as neighbours, patrons of their businesses, and social acquaintances. And we are trying, each in his own way, to become true northerners and members of a community that stretches far wider than the confines of Yellowknife but spreads across the one and a quarter million square miles of Canada's Northwest Territories. This cannot help having a tremendous effect on the attitude of northern residents towards our government and indeed the effectiveness with which we operate.[1]

The theory was obvious: government from Ottawa had been distant, alien, and unresponsive. Now that government was centred in Yellowknife, it would be close and responsive, and, thus, residents would begin to identify with it. All this was not as simple as it sounded.

It is true that there is a certain 'nordicity' in the NWT; indeed, residents of the region often comment about the North being distinct from the rest of Canada. The question is, in what way would this distinctiveness influence the evolutionary process occurring within the territorial government? A number of the Carrothers Report recommendations reflected the sense of this distinctiveness, emphasizing the need to develop strong local government institutions. This emphasis was necessary not only to socialize individuals into the Canadian polity but also to allow them greater opportunity to control their own destiny.

From the early years of developing the GNWT, there was a debate over the nature of the governmental process in the territories. Much of the debate centred on whether there should be a *centralized* or *decentralized* form of government for the region. The intensity of the debate ebbed and flowed, but it has been an integral part of the evolution of the GNWT. Indeed, even today, it is manifested in discussions about the powers of local and regional governments. Having Yellowknife as the capital did create expectations about a new governmental process.

GROWTH OF THE GNWT

Government officials used the Carrothers Commission Report as their battle plan for developing a provincial-like apparatus in the NWT. From 1967 to 1979, the growth in size and responsibilities for the GNWT was nothing short of phenomenal. In 1967, almost the entire staff and their families (seventy-five people) flew on one plane from Ottawa to Yellowknife. By 1979, there were 2,845 territorial employees, approximately 400 more than the number of federal employees working in the region.[2] Moreover, the operating and capital budgets of the GNWT went from $14,584,000 in 1967-8 to $282,167,000 in 1979 – almost a twentyfold increase.[3] Incidentally, during the same period, the federal government's budget quadrupled. The growth was driven primarily by the devolution of responsibilities from Ottawa to Yellowknife.[4]

Constructing the Administrative Apparatus

In 1967, the liquor board was the principal administrative organization of the GNWT. After the move to Yellowknife, two types of administrative organizations emerged as part of the new government structure: program and service departments. The departments were designed to service the growth of the territorial government (initially, they were to service the Mackenzie District). By 1970, the Keewatin and Eastern Arctic administrative districts were added to the responsibilities of the GNWT. Thus, after less than three years, the territorial government was administering one-third of the land mass of Canada.[5]

In the fall of 1967, three service departments were created almost instantly: Information, Finance, and Territorial Secretary. One program department, local government, was also established, as responsibility for local government was devolved from DIAND to the GNWT with the move to Yellowknife.

By 1970, three additional service departments had been added: Public Works, Legal Affairs, and Personnel. Three additional program departments also emerged: Industry and Development, Education, and Social Development. In 1973, a Crown corporation, the NWT Housing Corporation, assumed responsibility for territorial housing needs. By 1979, program departments had expanded to six, adding Renewable Resources and Health (Tourism had also been added to Industry and Development). Some of these departments, for example, Local Government and Education, exercised responsibilities in the NWT, that is, the federal government devolved powers to the GNWT, which assumed decisionmaking and administrative responsibility. But responsibilities such as health care and renewable resources were different. The federal government retained decisionmaking power, but the territorial government carried out certain administrative responsibilities.[6]

Jurisdictional responsibility poses a curious problem for a territorial government. On the one hand, de jure responsibiliity rests with the federal government. Under the amended Northwest Territories Act (1878) the federal government is responsible for administering the region. Presumably this will be the case until the region becomes a province or the NWT Act is altered. On the other hand, de facto responsibility rests with the GNWT. Within the parameters of devolution agreements, the territorial government actually governs as would any provincial government. Nevertheless, under the NWT Act, the federal government retains the power to disallow territorial legislation.

Thus, by 1979, the GNWT was well on the way to becoming a carbon copy of provincial governments in the South (Figure 12). With a budget of more than $250 million and about 3,000 civil servants, management of this administrative apparatus became crucial.

Executive of the GNWT

In 1967, the executive was dominated by the commissioner, who was responsible to the federal minister of Indian and Northern Affairs. In the Carrothers Report, the creation of an executive committee had been recommended in order to move policy responsibility to the GNWT. In 1967, the committee became operational, made up of the commissioner and his executive assistant and the deputy commissioner (Figure 13). With the evolution of an all elected Territorial Council (1975), the executive began to be transformed. Over time, the executive became an executive of the territorial legislature, chosen by and responsible to that legislature. The commissioner's de facto role declined to the point where, today, it is almost identical to that of a provincial lieutenant governor. In terms of de jure powers, because the NWT Act has not been changed, the commissioner remains the primary executive officer of the NWT. At the same time, however, the government leader of the territoral government, elected by the legislature, has powers similar to those of a provincial premier. The interesting constitutional transformation, which occurred almost totally by practice rather than by statute, is confirmed in correspondence between the minister and the commissioner.[7] Highlights of the changes are described in Figure 13.

The executive committee organized the delivery of territorial programs and services through administrative regions. Administrative responsibilities have been extended and reorganized to the point that, today, there are five regions: Kitikmeot, Keewatin, Baffin, Fort Smith, and Inuvik. The power of regional administrations, particularly regional directors, has been an issue in the GNWT since 1967. This power ebbs and flows, depending on whether the government is centralizing or decentralizing its responsibilities.

By 1979, it became clear that structural characteristics of the executive would follow the pattern of executives in provincial governments, with two important differences. First, political parties did not operate at the territorial level in the NWT, and, therefore, no partisan base existed by which ministers were chosen. Second, with no partisan

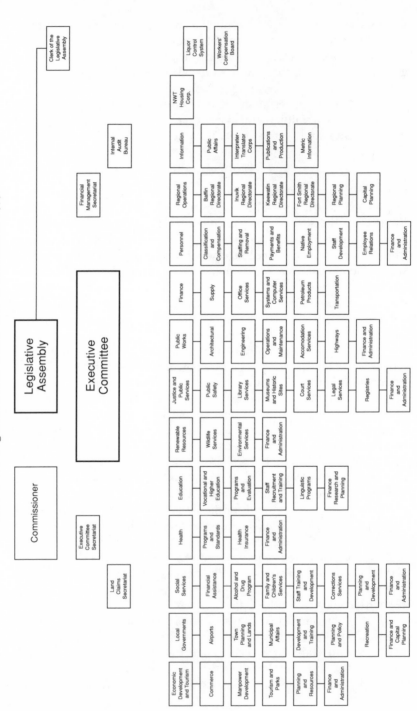

FIGURE 12: Organizational chart, GNWT, November 1979

SOURCE: GNWT, Department of Information, 1979

FIGURE 13
Executive branch of the GNWT:
evolution to responsible government, 1967-79

1967	Capital of NWT moved to Yellowknife and with it government of the Northwest Territories
1967-8	Executive Committee (GNWT)
	Commissioner - chief executive officer - chairman (Hodgson)
	Deputy commissioner
	Executive assistant (becomes assistant commissioner in 1969)
	Department heads and regional administration report to Executive Council
1969	Executive Committee: acquires permanent secretary
1971	Executive Committee: adds Executive Secretariat to co-ordinate 'the collection, analysis, and presentation of management information in a systematic and organized fashion'
1973	Executive Committee: second assistant commissioner appointed but removed after reorganization in 1975
1974	Federal minister authorizes two members of elected Territorial Council to be members of Executive Committee: after the 1975 election, council chooses these members
	Executive Secretariat grows: Audit Bureau; Financial Co-ordination and Program Analysis; Personnel Policy and Planning; Program Policy and Planning; and Petroleum Resource Development Project Group
1976	Executive Committee: adds third member of elected Territorial Council (named Legislative Assembly in 1976)
1978	Land Claims Secretariat becomes part of Executive Office
1979	Executive Committee: authorized 5 to 7 members of elected Legislative Assembly; after 1979 election, 5 selected; assistant commissioner's position phased out of Executive Committee in movement toward more responsible government. John Parker becomes commissioner.

SOURCE: GNWT, *Annual Report*, respective years

base for formulating and enacting policies, the system functioned on the basis of a 'consensus' of the MLA's. A successful relationship between the executive and the legislature depends on the ability of the executive members to 'persuade' non-government members of the legislature to support their policy proposals. This persuasion takes place without the influence of party discipline.[8]

An Evolving Legislative Assembly

Between 1951 and 1975, the Territorial Council was also transformed, changing from a federally appointed council to one elected by residents of the NWT. These changes were provided by statute, that is, parliamentary acts authorizing the number of elected council positions. For example, there were three in 1951, fifteen in 1975, and twenty-two in 1979. Since 1983, twenty-four elected MLA's represent constituencies throughout the territories. In 1976, the council changed its name to Legislative Assembly.[9]

A number of important changes accompany the evolution of representative government in the NWT. In the 1950s and 1960s, respectively, Inuit and Indians attained the right to vote, and many ran for seats in the Legislative Assembly. Since the election in 1976, Native representatives have held a majority of the seats in the assembly – the only jurisdiction in Canada where this is the case.

One unique feature of politics at the territorial level in the NWT is the non-partisan nature of the process. Political parties do function in federal elections, and, in the 1987 territorial elections, one unsuccessful candidate from Fort Smith ran as an NDP member. Normally, however, candidates for seats in the legislature run without party labels. Once elected, the twenty-four MLA's choose the eight-person executive, including a government leader.[10] The legislature then is divided between eight members who hold the government portfolios and the sixteen (fifteen and a speaker) non-government MLA's, usually referred to as 'ordinary members' or sometimes even called the 'opposition.' Without a partisan basis for politics in the assembly, the political dynamic between two groups is called 'consensus' politics.

Within the GNWT, as within any parliamentary process, there is the inherent tension and struggle between the eight-person executive and the sixteen MLA's without portfolios. Without political party discipline to control the struggle, there is an opportunity for an autonomous legislature to work. The legislature is autonomous in that the ordinary members hold a voting majority, and they are not bound by political party discipline. They can, and do, represent their constituencies. Although they could dominate the legislative process, rarely do they stand as a monolithic bloc and exercise absolute control with respect to the passage of legislative programs initiated by the executive.

The eight-person executive must persuade only five of the sixteen ordinary MLA's in order to attain a majority in the legislature. Moreover, the executive can use budgetary initiatives as a lever: spending programs proposed for communities can be a powerful persuader. As a consequence, it seems that a balance between the executive and ordinary members is usually found. While the process must still be classified as executive government, MLA's free of partisan controls can strike some tough bargains in order to trade their support for community programs. In the process, the executive does not enjoy the power base of a traditional political party. At the same time, ordinary members rarely find the unanimity which would enable them to dominate the executive. Consensus politics, then, may be a way around the rigidity of party discipline or the chaos of full legislative autonomy.

Part of the evolution of the legislative process has been the development of 'responsible government' in the territories. But responsible government in the GNWT is not responsible government in the conventional sense, where partisan governments sink or swim with their majority in the assembly. No conventional vote of non-confidence exists whereby a government, collectively, must resign. Responsible government lies in the fact that the legislature chooses ministers of the government, and the legislature can, when in session and on a formal motion, withdraw ministerial status. This form of 'responsible' government is distinctive to the GNWT.

The closest the legislature came to exercising this direct 'responsibility' occurred in 1985. After the 1983 territorial election, and the subsequent choosing of the executive, the assembly agreed to review their choices in two years. There was, then, a specified time in which autonomous legislative 'responsibility' would be exercised. The review took place in 1985, and two members of the executive were replaced by the legislature. The process was not institutionalized, however, because after the territorial election in 1987 it was agreed not to hold a review in two years.[11] This was a move away from exercising more direct assembly 'responsibility' and probably strengthens the role of executive government. After the 1991 election, the Twelfth Legislative Assembly voted to conduct a review of the government leader and members of the Cabinet at the end of two years. This move reinforced a degree of autonomy for the assembly.

Another move in 1987 to enhance the role of executive government consisted of granting the government leader the power to discipline members of the executive. The government leader can change portfolios within the executive or ask a minister to resign.[12] The assembly would then have to choose another member for the executive.

There are those who argue that consensus politics should be abandoned and a partisan process adopted. At the same time, there are those who argue that consensus politics is indigenous to the region, and that it should be maintained. Many of these individuals are opposed to a powerful executive, where party discipline can frustrate individual representation. The fact is, without political parties as a base for structuring NWT politics, members of the territorial legislature have worked out their own version of consensus politics, and it is a distinctive feature of the GNWT.

Local Governments in the NWT

Local government has had a significant place in the evolution of the GNWT. The special role of local governments in this evolution is influenced by two factors. First, Native people in the Eastern and Western Arctic are very community oriented and have a strong desire to be able to control their own affairs at the local level. Many of the small, isolated communities have remained traditional in their social and economic activities, and the isolation and persistence of tradition has generated a fierce desire on the part of these people to be masters of their own destiny. This is one reason members of the Carrothers Commission stressed the need to move away from an Ottawa dominated governmental process.

The second factor is that local governments enhance the idea of citizen involvement in government and politics. In theory, if local institutions were developed and local citizens were involved in that governmental process, those citizens would not only have greater control of their own affairs but would begin to perceive the governmental process to be legitimate. In short, gradually they would be integrated into the political process of the territories. Therefore, for members of the commission, *effective* local government institutions were crucial in the evolution of a governmental process.

Initially, local governments were under a five category classification: city, towns, villages, hamlets, and settlements. In 1967, some semblance of local government existed in two towns and two villages. By 1978, there was one city, four towns, two villages, eighteen hamlets, and twenty-seven settlements.[13] The first three categories were tax-based communities, raising some of their own revenue. Although their tax base was limited, tax revenues did provide the elected councils with some degree of fiscal autonomy.

Settlements were the first step in the formal political evolution of communities. Settlements were unincorporated but did elect a council. The election was considered an essential step in engendering a sense of political democracy in the region. These settlement councils also had some authority of their own. The GNWT gave block grants to each settlement council, $20 per capita annually, which could be spent at the discretion of the council.[14]

Powers differed somewhat between the five local government

categories established. Communities gradually were chartered, and, generally, local councils were empowered with responsibilities for local roads, water and sewage, garbage, fire prevention and ambulance service, business licenses, and public nuisance. By 1979, however, there was discontent with this distribution of powers. Subsequent proposals for Denendeh and Nunavut, for example, advocated including under community responsibilities services such as education, health care, housing, social services, policing, and economic development.[15] Many individuals thought that these responsibilities were critical to the welfare of the community, and that communities should have greater influence or control of such policies.

During the 1967-79 period, one of the more interesting initiatives by the territorial government was to launch a decentralization program in 1976. The argument was that just as the federal government had devolved powers to the territorial government, so the GNWT should in turn devolve additional powers to local governments. While the decentralization campaign may have generated more rhetoric than actual devolution, two important developments occurred that did have an impact on the nature of the governmental process.

One development was the enhancement of advisory committees at the community level.[16] Even before local governing institutions were established in many communities, organizations were created to advise government policymakers in Yellowknife. These committees were advisory, designed to give local residents an opportunity to voice concerns in matters such as education, health care, housing, or hunting and trapping. Many of the committees, such as local hunter and trappers associations (HTA's), have now evolved into very significant institutions in the communities. In the Inuvialuit region, for example, the HTA's have worked closely with the joint management organization given responsibility for managing renewable resources on lands affected under the Inuvialuit Final Agreement. The same model is being used in the Mackenzie Valley and in the Eastern Arctic in anticipation of land claim settlements.[17]

Over the past two decades, advisory organizations have fostered greater community participation. One problem, however, is that they have also fostered frustration; often communities felt their concerns, while voiced, were not being listened to by officials in Yellowknife. Also, individuals in communities frequently complained that there were too many special purpose committees, thus overextending the participation of more active citizens. In Pond Inlet, for example, at one point there were twenty-two of these advisory committees.

A second important development related to the decentralization policy was the creation of the Baffin Regional Council (BRC). The genesis of this regional body was the collective effort of thirteen communities on or around Baffin Island. The idea of a regional council was first discussed in the 1960s, but it began to be formalized at a workshop of settlement secretaries in Rankin Inlet in 1974. It was discussed again at conferences in Pond Inlet in 1974 and Igloolik in 1975. The Department of Local Government supported the concept, and an organizational meeting was held in Pangnirtung in April 1977. There, it was decided to hold the first meeting of the BRC in Arctic Bay in September 1977.[18]

Essentially, the BRC was an extension of community councils. Each of the thirteen councils chose one regional representative to serve for a year. Settlement secretaries, hamlet managers, MLA's from the region, or representatives of special groups could attend the meetings but could not vote. Thus, the BRC represented an indigenous aspect of constitutional development in the NWT, creating a third tier of government between local and territorial organizations.

Two explanations are usually offered for building yet another level of government in the region. First, many Baffin communities felt that Yellowknife was too far away and neither understood nor was responsive to problems in the Eastern Arctic. Moreover, because of the centralization of authority in the GNWT, many individuals in communities felt that expectations and needs of communities were being neglected, and that administrators were arbitrary in dealing with genuine appeals from local organizations. Thus, a regional body would offer more political clout than could be mustered by a single community.

The second reason was economic. It did not make economic sense for Yellowknife to devolve substantial responsibilities to each community – responsibilities such as education or housing. For example, it would be very expensive to operate a school board in each community. But it might be feasible, and logical, to operate a regional school board for a number of communities. The same argument can be made for regional hospital boards. While regional organizations might not operate as cheaply as would centralizing all operations out of Yellowknife, regional bodies were less expensive than were individual community bodies. In short, a cheaper but centralized and unresponsive organization would be traded off against a more expensive but responsive regional organization with more political muscle.

The Baffin region was the logical place for this type of entity to be conceived. The Eastern Arctic people did feel alienated from Yellowknife, almost two thousand miles away, and often had to travel first to Montreal, Ottawa, or Toronto in order to get there. And the Inuit in the Baffin region, with their cultural homogeneity, felt they could better respond to their own cultural needs than could administrators in the capital.

Therefore, the BRC was organized, with representation from each of the affiliated community councils. The council, with a budget and administrative staff, pioneered in the NWT the growth of a regional organization that could function on behalf of specific communities. The problem, of course, is that regional organizations also pose a threat to the powers in Yellowknife – bureaucratic and elected officials who exercise the responsibility of the GNWT. But the regional organization also poses a check on the concentration of power in the central government.

In spite of the problem of power, in 1977 the territorial government endorsed the concept of regional organizations. A representative of the territorial government, R.A. Creery, attended the Pangnirtung meeting. The position of the GNWT was 'to boost the transfer of government's programs to communities and the decentralization of authority and responsibility to the regional level ... Mr. Creery explained that the government's aim was to let people in the communities have a lot more control and influence over what the government does; it was up to the communities to decide for themselves how much they wanted to take over.'[19] Thus, at the time, the intent of the GNWT was, in fact, to decentralize. But the regional government issue was not settled in the 1970s, and it remains a significant constitutional issue today. Current positions on this issue will be discussed in Chapter 6.

The place of local government organizations has been one of the most important, and perhaps most controversial, problems involved in the constitutional evolution of the GNWT. The issue centres around different perceptions about the role of local governing bodies. Many Native people in small communities equated the development of local governments with the notion of self-government. In other words, as these institutions evolved, they would provide the vehicle for greater local control of their own affairs and less domination by officials in Ottawa or Yellowknife.

For others involved in the GNWT, and many individuals in the larger mixed communities, the evolution of local governments meant the development of a model similar to that in the provinces. For these people, no problem exists with a strong provincial type of government and dependent municipalities. Hence, arguments in the NWT concerning centralization and decentralization are critical. Most Aboriginal people advocate a more decentralized process, in which local councils perform a number of responsibilities now centred in Yellowknife. Non-aboriginals often argue, in the name of efficiency and equality, the need for a more centralized process working out of Yellowknife. The issue is one of dividing decisionmaking power, not just

administrative responsibility. The development of a strong, centralized GNWT is incompatible with creating strong, decentralized community governments in the more isolated settlements.

EVOLUTION OF NATIVE POLITICAL ORGANIZATIONS

Emerging alongside, and almost simultaneously with, the development of formal-legal, constitutional organizations in the NWT were the
informal Native political organizations. The principal Native groups
began to organize in 1969. By 1973 the Dene, Métis, Inuvialuit, and
Inuit had formed individual entities which took up the causes of their
respective members.[20] These organizations became an integral part of
politics in the region.

Three major factors provided a catalyst for Native people to organize
into groups, to uphold their rights against government intrusion, and
to provide protection against private economic development. In June
1969, the federal government issued 'A Statement of the Government
of Canada on Indian Policy,' the so-called White Paper on Native affairs. This statement was the work of many new advisors in the
Trudeau government and suggested the abolition of Native status under the Indian Act, with the federal government divesting itself of
responsibility for Native affairs. The provinces and territories would
then deal with Native people as they did with all citizens. The reac-
tion by Native people was firm and vocal in opposition to the suggestion.[21]

For Native people, the Indian Act was paradoxical. The act was a
problem because it placed them under the administration of DIAND.
At the same time, the act itself symbolized some degree of special status that Aboriginal peoples sought within the Canadian mosaic. In
1969, the federal government was still dragging its feet regarding the
recognition of the legality of Aboriginal rights. To abolish the Indian
Act at this point would only worsen the possibility of Native people
ever gaining special recognition of their rights within Canada. Native
people felt that by organizing into political groups they might have
a better chance of gaining these rights.

A second factor influencing the formation of Native organizations
was the increased oil and gas exploration in the Mackenzie Valley, the
Beaufort Sea, and the High Arctic. Oil companies had found significant gas reserves in the region, and there were rumors of a possible
pipeline being built down the Mackenzie Valley. Native people realized they had to organize in order to oppose this kind of proposal
and to have a say in the nature of economic development in the region.
A final factor was the core funding beginning to be offered by DIAND.

The funds provided a way of sustaining the organizations without having to depend on high membership fees. These were the main reasons behind the formation of the Indian Brotherhood in 1969.

The Dene Nation

A number of Dene chiefs ratified the Charter of the Brotherhood in 1970, and, soon after, James Wah-Shee became president, serving until his resignation in 1975. The Brotherhood received organizational funding from the federal government in 1971, and it became the principal vehicle for 'status' or 'treaty' Indians in the Western Arctic. It represented about 7,000 people in the early 1970s, that is, descendants of those involved in signing Treaty 8 (1899) and Treaty 11 (1921).[22]

The Dene, too, became activists in the politics of the NWT. In 1973, Dene chiefs filed a 'caveat' with the Supreme Court of the Northwest Territories, declaring their aboriginal rights to the land and claiming that the Canadian government could not develop this land without permission of the Dene. The case, Re Paulette et al. and Registrar of Titles (1974), was upheld in the territorial court, Justice William Morrow realizing that, indeed, through haste and misunderstanding, the Dene had never extinguished Aboriginal rights in Treaty 11. The right to apply for a caveat was overturned in the appeals court, and its position was upheld by the Supreme Court of Canada. But the ruling on the fact that the Dene had never extinguished their aboriginal rights was not challenged.[23] This fact leads to one of the most troublesome situations in the NWT. The federal government originally claimed, by virtue of the treaties, that the land in the Northwest Territories was Crown land. According to the courts, however, Native people have never given up their Aboriginal right to these lands. At issue then, is who owns how much and which lands. Developments in the current land claims issue in the NWT will be discussed in Chapter 6.

In 1975, the Dene published the 'Dene Declaration,' stating that as a nation they had a right to traditional lands, self-determination, and special status under the Canadian constitution. In spite of the way it was interpreted by many southern Canadians, the declaration was not a claim for absolute sovereignty. The declaration was followed in 1976 with a land claim presented to the federal government. In 1988, the federal government and the Dene-Métis Association finally arrived at an 'agreement in principle' on the claim, and a final agreement was initialled in April 1990. In the summer of 1990, however, many Dene disagreed with what they saw as 'extinguishment' of Aboriginal rights in the AIP. At the annual Dene Assembly in Hay River in July 1990, a motion was passed requesting a renegotiation of the agreement. The

Dene membership split on the issue, with some members seeking
regional negotiations with the federal government. The federal government, in November 1990, agreed to negotiate land claims in the
Western Arctic region by region. (Particulars of the current negotiations will be discussed in Chapter 6.)

In 1981, the Dene Nation and the Métis Association drafted a
proposal for creating three territories out of the NWT, one of which
would be 'Denendeh.'[24] The document was entitled *Public Government
of the People of the North*, and it was designed to provide a blueprint
for governing the homeland of the Dene. It advocated the use of powers similar to those of a province as the basis for governing the new
territory. The most troubling issue for the Dene was their minority
status should a Western Arctic territory be established. To protect Dene
minority status within the legislative process of Denendeh, they advocated a formation of a senate with guaranteed Dene representation.

The politicization of the Dene was also manifested in their participation in territorial elections. In 1975, they ran successful candidates
in the election. Early in the session of the new Legislative Assembly,
many of their people decided the territorial government was not working for the true interest of the Native people and, in fact, was little
more than an extension of the federal government. This led to the
resignation of George Barnaby (from Fort Good Hope) and James Wah-
Shee (representing the Great Slave Lake constituency), both of whom
had been elected in 1975. Many Native people still felt they could use
a majority of members in the legislature to attain their goals and
reversed their position in 1979. Four Dene were then elected to the
Legislative Assembly: Richard Nerysoo, Robert Sayine, Nick Sibbeston, and James Wah-Shee. After the election, Nerysoo and Wah-
Shee were appointed members of the executive, becoming ministers
of Social Services and Local Government, respectively. From this point,
the executive of the GNWT has included Natives and non-Natives.

The Inuvialuit and COPE

In January 1970, Native people of the Mackenzie Delta organized the
Committee for Original Peoples' Entitlement (COPE), and, in 1972, COPE
became an affiliate of the Inuit Tapirisat of Canada (ITC). Agnes Semm-
ler (a Dene) was the first president. In 1976, the organization was recon-
stituted, representing 2,500 Inuit of the Western Arctic (the Inuvialuit),
residing primarily in six communities: Aklavik, Inuvik, Holman Island, Sachs Harbour, Paulatuk, and Tuktoyaktuk. In 1979, Nellie Cournoyea, who had been active in COPE, was elected to the Legislative
Assembly, and, subsequently, she held a number of ministerial port-

folios and is now government leader.

The Inuvialuit presented their land claim to the federal government in 1977, and, in 1978, an agreement-in-principle (AIP) was reached. The original COPE claim included a proposal to create the Western Arctic Regional Municipality (WARM), a regional government with extensive municipal powers. The federal government, however, refused to combine negotiations on land claims and self-government within any new regional or territorial boundaries. In the agreement, a number of joint management committees and boards were formed, with jurisdictional responsibilty for, in particular, renewable resources. These organizations are in fact governing bodies in the region within the scope specified in the final agreement.

The claim was ratified in June 1984, the first comprehensive settlement in the territories. The essentials of the settlement were $45 million compensation, the equivalent of full title (including sub-surface rights to non-renewable resources) to 11,000 square kilometres of land in and around the six communities (Category I lands), and joint management rights (with the federal and territorial governments) on an additional 78,000 square kilometres (Category II lands). The Fisheries Joint Management Committee and the Wildlife Management Advisory Council (Northwest Territories) are examples of those joint management organizations. On Category II lands, oil and gas rights plus control of certain other materials remained with the federal government.[25] The Inuvialuit Regional Corporation was created as one of the organizations responsible for implementation of the claim.

The Inuit Tapirisat of Canada and the TFN

In 1971, the Inuit of Quebec, Labrador, and the Northwest Territories organized the Inuit Tapirisat of Canada (ITC), an umbrella organization for all Canadian Inuit. Most of the Inuit in the Central and Eastern Arctic were a fairly homogeneous group and had pushed for the formation of their own territory when division was debated in the early 1960s. In 1971, they advocated the formation of 'Nunavut,' a territory for all NWT Inuit other than the Inuvialuit. In 1976, they submitted a claim, including a proposal for the formation of Nunavut and its government. In 1977, the claim was re-submitted without formally including the Nunavut proposal, although the Inuit have never lost sight of their goal of forming a separate territory. Subsequent written proposals have included the Nunavut proposal.[26]

In the NWT there are four regional affiliates of the ITC: COPE, and the Baffin, Kitikmeot, and Keewatin regional associations. In 1982, the Tungavik Federation of Nunavut (TFN) became the organization of the

Inuit of the NWT (approximately 15,000 people) responsible for negotiating land claims. The Inuit signed an agreement in principle with the federal government in 1990 and land selections in the region have been completed. The Inuit have become extremely active in the political process of the GNWT, even though they have claimed that their first priority is the formation of Nunavut.

In the Legislative Assembly, the Inuit had six Central and Eastern Arctic constituencies in 1975. Peter Ernerk, for example, was elected from the Keewatin constituency and became minister of Social Development and then Economic Development. After the 1979 election, eight of the twenty-two seats in the Legislative Assembly were from the Eastern and High Arctic, where about 90 per cent of the residents of this region are Inuit. In 1981, Kane Tologanak, representing the Central Arctic, was chosen minister of Government Services.

The Métis Association

The Métis founded their association in April 1972. In the past, the federal government insisted on dealing with the two organizations – the Dene and the Métis. The Métis submitted their claim to the federal government in 1977. Later, along with the Dene, they proposed the formation of a province-like Denendeh in the Western Arctic. The federal government then agreed to resolve the land claims with one settlement and one Dene-Métis organization. In 1990, the Dene and Métis decided to again separate their organizations. Supposedly, regional land claim settlements apply to both groups.

There has been an interesting relationship between the Dene and the Métis. Within many communities the Dene and Métis argue that there is no distinction: they live as one people. But differences do exist, as is indicated by the rifts that have occurred between the leadership of the two organizations. In 1974-6, many Dene and Métis split on the industrial pipeline proposals aired before Mr. Justice Thomas R. Berger (the Mackenzie Valley Pipeline Inquiry). Those who felt the development should proceed were anxious to get on with resource exploitation in the region in order to facilitate economic development for their people. Most of the Dene opposed development, arguing that their land was the key to survival in the North, and, thus, land claims should be settled prior to resource development. In 1977, Judge Berger recommended a ten-year moratorium on the project in order to 'strengthen native society and the native economy through settlement of land claims'[27] The significance of the Berger Inquiry will be discussed later in this chapter.

The formation of Native organizations offered the opportunity for a forceful expression of feelings and arguments that had been repressed or not heeded for years. As one observer described the situation in the early 1970s, many non-Natives were very disillusioned with the strong Native position on development. They had felt, and hoped, that Natives and non-Natives together could work on development of the North.[28] Many of these people, however, did not realize the strong feelings inherent in the Native populations – feelings intensified by a colonial system that was very paternalistic in its treatment of Native people. Politicized Native organizations, then, have established their own political agenda as part of the governmental process in the NWT.

CHANGING ROLE OF THE FEDERAL GOVERNMENT

Between 1967 and 1979, growth of government in the Northwest Territories was impressive. The GNWT assumed full responsibility for education, housing, local government, and public works. At the same time, responsibility for economic development and tourism, health care, renewable resources, and social services was shared with the federal government. An elaborate administrative apparatus was being developed, and, within the next ten years, additional federal responsibilities would be assumed by the territorial government. While this was a remarkable transformation in many ways, it was not always a smooth one. The transformation faced institutional inertia in Ottawa and institutional expansion in Yellowknife. It also involved strong, conflicting personalities. Describing it as a remarkable transformation may be taking the high road, because it has been described also as 'war' between Ottawa and Yellowknife.[29] Regardless of one's interpretation of the change, it laid the groundwork for achieving in the NWT many of the objectives stated in the Carrothers Commission.

The question arises, with the build-up of the administrative apparatus in Yellowknife, was there a corresponding downsizing of Northern Affairs in Ottawa? This was not the case, because while DIAND was shifting responsibilities to the GNWT, it was expanding its involvement in developing non-renewable resources in the North and assuming a new role in attempting to resolve claims.

In the late 1960s and early 1970s, the federal government was confronted with an increasing number of Native land claims. These claims were of two kinds: comprehensive and specific. Comprehensive claims involved groups which had never entered a treaty or any legal arrangement with the federal government over land. Specific claims involved groups which had a treaty with the government but disputed, for example, different obligations under the treaty or the Indian Act.

The federal government was facing a growing number of claims from bands throughout Canada, and, after problems with the White Paper, it was obviously necessary to clarify the legal basis for the claims. In 1969, the Trudeau government appointed a claims commissioner, Dr. Lloyd Barber, to review the basis for the land claims. His mandate in 1971 was expanded to include an examination of the legal validity of the claims. After almost five years of study, in 1973 Barber strongly recommended the government settle the nagging land claims. 'Recently, I recommended that the Government receive and consider the Yukon proposal for negotiations and I would hope that this is a practical and meaningful demonstration of my belief that the Government must negotiate with native people in areas where land rights are a major issue.'[30]

While Barber's assessment was in progress, an important court decision was handed down that strengthened the basis for Aboriginal claims. *Calder et al. vs. Attorney General of British Columbia* (1973) involved the Nishga people in British Columbia. While technically the case resulted in a split decision, the judgments went a long way toward reinforcing Aboriginal title due to occupancy prior to colonization.[31] This case strengthened the hand of Native groups, and, in August 1973, the government changed its policy toward land claims. The new policy, articulated subsequently in an annual report of DIAND, 'recognized that non-native occupancy of land ... had not taken ... native interest into account, had not provided compensation for its gradual erosion, and had too frequently excluded native people from benefiting from developments that had taken place as a result of non-native settlement.'[32] This was quite an admission for the federal government, and it was followed, in 1974, with the creation of an Office of Native Claims in DIAND.

As mentioned previously, northern affairs had been split between two factions: those that pushed Resource Development and assumed that Native people would partake of the economic benefits, and those who stressed the need for education and other social benefits for Native people in order to enhance their economic development opportunities. The latter were often said to be more people-oriented, and the former were said to be more resource oriented. In 1968, the appointment of Jean Chrétien as minister of Indian Affairs and Northern Development was a boost to the people-oriented faction, because Chrétien was said to be a 'hands on' minister interested in working with Native people.[34] All of these events led to the Inuit, Dene, Inuvialuit, and Métis claims being submitted in 1976 and 1977. Two important initiatives by the federal government also significantly influenced politics in the NWT.

The Berger Inquiry

In 1974, the Trudeau government appointed Judge Berger to assess the impact of constructing a gas pipeline down the Mackenzie Valley. The Berger Report has been mentioned briefly, but note should be made of the meaning of the testimony of Native people before Berger.[35]

His commission travelled throughout the Western Arctic visiting all communities. Natives and non-Natives were offered an opportunity to explain their views on the construction of a pipeline. As one might expect in a public forum, individuals came at the problem from numerous perspectives. Two of the most frequent arguments voiced by Natives were:

(1) The pipeline should not be built because it would possibly destroy the land, and the land was a critical part of survival for many Dene and Métis. Moreover, settlement of land claims was mandatory before resource exploitation should occur on land the Dene saw as their own.

(2) Some degree of 'autonomy' or self-government should also be an integral part of any deal, because self-government would enable Native people to take control of their own destiny on their own lands.

For example, Alfred Tanoton of Fort Franklin, speaking at the Berger hearings through an interpreter, expressed very well how important land is for Native people: 'And he says that this land is practically our last resort – our last means of survival, and he says that we feel that since all this time all the minerals that the Government has received, we haven't received one cent from them ... '[36] Richard Nerysoo of Fort McPherson was even more emphatic: 'We see our land as much, much more than the white man sees it. To the Indian people our land really is our life. Without our land we cannot – we could no longer exist as people. If our land is destroyed, we too are destroyed. If your people ever take our land you will be taking our life.'[37] The land is considered to be the economic base for Native people. Charlie Chocolate of Rae Lakes and Ishmael Alunik of Inuvik said: 'This land is our industry, providing us with shelter, food, income, similar to the industries down South supporting the white peoples ... We do not think of our jobs as a substitute for living off the land. Jobs are another way to help us live. We still want to trap and eat the food from our land.'[38] The land is also integral to cultural survival. Alex Arrowmaker and George Erasmus made the point very clearly:

It seems that the government's intention is ... to persuade native people
to become like or act like white people. And there is no way that we
native people want to lose our culture ... There is no way they are going
to change native people or have them like the white man.

For us in the valley here, it's a decision: do we want to continue on
as Dene people? Or do we want to forget that and become like every-
body else? The decision before us, I think, has been made already, and
people are acting on it. Clearly we want to remain as Dene people. We
do not want to assimilate.[39]

Finally, land, an economic base, and cultural survival all depend on
self-government – the ability of Native people to control their own
lives on their land. Robert Clement of Fort Norman expressed the central issue: 'But look what has happened. Now the government gives
the people everything, pays for the water and the fuel and the houses,
the education. It gives the people everything, everything but one thing
– the right to live their own lives. And that is the only thing that we
really want, to control our lives, our own land.'[40] And Chief Jim Antoine of Fort Simpson reiterated the Native position: 'We think we are
smart enough and intelligent enough and we know what's going on
around us now, we are becoming aware of what the white man is all
about and ... I think we could decide for ourselves how we want the
future to be.'[41] Native people in the NWT saw their land as an integral
part of their economic and cultural survival. For this reason, Native
people needed to settle the claims and acquire self-government in order to be able to control the land. For many Native people, the idea
of self-government meant more powers for communities. It was spelled
out in the Denendeh and Nunavut proposals. Essentially, the power
of local councils was to be expanded to include greater control of
responsibilities such as education, health care, housing, social services, policing, and local economic development. Gaining greater control of these responsibilities would have given Native people a much
better opportunity to exercise control over the cultural dilemma they
were, and are, facing.

The Berger Inquiry was a profound expression of how desperate
the people felt as their culture was eroded. It is a heart-wrenching
story of how the predominant southern culture of most Canadians
was encroaching on the northern way of life. These statements explain why the land claims negotiations, coupled with self-government,
are absolutely vital for Native people in the North. It is only with these
tools that Native people themselves will have a choice in lifestyles.
The Berger Inquiry also had a significant impact in that it made many

Canadians aware, for the first time, of Native problems in the NWT. In fact, Berger's recommendations reflected a keen sensitivity to the cultural dilemma facing Native people in the Mackenzie Valley.

The Drury Report

A second significant factor in the constitutional development of the GNWT was the Drury Report. In 1977, the federal government appointed C.M. Drury as 'Special Government Representative for Constitutional Development in the Northwest Territories.' Part of his terms of reference included:

(i) to conduct a systematic consultation with recognized leaders of the Territorial Government, northern communities and native groups about specific measures for modifying and improving the existing structures, institutions and systems of government in the Northwest Territories, with a view to extending representative, responsive and effective government to all parts of the Territories and at the same time accommodating the legitimate interests of all groups in northern society, beginning with those of the Indian, Inuit and Métis.[42]

Drury was to report to the prime minister 'with recommendations for action by the Federal Government.' The final report came out in January 1980, and it was very significant and controversial. It was significant because Drury perceived, as perhaps few in the South at the time did, why all was not well with the new GNWT. It was controversial because at the time many people in the NWT were beginning to debate the issue of division of the territories, and there was much support, particularly in the Eastern Arctic, for division. Drury came out against division and the creation of Nunavut, and for that reason much of the remainder of the report never received the attention it might have.

Drury, like the Carrothers commissioners, travelled to more than twenty communities in the Eastern and Western Arctic and held more than 150 meetings with individuals and groups. His primary objective was to assess the constitutional process since the Carrothers Report and suggest changes as needed. Drury, like the Carrothers commissioners, also detected a strong sense of community orientation. But to his credit, he also recognized a great deal of frustration on the part of people in the NWT because they still felt dominated by a government that was alien to them. For example, at Frobisher Bay (now Iqaluit) he was told: 'Intelligent and community-minded people are not running for councils, locally ... because it is a frustrating experience and power to do things is very limited. Council really does not make decisions, they merely vote their approval to what Yellowknife has already decided.'[43]

Drury heard a great deal about the pull and tug between Ottawa and Yellowknife and between Yellowknife and the communities. But his focus was on constitutional development, and, therefore, he devoted a significant amount of the report to relations between the federal, territorial, and local governments in the region. A significant problem in the NWT was the relationship between the territorial and local governments. For Drury, part of constitutional development included a need to strengthen local governments rather than to divide the territories and create Nunavut. Many of his recommendations pertained to this issue. These recommendations were the core of the report and they represent a significant contribution to ongoing discussions about constitutional evolution in the NWT. The problem, as Drury saw it, was, in part, historical:

> Local government in the NWT follows the model of municipal institutions as it exists in southern Canada, with some adaptations for unique northern conditions. In the South, municipal political processes and institutions evolved over many years to meet the needs of the citizens. In the North, on the other hand, a comprehensive system of local government was centrally planned and has been largely implemented in the brief 12-year period since the Carrothers Report.[44]

At the same time, there was another important difference between the NWT and southern Canada:

> Government in the NWT has not emerged from the grass roots. It is the product of a progressive transfer of administrative and then political structures and authorities from Ottawa to Yellowknife and thence to the communities. Community authority is not seen to be the prime focus of the system of government, even though some decentralization may be considered as a desirable long-term objective. The result is that government in the NWT tends to be centralized.[45]

In the communities, the problem was seen to be one of power:

> Local councils and committees are perceived by the communities as possessing no real authority over those issues that are of vital importance to the lives of residents of the communities. The territorial and federal governments consider the local councils and committees to be their agents, or merely advisory bodies, and not part of a separate and distinct level of government. Thus, the same phenomenon occurs at the community levels as at the territorial level: despite the existence of fully

elected representative bodies, there is a sense of powerlessness and a feeling that government is being 'administered' from afar. The principles of accountable and responsive government are not being fulfilled.[46]

The current jurisdictional areas of municipal councils relate primarily to the physical operation of hard services and include services such as water, sewerage, garbage collection, road maintenance, zoning and community planning. The soft services, namely social and cultural matters, education and land management, are largely excluded from the local process of decision-making. Many residents of the smaller communities regard the soft services as being critical to their lives, but ones over which they have little influence.[47]

This was an interesting observation, reflecting grassroots feeling on the part of many residents of the NWT, particularly residents of the smaller communities. Also, it was a serious indictment after more than a decade of the development of the GNWT. For ten years, much energy and time had been spent constructing a territorial government, a province-like apparatus for all the region. There were many problems, but two stand out.

First, it was very difficult to get Ottawa to go along with giving up any power. There was inertia in the administrative apparatus, and it took some fancy manoeuvring and badgering to pry power from DIAND. Second, it was also very difficult to establish, in short order, an effective governmental apparatus that could meet the needs of some sixty diverse, isolated communities that had never been a part of the major economy of Canada. This was a Herculean task, and Stuart Hodgson, commissioner from 1967 to 1979, was the point man for this accomplishment.

At the same time, one must recognize that in the haste to put together and to empower this huge apparatus, there was the problem of concentrating power. Drury detected this problem and recommended the following as a solution:

Strong, autonomous government at the local level is critical to achieving citizen participation in government, responsive administrative and legislative bodies, and the accountability of government to the citizens. In the NWT the importance of the local level of government is of particular magnitude because of the cultural diversity and the vast distances between communities.

The suggestions made here are designed to strengthen community government in the NWT by increasing political authority and responsibility at the local level. For a number of reasons, movement in this direction is necessary and, indeed, crucial to political development in the NWT[48]

In Drury's view, local and regional governments should have a statutory base:

> The territorial and federal governments should recognize a real and distinct first tier of government at the local level. At such time as the NWT Act is revised, an article should be added that would explicitly recognize the municipal order of government in the NWT and specify those jurisdictions in which the communities would have paramount authority. Communities should, however, be permitted to choose to exercise such responsibilities as they feel ready to accept. The NWT Act should also permit communities to delegate any of their responsibilities to regional structures.[49]

In terms of the role of local governments,

> the GNWT should adapt its structures, functions and attitudes so as to foster and reflect the development of community government. As communities assume the major operations of programs now delivered by the GNWT, progressive reorganization and consolidation of territorial program departments will be required. Moreover, an extensive decentralization of community-related territorial functions will allow the GNWT effectively to advise and assist the communities to assume new responsibilities.[50]

Regional governments, nurtured by communities, figured significantly in the solution:

> Communities should have the choice of forming regional councils through voluntary delegations upward of community authorities.

> Communities should define the extent of authority to be exercised regionally through a regional council.

> Consistent with the conclusion that the incorporated community council should be the prime public body at the local level, a regional council, where it exists, should be the prime public political structure at the regional level.[51]

He had a straightforward recommendation for the GNWT. 'The Territorial Council and the GNWT should not hinder the development of regional councils, nor prohibit their use as valid forums for the expression of communities of interest.'[52] Addressing the problem of dividing power between Yellowknife and the communities, Drury included very important suggestions in terms of local finances, for

there would be little power at the local level without financial
resources:

> If settlements, hamlets and villages are to become more autonomous,
> community governments must exercise discretion and be held account-
> able for these expenditures.
>
>   The objective for all incorporated municipalities in their fiscal relations
> with the GNWT should be to provide communities with equal access to
> territorial financial support, consistent with the intent to eliminate the
> present hierarchical structure of municipal authorities. Authority to ex-
> ercise local responsibility should not be dependent on the ability to raise
> revenue.[53]

Drury then advocated 'block transfers' from the GNWT to community
councils. These funds would be allocated on a formula basis, enabling
local governments to plan 'according to local needs and interests.' He
also recommended that local councils be permitted to keep the taxes
which they levied rather than having them collected from Yellowknife
and returned to the communities.

These were powerful recommendations, especially given the nature
of territorial-municipal relations. Block transfers were the key: they
would provide local governments with the resources to attack
problems at the local level. This recommendation was, in itself, critical if, indeed, local authorities were to have any real power.

Thus, Drury, in his assessment of constitutional development in the
GNWT, illuminated one critical problem after a decade of evolution.
It was necessary to face head on the division of power not just between
Ottawa and Yellowknife but between Yellowknife and the communities. In fact, the problem had been festering in the NWT since the federal government began to move into the region in 1921. This problem
is a manifestation of the 'cultural' issue that bothered Natives for years
– the fact that they were not able to deal with their problems in a way
that reflected their values. Drury picked up on this issue and
addressed the problem.

Unfortunately, many Native people did not take advantage of
Drury's offer to visit communities and to listen to their views on
problems with government. Given the history of this kind of exercise
in the NWT, one cannot blame Native people for being skeptical. But
Drury did make the kinds of recommendations that would considerably strengthen the role of local governments. These recommendations, if enacted by the GNWT, would reinforce the power of local
governments.

On an initial reading of the Drury Report, some of what is suggested is not fully apparent. He was accused, for example, of 'a lack of imagination' in dealing with the problems.[54] However, on close scrutiny, his solutions were very subtle and reflected the experience of an individual who had spent a lot of time in public life. He had to make recommendations that would have a chance of being passed by Cabinet *and* that would be accepted by Native people. He compromised by opposing division and the creation of Nunavut because he knew it was unacceptable to most government officials. At the same time, he made an attempt to strengthen the hand of Native people by recommending a devolution of power to institutions at the local and regional levels.

Regardless of the reception of the Drury assessment, the substance of his work addressed squarely what was then, and is now, one of the critical issues in the NWT – the extent to which decentralization should occur within the GNWT.

CONCLUSION

Between 1967 and 1979, two major changes influenced political development in the NWT. First, the GNWT was moved to Yellowknife, beginning the evolution to a more autonomous territorial government. By 1979, Commissioner Hodgson had established with certainty a GNWT presence within and without the territories. The style of the commissioner was one of executive dominance, which was required to wrestle governing responsibilities away from the DIAND administration in Ottawa (an administration that had had its way in the North for almost fifty years). Hodgson was the man for the job at the time. Indeed, most powers equivalent to those held by the provinces were devolved to the GNWT and, by 1979, it was administering services throughout the region.

While the GNWT was closer to the people, it was not perceived to be a responsive government. From the testimony before the Berger Inquiry, from what Drury found, and from the desire on the part of Native people to divide the territories, it was clear that many Native people felt that the GNWT was as distant and as alien as had been the federal government. Nevertheless, it became a major player in setting the political agenda for the region.

The second major change involved Native people. By the early 1970s, the Dene, Inuit, Inuvialuit, and Métis had formed political organizations which also became major players on the NWT political scene. These organizations, not always acting in harmony, had their own political agendas.

An item common to each Native organization was 'self-government'

– a way in which Native people could gain greater control of their own affairs. This objective manifested itself in different ways in the NWT, but it was the underlying goal articulated in proposals for Denendeh, Nunavut, the Western Arctic Regional Municipality, and the Baffin Regional Council. In each of the proposals, it is clear that, for Native people at least, enhanced government power at the local and regional levels was essential. Thus, for individuals living in most of the small communities, the development of Native organizations was a critical step in gaining greater influence and control over public policies involving education, health care, housing, police, and economic development.

CHAPTER SIX

A More Autonomous Government of the Northwest Territories, 1979-91

After 1979, the government of the Northwest Territories consolidated its province-like constitutional powers. Having an elected Legislative Assembly enabled the government to strengthen the executive apparatus. And the administrative apparatus was expanded to accommodate the devolution of powers from the federal government. In fact, during John Parker's time as commissioner, 1979-89, commissioner-in-council government was transformed to responsible cabinet government.

While constitutional development was progressing, public finance in the territories was a problem. The territorial government still derives slightly more than 80 per cent of its revenue from the federal government. Indeed, the tax base in the NWT is a questionable source of revenue, because, economically, the region is one of the most underdeveloped regions in Canada. There is hope for some change in the revenue situation because the federal government has agreed, in the 'Energy Accord' (signed with the GNWT in 1988), to share federal benefits from non-renewable resource development. While the revenue derived from resource extraction may never be a substantial portion of the total GNWT revenues, controlling this part of their funds would remove yet another symbol of the past colonial experience.

On the other hand, the development of the precise nature of the government process *within* the territories remains an important constitutional issue. The central question is, now that the GNWT has power, can it engender a sense of legitimacy and support from residents of the NWT? Or will residents of the region reject the present territorial government and opt for division of the region into smaller constitutional jurisdictions? Individuals in the Central and Eastern Arctic clearly prefer a Nunavut government as opposed to the present GNWT. In the Western Arctic, opinions are more evenly divided, although many people in small communities supported division in 1982 (the division issue is discussed at the end of this chapter). Constitutional development within the NWT is, therefore, a critical and complex issue. To put this constitutional issue into its current context, one must appreciate the political changes of the last decade.

CONSOLIDATING POWER IN THE GNWT

Two decades after moving the seat of government to Yellowknife, the GNWT does resemble provincial governments in the South. With two important exceptions, it has assumed responsibilities equivalent to those of the provinces. First, neither of the territorial governments are involved in amending the Canadian constitution. This fact, of course, was one of the reasons northerners in the NWT and the Yukon were adamantly opposed to the Meech Lake Accord. They claimed that the process of first ministers proposing amendments to the constitution created two classes of Canadians – those who were represented by their premiers at the table and those who were not. Territorial government leaders being denied formal representation at meetings involving constitutional changes was particularly offensive to northerners and did little to encourage northern integration into the Canadian polity.

A second point is that neither of the territorial governments have powers equivalent to the provinces regarding control of non-renewable resources. Most northerners accept the fact that revenue from resources in the region should not go solely to residents of the NWT or the Yukon; they know that with small populations it would be ludicrous to assume that all benefits would accrue to northerners only. At the same time, however, they feel they should have a proportional share of benefits from their resources. The federal government's position is that most of the GNWT's revenues come from Ottawa transfers, and this is far more money than the region could derive from land sales and royalties on non-renewable resources. Residents of the territories, however, would like to share directly in these benefits rather than have them cycled through the federal government. Revenue sharing, regardless of its amount, would represent an autonomous source of funds for the territorial government.

Legislative Committees

With the territorial election of 1975, all federal appointees to the Territorial Council were eliminated. Residents of the region for the first time had an all-elected assembly. This assembly, now with twenty-four MLA's representing constituencies throughout the territories, has become the heart of the governmental process. As can be seen in Table 14, there is now representative government in the NWT. Responsible government, however, is evolving in a different way.

TABLE 14
General elections: Legislative Assembly, NWT
(NWT Council until 1975)

Year*	Appointed members	Elected	Total votes	Per cent of electors voting	Constituencies
1967	5	7(1)†	6,463	64.6	(4) Mackenzie Valley (3) East, Central & Western Arctic
1970	5	10(1)	9,169	69.2	(4) Mackenzie Valley (4) East, Central, High & Western Arctic (1) Keewatin District (1) Yellowknife
1975	—	15(1)	10,813	63.9	(6) Mackenzie Valley, G. Slave & G. Bear lakes (4) Central, High & Western Arctic (2) Baffin Island (1) Keewatin District (4) Yellowknife
1979	—	22(1)	12,586	62.1	(9) Mackenzie Valley, G. Slave & G. Bear lakes (4) East, Central & Western Arctic (3) Baffin Island (3) Keewatin & Hudson's Bay (3) Yellowknife
1983	—	24(2)	15,764	69.7	One new constituency in the Western Arctic, one in the High Arctic
1987	—	24(3)	15,775	70.9	Constituency boundaries roughly the same as 1983

TABLE 14 (continued)

Year*	Appointed members	Elected	Total votes	Per cent of electors voting	Constituencies
1991	—	24(6)	21,021	76.4	Constituency boundaries redrawn; Pine Point constituency eliminated, Yellowknife-Fram Lake created, and a number of changes in the Eastern Arctic, e.g., Sanikiluaq incorporated into South Baffin

SOURCES: Government of Canada, 'Report of the Chief Electoral Officer on the General Election of Members to The Council of the Northwest Territories,' Ottawa, respective years; for 1991 results: *Nunatsiaq News*, 18 October 1991, 2

* By-elections not included
† ( ) number of members elected by acclamation

The Legislative Assembly is structured like provincial legislatures. For example, the assembly is broken down into standing and special committees. Standing committees deal with business of an ongoing nature while special committees are established to deal with specific issues.[1] Standing committees now include committees on: finance, public accounts, legislation; management and services boards; rules, procedures and privileges; and agencies, boards, and commissions. With minor exceptions, the government leader and ministers are not members of these committees.

Special committees deal with particular problems facing the legislature. The Tenth Assembly (1983-87) created two special committees, one on rules, procedures and privileges, to review 'the powers and organization of the Legislative Assembly,' and one on housing, to examine the problem of territorial housing and 'operation of the NWT Housing Corporation.'[2] The Eleventh Assembly (1987-91) established three special committees: one on the northern economy, one on Aboriginal languages, and one on constitutional reform.

Where the Legislative Assembly differs from its counterparts in the South is in the relationship between the executive and the committees. This relationship is influenced, of course, by the absence of political parties. Without partisanship forming the basis of support for the executive, the assembly committees have more autonomy than is the case in most provincial legislatures. For example, in explaining the role of the 1983 Committee on Finance and Public accounts, 'The Minister of Finance, who holds no power of party loyalty to gain approval of the budget, must seek the Committee's support when he tables his Main Estimates and his money bills.'[3] A former MLA, Linda Sorenson, in writing about the role of backbenchers in this process, says:

> With the assistance of simultaneous translation, constituency assistants, research and typing services, and a modest budget, the ordinary MLA has been able to better represent constituents, hold government and the Executive Council accountable, and influence government spending of taxpayers' dollars. The committee system has grown and strengthened with the introduction of support staff and, more importantly, credibility.
> The lack of political parties, the minority position of the Executive Council in the legislature, and the enthusiasm with which members raise issues in the legislature have all combined to create a unique style of governing ...[4]

Thus, one feature of the NWT legislature is that it does not function in the partisan, 'majoritarian' style of the provinces. Legislative committees can bargain with the executive without the constraints of political party discipline.

Development of Cabinet Government

Over the past two decades, the GNWT has assumed primary responsibility for delivering services in the territories. This was a stated objective expressed in the Carrothers Report, and it was the intent of Commissioner Parker to pull back the commissioner's role in the process of government.[5] The transformation of the executive to what can be termed 'Cabinet government' is a fact. Highlights of this evolution are described in Figure 14.

Eight of the twenty-four MLA's form the Cabinet of the GNWT. They are selected by the Legislative Assembly and, as ministers of the Crown, are responsible to the assembly. The physical arrangement of the Legislative Assembly even follows the Westminster model – government ministers sit to the right of the speaker and ordinary MLA's to the left. And the give and take between ministers and ordinary members is patterned along the lines of a question period in Parliament. Thus, except for party discipline, structures and procedures represent all the characteristics of a parliamentary process. The

lack of political parties, however, does create a different legislative
process.

As mentioned in Chapter 5, procedural changes after the 1987 elec-

---

FIGURE 14

Executive branch of the GNWT:
evolution to responsible government, 1980-91

1980   Two additional Legislative Assembly members elected to Executive
Council
Commissioner, deputy commissioner, 7 elected members
(Legislature agreed that one member of elected executive serve as
elected executive leader)

3 executive committees formed:
Priorities and Planning: George Braden, chair
Financial Management Board: Commissioner John Parker
Legislative and House Planning: Richard Nerysoo

1981   Elected member becomes minister of Finance: commissioner remains
chair of Financial Management Board

1983   Executive Council:
Leader of elected executive takes deputy chairman, Executive Council
Minister of Finance becomes chairman of Financial Management
Board
Deputy commissioner no longer sits on Executive Council (one
more seat to be elected, total of eight)
Executive Committee becomes Executive Council

1984   Leader of elected executive called government leader: Richard Nerysoo

1985   Two of the eight executive members replaced by assembly after interim vote, representing a type of 'responsible government.' Nick
Sibbeston is chosen government leader

1986   Government leader becomes chairman of Executive Council
Government leader takes over management of Public Services, last
formal administrative responsibility of commissioner

1987   Dennis Patterson chosen government leader

1989   John Parker retires as commissioner; Daniel L. Norris, resident of the
Western Arctic, is appointed commissioner

1991   Nellie Cournoyea chosen government leader

SOURCE: GNWT, *Annual Report*, respective years.

tion were designed to strengthen the power of the government leader. After the 1991 election and the formation of the Twelfth Legislative Assembly, members met to choose the government leader and members of the Cabinet. In this case, the process was held in public. Members declared their candidacy and, after delivering speeches in the assembly, were chosen by the entire assembly. This was in contrast to the MLA's meeting in camera, after which they later declared the winners. A motion was made to have the government leader choose her Cabinet. It was defeated and the Legislative Assembly chose the remaining seven members. The leader then assigned ministerial portfolios. The Legislative Assembly retains a degree of autonomy because it elects the Cabinet and reviews in two years the performance of the government leader and all members of the executive.

While the leader does not choose members of the executive, he or she can change a minister's portfolio and members of the executive can be 'disciplined.' Thus, the leader does have some clout in the executive. But the fact that all members of the executive must answer to the entire assembly creates a kind of non-partisan 'responsibility' of its own. These ministers, however, are not responsible in a collective sense, as would be the case for a cabinet in a partisan system. Cabinet responsibility in the GNWT, then, is another distinctive feature of that government.

This process has developed a dynamic of its own. Government ministers, for example, must take care of their constituents if they hope to be re-elected. At the same time, they must take care of the ordinary members if they aspire to retain a ministerial portfolio. This makes it sound as if the backbenchers have all the clout in the legislative process. If, however, ordinary members are going to enact policies that will effect their constituencies, they must work with members of the the Cabinet. This basis for trade-offs without the influence of political parties is the way cabinet government has adapted to consensus politics.

The Administration

One obvious characteristic of the GNWT is its growth. In 1979, for example, there were 2,845 territorial civil servants. By 1989, there were 6,140. In addition, there were 1,354 municipal and 1,524 federal officials in the territories.[6] On a per capita basis, the NWT has more public officials than any jurisdiction in Canada. Government has become a growth industry in the territories. The devolution of responsibilities from Ottawa to Yellowknife has been behind much of this growth.[7]

Highlights of this devolution are described in Figure 15. The administrative structure of the GNWT today resembles that of most provinces. But the growth is not only in the civil service. As a measure of growth, government budgets are even more impressive. In twenty-five years (1967-91), the operating and capital budgets have increased almost 700 per cent (Table 15). But the point to remember is that these figures represent the equivalent of provincial *and* municipal government spending in the South. A good portion of the latter, of course, goes for services which are locally funded in most provinces. But the low levels of economic development in many NWT communities requires that most local services be funded by the territorial government. This fact has a positive and a negative side; while it increases the number and quality of services provided to communities, it also increases dependency. Local governments have been, and remain, financially dependent on the Yellowknife administration.

FIGURE 15
Evolution of administrative responsibilities, 1979-89

1979 Department of Nature and Cultural Affairs renamed Department of Renewable Resources

Department of Public Services renamed Department of Justice and Public Service

1984 Transfer of intra-territorial road construction programs from federal government

1985 Department of Information renamed Department of Culture and Communications

Department of Justice and Public Service renamed Department of Justice

1986 Department of Local Government renamed Department of Municipal and Community Affairs

1987 Forest management and Fire Suppression responsibilities devolved to Renewable Resources

1988 Final health care responsibilities transferred to GNWT

Northern Canada Power Commission and Northern Scientific Resources transferred to GNWT

1989 Creation of three new departments: Safety and Public Services; Transportation; Energy, Mines and Petroleum Resources

---

SOURCE: GNWT, *Annual Reports*, respective years

TABLE 15

Operations, maintenance, and capital expenditures of the GNWT, 1967-92

Year	Amount
1967	$ 14,332,487
1968	14,584,000
1969	20,218,000
1970	41,279,318
1971	72,237,464
1972	90,957,473
1973	111,651,974
1974	128,455,876
1975	139,466,447
1976	167,667,750
1977	217,694,184
1978	247,637,618
1979	282,187,000
1980	307,530,000
1981	335,027,000
1982	406,136,000
1983	475,996,000
1984	486,772,000
1985	535,785,000
1986	633,931,000
1987	093,011,000
1988	797,653,000
1989	858,041,000
1990	1,006,243,000
1991 (forecast)	1,078,932,000
1992 (estimates)	1,127,991,000

SOURCES: GNWT *Annual Report*, 1967-88; figures for 1989 and 1990 from GNWT, Michael A. Ballantyne, Minister of Finance, 'Budget Address,' 37, and 'Budget Address, 1991-2,' 25

Financing the GNWT

Securing financial resources is an integral part of the evolution of the GNWT. Indeed, without a constant source of public revenue, the territorial government will not be able to respond to problems in the region, and without developing a revenue base of its own, the 'autonomy' of the government will always be in question.

In regard to GNWT finances, two points need to be made: most public funds come from the federal government, and, over the past decade, this source of funding has been stabilized. On the revenue side, for example, in 1989 total revenues for the GNWT were $912,751,000. Of this amount, $675,499,000 (72 per cent of total revenue) was an unconditional grant from the government of Canada. In addition, the federal government provided basic transfers to all jurisdictions, and the NWT portion of the Established Program Finances (EPF) and other transfers and recoveries amounted to $125,788,000 – 13.8 per cent of total revenue. On the other hand, territorial tax revenues were $64,999,000 (7 per cent of revenues), and another 7 per cent ($64,566,000) was raised from transactions, including the liquor control system.[8]

On the expenditure side, operating and capital funds expended in 1989 were $858,041,000. The breakdown of these operating expenditures by departments is outlined in Table 16. Departments with the largest budgets were Education, Health, and Public Works, followed closely by the Territorial Housing Corporation, Municipal and Community Affairs, and Social Services.

While it may appear that Ottawa is generous with funding for the NWT, two things must be considered. First, all provinces depend on the federal government to some extent. Ottawa funds about 45 to 55 per cent of the total revenue in most Maritime provinces, and about 12 to 15 per cent in Alberta, British Columbia, and Ontario. Therefore, depending on the strength of provincial economies, Ottawa *does* vary its transfer payments. Given the condition of the NWT economy, Ottawa's transfer payments will be high.

Second, the NWT to this point has not received benefits from the rather considerable resource extraction in the region. For instance, the value of mineral shipments from the region in 1989 was $1,129,928,000.[9] Since 1977, shipments of metals and fuels totalled more than $8 billion (Table 17). Rents and royalties in the NWT may never amount to a great deal of revenue for the GNWT. However, sharing the resources will provide a greater degree of autonomy for the territorial government.

In the last ten years, one advantage for the territorial government has been formula financing, established for a five-year period. Until 1979, grants were on a year to year basis. Mr. Drury, in 1980, suggested that financing be extended over a longer period of time in order to facilitate planning. The first change was to extend grants to a three-year period. In 1985-6, the GNWT and the federal government negotiated a five-year 'Formula Financing' arrangement. This arrangement, while perhaps not perfect, was considered crucial to stabilizing programs devolved from the federal government. As an official in the

Fiscal Policy Division of the GNWT has said, 'Formula financing was a vital step in the evolution of responsible and accountable govern-

TABLE 16

Expenditure summary by program, 1987-8 to 1991-2 ($000)

Program	1987-8 Actuals	1988-9 Actuals	1989-90 Actuals	1990-1 Revised forecast	1991-2 Main estimates
Legislative Assembly	$ 5,108	$ 5,966	$ 9,079	$ 8,959	$ 9,209
Executive	13,131	14,901	15,778	18,409	18,345
NWT Housing Corporation	74,168	70,880	82,555	79,992	82,956
Finance	10,663	18,701	20,989	21,408	21,120
Culture & Communications	7,698	7,532	9,619	12,355	13,621
Personnel	25,225	27,081	30,109	33,299	29,852
Justice	28,799	32,962	35,179	39,564	40,006
Safety & Public Services	3,428	3,926	5,043	5,799	6,282
Government Services	21,441	21,833	24,132	23,590	22,404
Public Works	96,655	105,121	105,952	118,799	120,952
Transportation	35,411	32,529	38,046	49,060	63,187
Renewable Resources	39,061	38,631	53,495	44,453	45,107
Municipal & Community Affairs	90,693	77,410	94,269	107,891	96,756
Health	97,888	149,323	161,579	178,444	173,559
Social Services	61,980	73,202	78,417	89,630	92,292
Energy, Mines & Petroleum Resources	1,564	2,678	3,800	3,965	2,710
Economic Development & Tourism	25,968	28,826	33,370	45,494	43,102
Education	158,742	146,539	170,587	187,507	196,514
Total O & M and capital	$797,653	$858,041	$971,998	$1,068,618	$1,077,983

SOURCE: GNWT, Michael A. Ballantyne, Minister of Finance, 'Budget Address, 1991-2,' 25

TABLE 17
Value of metals and fuel shipments from the NWT, 1977-89 ($000)

Year	Metals (TS685)	Fuels (TS695)	
1989	$ 950,857	$ 179,071	
1988	805,636	130,410	
1987	696,258	155,809	
1986	642,118	119,835	
1985	588,038	223,209	
1984	666,090	38,964	
1983	496,552	37,682	
1982	383,384	34,716	
1981	304,017	50,414	
1980	367,339	57,162	
1979	383,299	51,679	
1978	270,953	38,686	
1977	216,439	39,220	
Totals	$6,987,419	$1,122,857	= $8,110,276

SOURCE: GNWT, Statistics Quarterly 12 (1990):109

ment in the north.'[10]

At the heart of the 1985 agreement was a formula based on a national average of provincial and local government spending, and the figure recognized 'the need to insulate the Government of the Northwest Territories from the volatility of tax collections.'[11] The new formula negotiated in 1990 does away with this insulation, and it now also factors in 'changes in provincial and local government tax efforts.'[12] For many residents of the NWT, the new formula is not as beneficial as was the 1985 arrangement. Nonetheless, formula financing remains one more milestone on the road to a more autonomous GNWT. A concern for territorial officials, however, is the federal government's pronouncements that, in the future, provinces and territories may receive less not more financial support from Ottawa. This poses a real cloud on the horizon, as the territorial government has relied heavily upon federal funding to maintain basic services in the region. If the cuts materialize, it would be very difficult for the government to make up the shortfall, especially given the state of the economy in the region. An examination of education and housing policies offers an indication of how well the territorial government is fulfilling its responsibility for delivering services.

EDUCATION POLICIES

Problems with the education system in the NWT are complex indeed. In fact, education poses a troubling dilemma. On the one hand, economic growth and development in communities hinges on an educated population. On the other hand, schools in the territories are not meeting the needs of young people. As noted in a recent report by the Special Committee on the Northern Economy: 'No matter what programs we try to introduce, we can't keep up with the number of young people who quit school before acquiring the basic skills needed in the workplace.'[13] In trying to explain the dilemma, critics often point the finger at the GNWT.[14] But the problem is not an easy one to resolve. Constructing a viable program for over sixty scattered communities in which people use at least nine different languages or dialects would be a challenge for any administration.

As noted in previous chapters, education policies have changed greatly in the NWT. Initially, the churches, with government support, provided elementary education in scattered day and residential schools. After the late 1940s and early 1950s, the government assumed responsibility for education and increased substantially its commitment to the system. There was great emphasis upon making schools available for residents in all communities. By the 1960s, with a growing emphasis on wage employment, schools were constructed in most communities, usually offering grades one to nine. For most communities, completion of high school required that students go to residential schools in Inuvik, Yellowknife, Iqaluit, and, more recently, Rankin Inlet. Thus, in terms of plants and equipment, today northern schools are equal to most school districts in the South. Elaborate gymnasiums and computers have become integral parts of the program, and the GNWT's Department of Education spends about 20 per cent of the territorial budget – approximately $130 million in 1989.

In spite of the many initiatives and developments by the federal and territorial governments, numerous problems still exist with the NWT education system. For example, the number of young people completing grade twelve in 1983 was greater than in 1990.

TABLE 18
High school enrolment and graduates, NWT

	1989-90	1987-8	1982-3
Total enrolments	13,748	13,386	12,761
Senior high	1,487	1,391	1,181
Senior high graduates	162	226	179

SOURCE: GNWT, Statistics Quarterly 13(1991):13, 14

While Native students represented approximately 70 per cent of total enrolments in 1987-8, only 31 per cent of those awarded diplomas were Native students.[15]

But the problem is not just high school graduates. As one report noted in 1989: 'Thirty-three per cent of our total population, and seventy-four per cent of our native population are functionally illiterate in English (with less than a Grade 9 education).'[16] The realization that something was wrong was not a recent revelation. Over two decades ago the problems were known by a number of people working closely with Native people. For example, in a 1967 report to the superintendent of adult education, Keith J. Crowe wrote:

> What is needed is integration, as far as possible, of all programs, and involvement of Eskimos at all levels of settlement planning, whatever the short-range costs in terms of time and efficiency.
>
> We need to increase the available educational literature in the Eskimo language.
>
> I believe that if we fail to develop a combined educational and administrative method that reflects the realities of Arctic community life, then we will support for a long time a demoralized adult population, and this in turn will negate the purposes of our schools.[17]

Although he was talking about the situation in the Keewatin District, Crowe's comments touch upon problems common throughout the NWT. He first of all linked the educational system with community life. The two had to be synthesized. Second, there had to be greater community involvement in the school system. And, finally, the curriculum had to reflect the languages of the community.

The problem of involving local residents in the education system was bureaucratic. From the outset the school system in the NWT was imported, and it was administered from the top down. In setting up the education system, initially the department in Ottawa and later the department in Yellowknife established and administered a system that resembled schools in the South. The difference was that in the South, school systems usually evolved the other way; local citizens formed a board, and, in some cases, with provincial, or perhaps federal, financial assistance, a school program was launched. In the North, the school system was the product of an Ottawa or a Yellowknife administration. While individuals in the communities saw the value in education and certainly desired schools, until the 1970s (with the exception of Yellowknife) there was little opportunity for community input into shaping the nature of the educational system. The input that did occur by the mid-1970s was in an 'advisory' capacity, and control of the process remained in the hands of departmental 'experts.'

At the same time, the education system in the NWT followed the Alberta curriculum. In other words, the language and examples used in the school system were those designed for Alberta students. Needless to say, discussions about elevators in skyscrapers, agricultural production, or turkey dinners did not always make a lot of sense to children in small northern communities.

By 1977, there were pressures from the communities for change. Many people felt that local needs and concerns should be addressed in the curriculum. In that year, the GNWT responded with a new education ordinance, which, among other things, permitted communities to elect members of a Local Education Authority (LEA's). This response did not meet all local demands, and, in 1980, the Legislative Assembly created a Special Committee on Education. The report of that committee, 'Learning: Tradition and Change in the Northwest Territories,' was revealing. In the 'Overview' of the report, committee members said: 'We have been deeply impressed by our people's interest in the system and by their conviction that it should serve the student's needs far better than it does at present.'[18]

This community feeling was expressed very vividly by local residents. In public hearings in Inuvik it was suggested that: 'The school system is not reaching out to the community and getting feedback from the people and parents in the community.'[19] In Igloolik, one person went right to the heart of the issue: 'We don't want to drop the school system, we just want a system appropriate to our needs.'[20]

The committee responded with forty-nine recommendations, which addressed structural and curriculum problems. For example, it was suggested that the minister of education should delegate responsibility for education through grade nine to ten divisional boards of education, and each community should have representation on one of those boards. In terms of the curriculum, local education authorities could 'determine the language to be used in the classroom,' and, accordingly, funds would be made available to develop teaching materials.[21]

The Department of Education has responded to the recommendations. The new lines of responsibility under the Department of Education are described in Figure 16. The diagram reflects three different types of local involvement in the school system. For example, there are two types of Local Education Authorities – committees and societies. Local committees advise the superintendent. Societies, on the other hand, have greater responsibilities. They can be involved in the process of hiring local teachers, and they have some discretionary funds from the department which they can spend.

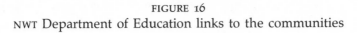

FIGURE 16
NWT Department of Education links to the communities

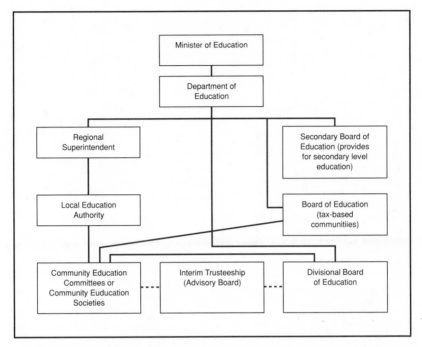

SOURCE: GNWT, Department of Education, 'Public Control of Education: How it Works in the Northwest Territories' (Yellowknife, 1988)

The divisional board represents the second way in which local residents can participate in the school system. Several communities can participate under a divisional board which has additional responsibilities: hiring a superintendent, teachers, and staff, developing programs, choosing the language of instruction, and determining the school year. Baffin Island communities established the first divisional board in 1985.

The third organization on the chart is the Board of Education in tax based communities. These boards are required to raise 25 per cent of their funds from local taxes, and they are responsible for all aspects of the school system. Yellowknife has the only school boards: a separate and a public board. These structures reflect the fact that local residents are taking a greater part in running local schools. The way in which communities in the NWT have moved from committee to society is described in Table 19.

The curriculum also poses a problem in NWT education. Much

TABLE 19

Designated education committees and societies by superintendency and education division, 1978-87

Superintendency/Division		1978	1979	1980	1981	1982	1983	1984	1985	1986	1987
Baffin - 15 districts	Societies	—	—	2	2	5	6	6	6	6	6
	Committees	15	15	13	13	10	9	9	9	9	9
Inuvik - 11 districts	Societies	—	—	—	—	—	1	1	1	1	1
	Committees	11	11	11	11	11	10	10	10	10	10
Kitikmeot - 6 districts	Societies	—	—	—	1	1	1	2	3	4	5
	Committees	6	6	6	5	5	5	4	3	2	1
Keewatin - 7 districts	Societies	1	1	2	3	3	3	5	5	5	5
	Committees	6	6	5	4	4	4	2	2	2	2
Fort Smith - 18 districts	Societies	—	1	1	1	1	2	3	4	6	7
	Committees	18	17	17	17	17	16	15	14	12	11
Yellowknife - 1 district	Societies	—	—	—	—	—	1	1	1	1	1
	Committees	1	1	1	1	1	—	—	—	—	—

SOURCE: GNWT, Department of Education, 'Public Control of Education: How it Works in the Northwest Territories' (Yellowknife, 1988)

adaptation has been required to make the school program relevant for NWT students. Materials had to be adapted to the cultural needs of communities or districts. Changing the language of instruction in the first four grades was desirable in many communities. The department has worked to provide curriculum support material to meet the needs of all students. For example, the science curriculum is being supplemented by materials that include animals and plants indigenous to the NWT.[22]

There is also a need to hire teachers locally. This is not easy, because there is a shortage of qualified teachers who are residents of the territories. Hence, outsiders often come to the communities for only a short time and have little opportunity to adapt to the NWT cultures. Or some individuals may be insensitive to local cultural traits. This problem has been addressed to some extent by the Department of Education in hiring teachers' aides locally. On Baffin Island, for example, nine years ago 3 per cent of the teachers came from the region. Today it is about 30 per cent, and, in ten more years, it could be that 75 per cent of the teachers in the region will be Inuit.[23] Arctic College, at its main campuses, is placing a great deal of emphasis on teacher certification programs.

These adjustments having been made, why is there ongoing criticism of the school system in the NWT? What are the basic problems with the system and with the department? Colin Irwin, probably one of the strongest critics of education in the territories, suggests in his *Lords of the Arctic: Wards of the State* (1988) that education in the NWT should prepare individuals to live in two worlds – the world of southern industrialized Canada and the more traditional world of hunting and trapping in the NWT.[24] Irwin suggests that in fact Inuit are getting 'the worst of both worlds and the best of neither.'[25] Part of the problem is that, since 1968, the department has failed to develop an adequate curriculum and has thus failed to get an adequate number of Inuit teachers in the program. If these failures continue, southern whites 'will continue to dominate the higher levels of management in both the private and public sectors.'[26] The gist of his argument is:

> The generation of Inuit who were born, grew up, and went to school in the settlements established in the 1960s have acquired neither the tradition nor the formal education possessed by their older brothers and sisters. They find it very difficult to live on the land, to develop a career, or to complete a program of higher education. They are a lost generation, whose education and enculturation provides them with little more than the skills required to live out their lives as wards of the state.[27]

The department countered, naturally, saying that Irwin did not take into account what the government was doing to improve education. The argument was made that Irwin's research was too narrow, and that his generalizations were based on findings from a small part of the entire system. The government's position was that its approach was right and that, in time, difficulties in the system would be overcome. Irwin was saying that, given present trends, the system would remain a problem for the next generation.

There is probably truth in both positions. Education remains a critical problem in the NWT. It is one of the key areas in which suppositions are made regarding a better life for residents of the region. Yet Native young people, particularly, are not taking advantage of the system. Because of this fact, job prospects for a growing population are not good. At the same time, the Department of Education has recently introduced a number of changes: some decentralization, local languages used in instruction, and so on. The point is, it may be a decade before the consequences of these changes are felt. In other words, the true test for current changes will be demonstrated in the number of today's elementary students who graduate from high school.

In the NWT education system, the curriculum must be, as Irwin points out, sensitive to the cultural needs of northern students. Part of the problem is that a large government department may be better at building plants and equipment than it is at supporting the cultural needs of the different groups in the NWT. There are, then, two problems with incoporating northern cultural materials into the curriculum: (1) decisions made influencing cultural content in the curriculum and (2) finding funds to support the changes.

The first is a problem inherent to a large bureaucratic organization. Will officials in Yellowknife give communities and divisional boards the leeway to develop curriculum materials? One positive example has been the Arctic Institute's Gwich'in Language and Cultural Project. This is a pilot project designed to train individuals in Fort McPherson who can teach people in the community to read and write in their Native language. A primary goal of the project is to enhance the skills of Native people so that they can gain 'local control of education and ... start on the road to self-government.'[28] According to Joan Ryan: 'Biculturalism implies a need for bilingualism.'[29] Therefore, the project designed to educate individuals in their indigenous language and to develop culturally related materials should strengthen Fort McPherson's school curriculum.

This project is unique because from the start it was supported by a mixture of private and public funding, and it meshed conveniently with objectives of community leaders in Fort McPherson. For the first three years, it was a joint venture project of the Arctic Institute, the community, and the Department of Education. This kind of autonomous project may be the best kind to use to foster the development of culturally based curriculum changes. However, it may be difficult for the territorial department to initiate such projects for each community or school district.

It is also difficult to secure funding for this type of project. It would not be easy for each community or each school district in the NWT to find external funding to expand cultural materials. While the Department of Education is set up for funding capital and operating expenses, it may be reluctant to provide a variety of groups unconditional grants with which to work on local curriculum needs. Thus, to best support local cultural projects, increased block funding by the Department of Education to communities or districts could strengthen the curriculum for local schools. Where the needs are quite diverse, increased block funding would enable the Department of Education to assist further all school jurisdictions altering the cultural mix of educational materials.

The problems inherent in education in the NWT are problems involved in any bureaucratic organization – the difficulty being devolving decisionmaking responsibilities to local organizations. Changing the organizational orientation from top down to bottom up is a difficult task. Yet it is a critical task if the residents of communities are to have meaningful involvement in shaping the local curriculum. This is not to say that, with more local control, the curriculum will necessarily move in the direction of more Native cultural content. Nor is it to say that the curriculum will necessarily remain as it is now. But these are decisions to be made locally. The NWT education system has a problem, particularly with Native children, in encouraging the completion of high school. If greater cultural content helps, perhaps it should be tried. However, the real challenge for the education system is to provide a curriculum for students so that they will have a choice of lifestyles: living the modern, industrial way; living the traditional way; or trying to strike a balance between the two.

HOUSING POLICIES

Housing for residents of the NWT is an extremely controversial issue. Adequate housing in the region is essential, of course, given the climate. And housing is an issue because of northern construction costs. Housing is also a public policy issue because of 45 per cent of the NWT housing is government supplied, 31 per cent is social housing, and 14 per cent is federal or territorial government housing.[30] Thus, the controversy surrounding this issue involves meeting the housing needs of a rapidly growing population (particularly in small communities), providing appropriate housing, and involving individuals in the decisionmaking process concerning housing policies.

In the late 1950s and early 1960s, the federal government established permanent settlements for NWT Natives. Home construction was a big part of this policy. Problems arose almost immediately, as most families were large and were expected to live in very small residences. In 1963, the standard plan was a house with 288 square feet. By 1972, the standard rental house was 768 square feet.[31] Over the years a number of home ownership and rental programs have been established. The initial intent was to assist in ownership. By 1965, however, because it was obvious that many NWT residents had difficulty with mortgage requirements, the rental programs were initiated (Figure 17).

With the movement of the GNWT from Ottawa to Yellowknife in 1967, housing responsibilities soon followed. By 1969, the territorial government took control of delivery of housing in the region. The Department of Local Government became involved in housing because it was an issue of prime concern to people in the new communities. In 1971, the Territorial Council established a task force on housing, and in its report two principal recommendations were made:

(1) the responsibility for all housing programs be placed under the control and policy direction of the Government of the Northwest Territories.

(2) a Northwest Territories Housing Corporation be established and head-quartered at Yellowknife, to create, co-ordinate and give direction to housing programs based on need, environment and research, so as to make available an adequate standard of housing to all residents of the Northwest Territories.[32]

The Northwest Territories Housing Corporation (NWTHC) began operation on 1 January 1974. The corporation 'develops, maintains and manages social housing and other housing programs for the benefit of all residents of the Northwest Territories.'[33]

The problems facing the corporation were numerous – for example, size, design, and delivery of the product. They were discussed in a conference-workshop, 'Building in Northern Communities,' held in February 1974. In the report of the conference, Margaret McGee, then an administrator in the corporation, noted the problem with design: 'The Housing Association is responsible for recommending to the local Settlement Council the location of the new houses to be constructed. After that the Housing Association has no involvement what-

FIGURE 17

Chronology of major housing programs in the NWT, 1952-86

1952 Welfare Housing (Indian Affairs Branch)	
1959 Eskimo Housing Loan Program (Indian Affairs Branch - East)	
1961 Territorial 2nd Mortgage Loans (NWT/CMHC)	
1962 Territorial 1st Mortgage Loans (low Cost Housing Ord. - NWT/CMHC)	1965 Eskimo Rental Housing Program (Indian Affairs Branch)
1968 Indian Off-Reserve and Eskimo Reestablishment Program (Indian Affairs Branch)	1968 Northern Rental Program (Indian Affairs Branch)
1968 Northern Purchase Housing Program (Indian Affairs Branch)	1968 Northern Rental Program (Indian Affairs Branch)
1969 Territorial Purchase Housing Program (NWT)	1969 Territorial Rental Housing Program (NWT)
	1969 Public Housing (NWT/CMHC - NHA 16, 35)
1973 Country Home Assistance Grant Program (NWT)	
	1974 Public Housing (NWTHC/CMHC - NHA 43, 44)
1976 Rural and Remote program (NWTHC/CMHC)	
1977 Small Settlement Home Assistance Grant Program (NWTHC)	
	1980 Public Housing (NWTHC/CMHC - NHA 40)
1983 Homeownership Assistance Program (NWTHC)	
1986 Homeownership Assistance Program (NWTHC/CMHC)	

SOURCE: NWTHC, 'Study on Housing Policy and Program Coordination,' Steve Iveson, Director Policy and Evaluation, 26 April 1990

soever with the project until the houses are signed over to the Chairman of the Association. What is needed is more local input in the
design of the units.'[34]

At the same time there was a problem involving ownership and
rental housing. Victor Allen, a resident of Inuvik, commented at the
same conference: 'The government comes along and says, you've got
poor housing; we will give you a low rental ... Under the government
plan he is not dependent on himself anymore. He suddenly finds out
that he felt pretty happy until the government officers came along.[35]
There was the problem of demand. Never have there been sufficient
resources for governments to meet the demand for housing in the NWT.
'The Northern Rental Housing Program provided for 1,558
three-bedroom houses to be built in 43 northern settlements by 1973.
At the close of the 1971 construction year, 1,378 houses had been built
under the program. Even with the program spanning the Arctic from
east to west, the demand outpaced the supply.'[36]

Thus, the Territorial Housing Corporation faced a formidable task.
According to a number of reports, however, the corporation was not
the panacea for housing problems. In 1977, the Legislative Assembly
adopted an 'Integrated Housing Policy' for the NWT. The policy was
designed to resolve a host of housing problems, including shortages
in new house construction and home ownership.[37] In spite of good
intentions, many problems remained with the corporation. For
example, 'in 1978, there was a senior management change in the NWT
Housing Corporation. Funding by way of the Treasury Board submis-
sion was not achieved. And the goal to integrate programs with other
agencies, including Territorial government departments, was not
pursued.'[38]

By 1980, a number of communities were taking it upon themselves
to work on housing problems. In the Keewatin, for example, a proposal
was made by which the

> Housing Corporation District office functions [would] be delivered by
> the regional federation. A District Manager trainee was selected and the
> process for transition was instituted. It never came about.
>
> In 1981 there was another change in the senior management of the
> NWT Housing Corporation and the direction of the Corporation shifted
> away from a community development approach, consistent with the
> Government of the NWT move towards devolution of local government
> program delivery and responsibility. This was evident in the 1981 Western
> Arctic Housing Corporation in Inuvik where viewpoints of community
> representatives and CMHC-NWTHC staff clashed.[39]

These bureaucratic problems were particularly frustrating for individuals, community leaders, and territorial politicians. Popular pressure for change was focused on the Legislative Assembly, and, in 1984, a special committee on housing was formed. In the course of holding public hearings in thirty-five communities, the frustrations with the process were evident. Peter Koonilusie spoke at the Clyde River hearing:

> I don't like the (NWT) Housing Corporation. I just got out of the Housing Association last fall. I was the Chairman of the Housing Association for a year. When we have gone to the Housing Federation Conference – the Housing Federations seems like a committee of the Housing Corporation and when the Housing Federation wants to do a major project there has never been a representative from (NWT) Housing Corporation attending the Housing Federation Conferences.[40]

And George Barnaby of Fort Good Hope was even more critical:

> As was mentioned before, there has always been a problem with housing, especially since the territorial government got involved in it. If you look back to before the government moved North, I mean everybody owned and built their own houses and had responsibility for everything they decided. They did it for themselves. About 1968 or 1969, there was a big push by the government to change everything around ... I guess it involved everything, but it also involved housing. There was a lot of time and money spent introducing a new rental program of housing. At that time people were promised that they would pay a couple of bucks a month and they would have a lower rental unit, that is what they were called. So that was a pretty good deal, you get all your electricity and fuel oil plus the house for two dollars a month.
>
> Along with that a lot of the old houses were destroyed. At that time there was no Council, nothing to advise the territorial government. They did not recognize the band councils. They did not talk to them. So a lot of the houses were destroyed. Some of them were pushed over with cats. Some of these people still do not have houses. Their houses were never replaced. Also they would have no choice but a rental house. That means their houses were taken away from them and then they would have to rent from the people who took them away.[41]

Obviously, there was a communication problem between the corporation and the communities. One problem fueling frustrations was the housing backlog. In 1985, the special committee report was published. It stated that 1,000 public housing units would be needed over the next five years.[42] By 1990, however, the minister responsible for the NWTHC reported that there was a need for 3,000 housing units. Furthermore, 'in 1989-90 the corporation built or assisted in the construction of 400 new houses and wrote off 100 old northern territorial rentals for a net gain of 300 units. At this rate, it will be at least 20 years before we catch up on current demand.'[43]

Growth in the population compounds the problem for the corporation. For instance, during the 1961-86 period, the territories grew 127 per cent while growth in the Canadian population increased by 38.77 per cent. From 1981 to 1986, population in the NWT increased by 14.2 per cent while growth in Canada was 3.97 per cent. The growth was not due to in-migration. Between 1982 and 1988, a net of 3,187 people left the territories, while the population grew by an estimated 7,000.[44] Clearly, the increase is caused by a high birth rate, which compounds the housing problem.

Another, more complex, problem involves the use of house construction to head off some of the economic problems in communities: 'It is certainly safe to say that the construction of new housing to alleviate the housing shortage would generate substantial economic activity in the communities.'[45] The point was made again in a NWTHC 'study' in 1990. Steve Iveson said:

> Housing presents a unique opportunity to further government policy objectives (such as the Economic Development Strategy, Employment Development Strategy, Community Self-Govt Initiative, etc.) because of the significant and relatively constant levels of funding, the fact that it can provide a training ground for a wide array of business and job skills (from construction to administration), and due to the range of industries and businesses that participate directly or indirectly in the provision of housing and housing services.[46]

There was a link between economic development and housing. In the first place, local contractors (or at least local labour) had to be used. Although this seems an obvious point, the corporation was hiring outsiders to construct housing while local unemployment was a major problem.

By 1987-8, the corporation was making an effort to respond to some of these criticisms. According to Stephen Kakfwi, then minister responsible for the NWTHC, a number of initiatives were launched to address the problem. The corporation began a process of community consultation to improve housing, and a design team visited twenty communities. Also, some block funding agreements were made with communities for delivery of Homeownership's Assistance Program

(HAP) housing.[47] Most importantly, in 1989-90 the corporation under-
took demonstration projects in Fort Mcpherson and Snowdrift. These
projects involved the corporation sending in the materials and a fore-
man and the community providing the labour. Tom Butters, the last
minister responsible for the Housing Corporation in the Eleventh
Legislative Assembly (1987-91), spoke very highly of the results and
said the experiment would be expanded to Pangnirtung and Coral
Harbour.[48] The corporation finally appears to be moving toward a more
decentralized process. With block funding and local people working
on housing, communities may be able to affect their housing problem.
While a decentralized process may overcome some of the bureaucratic
problems which have plagued the NWTHC, the success or failure of
any new initiatives will depend on the financial resources available.

There are problems with the GNWT's education and housing policies.
Part of the problem is rooted in the highly centralized government
process by which decisions are made and services delivered. Over
the years, individuals in communities have reacted strongly to this
centralized process. They argue that education and housing policies
can be improved significantly if the governing process is decentralized
and local officials assume more responsibility for decisionmaking.

ECONOMIC DEVELOPMENT

Economic development in the NWT has special meaning. Economic
development for the region does not necessarily mean launching more
megaprojects in the North. Over the years, the North experienced its
share of megaprojects: the Alaska highway, DEW Line construction,
and non-renewable resource extraction developments. At the same
time in economic terms, most small, isolated communities remain
almost untouched by these projects.

Economic development in the North poses a tragic paradox. The
region is a vast storehouse of mineral wealth. Over the past half
century, it has supplied a significant amount of gold, silver, copper,
lead, zinc, cadmium, tungsten, and oil and gas (there is one gas well
near the BC border). Now there is great potential in gas reserves. At
the same time, Native people in the region have severe economic
problems. Their annual incomes average half those of Canadians as
a whole, and their annual unemployment figures are two to three
times higher than the national figures. Rarely have Native people
benefitted directly from the exploitation of non-renewable resources
from lands that remain disputed.[49]

Why has the federal government, which controls the land, not per-
mited Native people to share in at least a portion of the non-renewable

resource revenues taken from lands to which they have a claim? There is no simple answer. No doubt at least part of the answer lies in the attitude that has prevailed since 1920. Economic development in the NWT has been the primary function of the various federal departments responsible for northern development, and economic development was equated with resource extraction. In fact, an assumption prevailed that the more extraction, the more development.

The problem with Native people in the region was troublesome but was secondary to the central objective of non-renewable resource extraction. Initially, it was thought there could, in effect, be two Norths; resources could be extracted and Native people would continue to live, largely, a traditional way of life supported by hunting, fishing, and using the benefits of trapping to support their basic needs. By the 1950s it was obvious that change had penetrated the lives of Natives in the NWT, and the government changed policies dramatically. Through the intervention of the state, northern Natives would be provided most amenities available to southern Canadians, and the state would structure conditions whereby Native people could live in a wage economy. By adopting this policy shift, it was also assumed that non-renewable resource extraction projects would provide the economic base for a northern wage economy, and Natives taking advantage of this opportunity would be assimilated into the mainstream of the Canadian economy.

This policy has not succeeded. The resource industry has not provided the vehicle through which a wage economy is available to NWT Natives. In fact, today many Native people face severe economic problems. Hence, when one speaks of economic development in the region, one must focus not only on non-renewable resource extraction but also on economic development for the bulk of the population – the people living in the small communities throughout the territories. Economic development for the region implies finding a way to strengthen the economic base of the small communities.

As the following figures indicate, economic development in the NWT has by-passed most Native people in small communities. The evidence is very stark. In terms of unemployment, education, and income, annual averages for most Native people are very different from those of Canada and even from those of the Northwest Territories as a whole.

For example, for persons fifteen years and older in the NWT, 70 per cent participate in the labour force (Table 20). For Native people, however, the figure is only 56 per cent. For the Inuit, the participation rate is 53 per cent and for the Dene 54 per cent. On the other hand, for non-Natives, 88 per cent are involved in the work force. In other words, only 12 per cent of non-Natives fifteen years and older are not a part of the labour force. In Native communities, however, the rate would be 44 per cent. Thus, almost one half of Native people over fifteen years are not involved in the work force.

The official unemployment figures for the territories is 16 per cent. For Native people, it is 30 per cent; 31 per cent for Inuit and 35 per cent for Dene. The non-Native unemployment rate is 5 per cent. It is obvious that work situations for Native people are considerably worse than are those for non-Natives.

One factor that correlates with high unemployment is a lack of education. Again, in the fifteen years and older Native work force, 54 per cent of the work force of 19,611 individuals have a grade eight or less education, and an additional 19.3 per cent have grade eleven or less (Table 21). Unemployment figures in these two categories are 30 per cent and 41 per cent, respectively. For non-Natives with a grade eight or less education, the unemployed figure is 8 per cent, and for those with grade eleven or less it is also 8 per cent. The disturbing fact is that 73.3 per cent of the Natives in the work force have grade eleven or less, whereas 16.8 per cent of the non-Natives are in the same category.

In terms of average annual income (for individuals working), the figures are also telling. Averages for males in Canada and the NWT are very close; $23,265 and $23,900, respectively. The figures in most predominantly Native communities are about 60 per cent of these figures. For males in communities listed, the low is $11,906 in Fort Providence and the high is $16,334 in Fort Good Hope. And these averages are only for the working portion of the labour force – 56 per cent for Native people (Table 22).

In Yellowknife the average income for males is $31,307. While this figure is higher than Canadian or NWT averages, it reflects to some extent the cost of living in the North. A high portion of those employed in the city are civil servants, working for the federal or territorial governments. Their salaries usually include a cost of living allowance. The fact that the cost of living for Native people is just as high makes their average look even worse. Generally, it is between 40 and 45 per cent of the Yellowknife figure.

The terrible contradiction in the North is that, while most Natives are involved in a subsistence way of life in small communities, non-renewable resources from the region generate a great deal of wealth. For example, from 1977 to 1989, mining companies shipped a total of almost $7 billion worth of metals (Table 17). Oil companies, principally Imperial Oil from Norman Wells, shipped over $1 billion worth of fuels. In other words, in a thirteen year period, over $8 billion worth of resources was extracted from the region. Native people have

TABLE 20

Male and female labour force activity by ethnic group in the NWT

	Persons 15 years & over (no.)	Labour force (no.)	Participation rate (%)	Employed (no.)	Unemployed (no.)	Unemployment rate (%)	Job wanted (no.)	Worked in 1988 (no.)
Northwest Territories	34,650	24,250	70	20,328	3,922	16	8,776	26,216
Males	18,213	13,850	76	11,512	2,338	17	4,685	14,889
Females	16,437	10,399	63	8,815	1,584	15	4,091	11,327
Natives	19,611	10,990	56	7,668	3,322	30	7,782	12,430
Males	9,981	6,175	62	4,172	2,003	32	4,166	7,035
Females	9,630	4,815	50	3,496	1,319	27	3,616	5,396
Inuit	9,662	5,166	53	3,540	1,626	31	4,407	5,970
Males	4,898	2,925	60	1,989	936	32	2,279	3,498
Females	4,764	2,242	47	1,551	691	31	2,129	2,471
Inuvialuit	1,797	1,055	59	766	289	27	579	1,279
Males	919	587	64	411	176	30	317	701
Females	878	468	53	355	113	24	262	578

Dene	5,715	3,059	54	1,975	1,084	35	2,236	3,295
Males	2,879	1,695	59	997	698	41	1,250	1,791
Females	2,836	1,364	48	978	386	28	985	1,504
Métis	2,437	1,709	70	1,387	322	19	560	1,887
Males	1,285	968	75	775	193	20	320	1,044
Females	1,152	741	64	612	129	17	240	843
Non-Natives	15,039	13,259	88	12,659	600	5	995	13,785
Males	8,232	7,675	93	7,340	335	4	520	7,855
Females	6,808	5,584	82	5,319	265	5	475	5,930

SOURCE: 1989 NWT Labour Force Survey, 13, 14

TABLE 21

Labour force activity by highest level of schooling and by ethnic group in the NWT

	Persons 15 years & over (no.)	Labour force (no.)	Participation rate (%)	Employed (no.)	Unemployed (no.)	Unemployment rate (%)	Not working (no.)	Job wanted (no.)	Worked in 1988 (no.)
Northwest Territories	34,650	24,250	70	20,328	3,922	16	14,322	8,777	26,216
Grade 8 or less	11,152	4,960	44	3,056	1,904	38	8,096	4,746	5,539
Grade 9 to grade 11	5,715	3,774	66	2,962	812	22	2,753	1,920	4,432
High school diploma	5,307	4,449	84	4,109	340	8	1,198	650	4,827
Certificate or diploma	8,394	7,434	89	6,667	767	10	1,727	1,227	7,696
University degree	3,611	3,429	95	3,381	48	1	230	70	3,452
Not provided	471	na	na	na	na	na	na	na	na
Natives	19,611	10,990	56	437,668	3,322	30	11,943	7,782	12,430
Grade 8 or less	10,568	4,570	43	2,698	1,872	41	7,870	4,699	5,150
Grade 9 to grade 11	3,776	2,269	60	1,577	692	30	2,199	1,704	2,806
High school diploma	1,246	976	78	822	154	16	424	282	1,087
Certificate or diploma	3,494	2,893	83	2,340	553	19	1,154	933	3,054
University degree	130	130	100	130	–	–	–	–	130
Not provided	396	na	na	na	na	na	na	na	na
Non-Native	15,039	13,259	88	12,659	600	5	2,380	995	13,785
Grade 8 or less	584	390	67	358	32	8	226	47	389
Grade 9 to grade 11	1,938	1,505	78	1,385	120	8	553	216	1,627
High school diploma	4,061	3,474	86	3,288	186	5	773	368	3,740

Certificate or diploma	4,900	4,541	93	4,327	214	5	573	294	4,643
University degree	3,481	3,300	95	3,252	48	1	229	70	3,322
Not provided	75	na	na	na	na	na	na	na	na

SOURCE: 1989 NWT Labour Force Survey

TABLE 22

Average annual income for workers by selected communities in the NWT

	Canada	NWT	Clyde River	Pang-nirtung	Cape Dorset	Fort Provi-dence	Rae-Edzo	Fort Good Hope	Fort McPher-son	Copper-mine	Baker Lake	Eskimo Point	Yellow-knife
Males, 15 yrs. and older	23,265	23,900	13,830	13,847	13,463	11,906	13,923	16,334	14,708	15,543	13,195	15,397	31,307
Females, 15 yrs. and older	12,615	15,037	11,409	11,409	10,845	8,605	10,845	9,381	10,579	10,474	8,699	9,036	13,777
Family	34,261	40,271		23,600		26,172		32,000	28,326	24,181	26,209	26,209	52,680

SOURCE: Statistics Canada, Catalogue 94-124, *Profile*, Northwest Territories: Part 2

had few opportunities to share directly in this wealth.

These minerals and fuels come from lands which are disputed. Since Justice Morrow's ruling in the *Paulette* case (1973) and subsequent appeals, it has been understood that any surrender of lands under treaties 8 and 11 was not altogether valid. Certainly, by 1975, the federal government had its land claims office in operation and was willing to negotiate a comprehensive claim with the Dene-Métis, Inuit, and Inuvialuit. But in the fifteen year interim, billions of dollars of resources have been extracted. The slow pace of the federal government to work on these claims has led to a great deal of frustration on the part of Native people – a frustration summed up by Johnny Washie, who writes for *The Native Press* (now *The Press Independent*):

> Over the years when we look back as native peoples in this country, we have already given up way more land to non-natives than we have received.
>
> In our land we have gold, minerals and fuel to make a good profit, much more than a golf course in Oka, Quebec, but reaching an agreement with the federal government is a very slow task. A lot of Dene/Métis people are getting frustrated. Land issues and many others just hang up in the air and nothing seems to be done.
>
> In 1921, the government of Canada took advantage of our native people and took all their land away. Our Dene people were not educated – unable to speak English or write their names on a piece of paper.[50]

It is frustrating for Native people to see a dual economy in the NWT. On the one hand, they are living a subsistence way of life. In fact, many are wards of the state. On the other hand, the non-renewable resource economy of the territory has flourished. The mining and oil companies have extracted substantial resources for use in the South or for export. It is strange that while the federal government has pushed economic development in the region and has pushed for Natives to become part of the wage economy, a way has never been found by which Native people could become integrated with the non-renewable, resource extractive economy.

In the NWT, mining and oil make up 26 per cent of the Gross Domestic Product (GDP).[51] But these industries employ only about 14 per cent of the industrial labour force.[52] In other words, the extractive industry generates a lot of capital, but it is not labour intensive. These industries, in 1988, were employing between 2,500 and 3,000 workers, most of whom were non-Natives.

There is little reason to look to the non-renewable resource industries as a panacea, as a way of suddenly turning around the economies of the small communities. Is there any hope for improving economic conditions in these isolated, predominantly Native communities? Is there something that can be done to develop their economies, or are these people destined to become increasingly more dependent on governments?

There are possibilities for these communities but they may require an entirely different approach to the problem. In the past, much of economic development theory in the North was predicated on the assumption that the non-renewable resource economy would generate employment; that expanding this sector of the economy would have a spill-over effect, enabling Native people to become a part of the wage economy. Obviously, this has not happened in the past four decades – a period of great expansion in the extractive economy.

There are those who argue that the problem should be approached from the community level rather than as a problem solely for the non-renewable resource industries.[53] In other words, attempts should be made to tackle the problem from the bottom up not just the top down – to build on strengths of the local communities rather than to depend only on the whims of larger commodity market forces. Working on the problem from the local perspective is not apt to create a quick fix either; on the contrary, it may be slow and employment may grow in a very incremental fashion. However, it may represent a more sustainable process of economic development. Perhaps, most importantly, it would involve the people in the communities working on resolving problems that have plagued them for years.

Using the 'bottom up approach,' the idea is to create small businesses in the communities – small businesses that fill needs which have not been met and which result in the importation of goods and services from the South. The underlying assumption behind such an hypothesis is that many small communities lack services that exist in most small communities elsewhere. These services may include a bakery, a hairdresser, a wood cutting operation, a tannery, or a local construction and maintenance company. Small businesses like these may not have developed in the past due to a lack of capital resources or to a lack of expertise.

One example of local involvement is the formation of a construction company, mentioned in the previous section on housing. In many cases, the materials and labour were brought into the community when, obviously, there was a surplus of labour, and, in the Western Arctic, local materials (logs) were available. This lack of local involvement was tragic, especially when housing was such an important concern in every community. Currently, hamlets, local entrepenuers, or Native development corporations are forming construction enter-prises. The fact that any experiment like this was so long in coming reflected a certain colonial attitude within the housing corporation.

This attitude was also reflected in a proposal for the importation of carving stone from Montana and Virginia. The Department of Economic Development and Tourism was reported to have ordered approximately $200,000 worth of stone to supply carvers in the territories.[54] But good stone exists in quarrys throughout the NWT. It does not make sense for people in Virginia or Montana to be employed to supply northern stone carvers if NWT individuals could supply the same product. Such a colonial attitude must be changed if, indeed, the responsibility for development is to be shifted to the communi-ties. If financial resources were made available to communities, then local communities could be responsible for their own housing needs or for supplying their own stone. In the past, departments in Ottawa and Yellowknife have tended to initiate and control policies and solu-tions. Now human resources *do* exist in the communities. The problem is to place financial resources at the disposal of local communities and regions so that they can take over responsibility for resolving local problems.

Three sources of capital might provide the financial resources for small business expansion in communities. The first is money from land claims – money that can be utilized in two ways.[55] Part of the land claim finances will and should be directed into Native develop-ment corporations. These corporations exist and are operational in the different regions of the NWT. It is important that they take on projects, such as road maintenance, which are not done by local private com-panies or community organizations. Liard or Fort McPherson are examples of where this type of innovation is occurring. There is no reason for Public Works in Yellowknife to hire Alberta or Quebec bus-inesses to perform road construction or maintenance in or around local communities. With land claim settlements, the Native Development Corporation will have the resources to purchase the necessary equip-ment to do the jobs locally that, in the past, have been contracted to outside firms. New capital channelled into the Native development corporations can and will affect local employment opportunities.

Another part of the claim settlement money could be invested in a trust fund to create dividends for all beneficiaries of the regional claims. The idea is to have investments that would generate dividends to be paid to community members annually or semi-annually.[56] Increased income in communities would also increase spending, thus enhancing the economic environment in small communities. Increas-ing cash flow in communities would provide greater opportunities for small businesses to employ a few local people, thus helping improve the local employment picture. Capital resources from land claims established as a trust fund would generate additional cash flow in communities, which would strengthen the economic base for developing new small businesses.

A final source of new capital to influence local economic development could come from GNWT organizations like the new Economic Development Corporation.[57] Formed in 1990, its objectives are to support investments in local businesses. This corporation's first project was support of an arts and crafts industry in Pangnirtung. This organization holds a great deal of potential for assisting community development, if, indeed, it can supply the capital resources and let local individuals and organizations work the capital.

The burden of economic development should be shifted to communities and regions. Economic development of communities is still a very complex undertaking. It will involve the resources of the community, the Native organizations, and the GNWT. But, in the past, the engine for economic development has been driven principally by the federal and territorial governments using non-renewable resources as the base.

The GNWT's Department of Economic Development and Tourism is focusing on the development of renewable resources. The ideas are outlined in the department's paper, 'The Renewable Resource Strategy.' While the renewable resource sector constitutes only about 5 per cent of the territorial GDP, it holds great potential for influencing employment in small communities:[58] 'The opportunity for Northerners to commercially harvest local renewable resources helps strengthen and support the subsistence economy. It also provides income and job experience to Northerners.'[59] Emphasis is being placed on the commercial development of fisheries, forestry, fur, agriculture, and wild meat. Moreover, the department is asking residents in communities to come forward with proposals for increasing commercial development of these resources.

The change now needed is for that engine to become community driven. Obviously, there is a role for the public sector, for there is no way that development can be maximized unless all parties are involved in the process: individuals, communities, Native organizations, the GNWT, and the federal government. In the past, federal and territorial administrators were apt to come in and say: 'This is how it is to be done.' Administrators now are more sensitive to local input. At the same time, it is often difficult for them to take a supportive role and to let communities initiate policies wich they feel are necessary to get economic development underway.

Shifting the role of the bureaucracy may sound easy. But anyone who is a student of public administration or an observer of the behaviour of large bureaucracies, public or private, realizes that changing the course of this institution is very difficult. It takes a lot of guts on the part of a strong political leadership to move the bureaucracy to respond to development needs by providing capital resources and expertise when needed, while the initiatives come from the people in communities. Decisionmaking responsibility has to move from Yellowknife to communities and the regions, with administrators providing a supportive role. In the meantime, a complicating factor is that the GNWT will remain heavily dependent on the federal government for much of its operating revenue. This does not bode well for creating a more autonomous GNWT or for it readily devolving some of its power to local and regional governments.

THE LOCAL AND REGIONAL GOVERNMENT ISSUE

The role for local and regional governments in the NWT is a contentious issue. In fact, it is the key controversy in constitutional development in the Northwest Territories. The problem is that there are at least two conflicting models of the responsibilities of local and regional governments. On the one hand, there is the conventional, southern model, which provides the basis for dividing territorial and municipal powers. In this case, the territorial government (like provincial governments in the South) would charter local governments and provide a great deal of the financial resources for their operation. Local governments in the South do, however, raise about half their revenues and thus have some degree of autonomy in their expenditures. Nevertheless, local and regional governments are often referred to as creatures of the territorial governments. This is the model advocated by many northerners, who see the GNWT emerging as a mere copy of provincial governments in the South.

The second model is one in which local and regional governments have much more autonomy. In this case, municipal powers are extensive, designed to take care of most public services for residents of a community. Powers would include responsibilities normally under the jurisdiction of municipalities in the South, including institutions such as local education and hospital boards. Within this model is the option for a number of municipalities, when they desire, to form regional governments with powers delegated by municipalities. Advocates of this model also recommend greater unconditional grants by the GNWT to local governments. Those who push for this mode of local government are usually Native people, particularily those in smaller communities. For years they have felt that the federal and territorial governments intruded far too much into what should be municipal and regional affairs. Proponents of this model feel that local and regional problems are better resolved locally than by having solutions imposed by officials from Ottawa or Yellowknife.

At the heart of the local government issue is the question, will the GNWT decentralize its operation? Will the territorial government devolve decisionmaking powers to local or regional governments? Or will it continue central control for most functional responsibilities? Katherine Graham has an interesting way of describing this issue. She says: 'A gap exists between the aspirations of community governments to enhance their ability to take on additional responsibilities and service their residents according to local needs and priorities and the willingness or ability of the GNWT to devolve additional powers to the local level.'[60]

In fact, for more than a decade discussions have gone on within the GNWT about 'devolving' more powers to local governments. Graham also tracks the GNWT's record on the issue and suggests that 'the Government of the Northwest Territories has sustained a policy stance on the development of local government that holds much promise. However, this promise is yet to be realized.'[61]

The policy of the last government (1987-91) to send out conflicting signals for residents of the NWT. On the one hand, there are suggestions that local governments should have 'prime public authority' (PPA).[62] While PPA has not been defined by the territorial government, one can only surmise that *prime* authority means first authority. Local councils have PPA in regard to what Drury called the hard services, water, sewage, garbage, sidewalks, fire protection, and so on. To implement greater PPA, the GNWT would have to designate additional powers to be devolved to local councils, noting the council as the first and highest authority in regard to these responsibilities. The problem is that while officials of the GNWT used the term, they never spelled out any change in the division of powers between the GNWT and local councils. To attain greater PPA would require granting municipalities a great deal more authority than they now have. Most people would argue that today municipalities in the NWT have limited authority.

On the other hand, there were suggestions that local governments are diffuse and expensive. One of the best statements by the GNWT on this issue is contained in a discussion paper entitled 'Political and Constitutional Development in the Northwest Territories.'[63] The paper begins with a statement on the high cost of delivering public services in the NWT:

It is estimated that there are over 1,500 elected politicians in the Northwest Territories. As well, there are at least 800 statutory and other GNWT
sponsored bodies operating in our communities. These include community and municipal governments, local education authorities, hunters and
trappers' associations, youth and justice committees, radio and televi-
sion societies, housing associations and various kinds of social service
committees to name only a few.

In non-tax based communities alone, there are over 320 special purpose
bodies costing about $66 million a year.

In addition, at the regional level there are regional and tribal councils, health, wildlife and education boards and aboriginal organizations.
At the Territorial level there are boards and agencies, the Legislative
Assembly and the GNWT, as well as the Territorial aboriginal organizations and other government-funded special interest bodies.

The cost of supporting these groups is deflecting public funds from
the actual provision of public services such as education and housing.
The proliferation of authorities is confusing to the electorate and in some
constituencies it detracts from the role of the MLA.[64]

This implies that a more centralized system of constitutional authority
is cheaper and more effective to operate than is a more decentralized
system.

The paper, nevertheless, goes on to reiterate support for PPA: 'In
addition, government policies on devolution and delegation of responsibilities to community government and the introduction of the Prime
Body (PPA) concept are designed to further strengthen this level of
government. This approach allows communities to assume responsibility for a broader range of programs and services than has been traditionally assumed by local governments elsewhere in Canada.'[65] One
option for the Legislative Assembly is strengthening PPA: 'Municipal
and community governments in the Northwest Territories will get
additional direct responsibilities. An increased measure of control and
planning would give full meaning to the prime public authority at
the local level.'[66] Regional organizations do not fare as well in the
discussion paper:

Regional and Tribal Councils developed in the early stage of ministerial
government out of periodic meetings between government representatives, local mayors and local chiefs. As early as 1980, the Baffin Regional
Council was legally recognized. And then, in 1983, the Legislative
Assembly passed the Regional and Tribal Councils Act in order to create
a similar regional focus amongst communities and bands elsewhere in
the NWT. The councils mainly act in an advisory role and serve as a use-

ful focus for the exchange of information and ideas on common concerns
and problems.

Regional bodies, through the delegation or devolution of responsibilities from the GNWT and communities, would exercise prime responsibility in certain areas of jurisdiction. An issue for the Legislative Assembly,
with this option, is how MLA's can retain their authority, accountabili-
ties and responsibilities to electors in those areas that are delegated or
devolved to regional bodies.[67]

Regional organizations were not to be an integral part of the constitutional design of the GNWT.

At the end of the paper, under a discussion on 'choices' for the
government, mixed messages again emerge: 'The proliferation of
regional and local special purpose bodies has lead to confusion in
responsibilities and costly duplication. This duplication serves to divert
scarce resources away from the development of new, or the enhancement of existing programs and services being demanded by northern
residents. The accountability of the Legislative Assembly is being
affected.'[68]

One point in all this is that there will never be any absolutely clean
division of powers between territorial and local and regional governments. In the provinces, MLA's are constantly faced with local school
boards or local hospital boards which have a great deal of autonomous power. The responsibility of these boards to the provincial
government is principally fiscal. Therefore, devolving decisionmaking
powers to local or regional organizations should not challenge the
authority of MLA's or challenge the accountability of the Legislative
Assembly. Such a challenge will exist only if all power is centred in
the GNWT. A division of jurisdictional powers exists in most governments, and in the NWT the authority of the territorial government
should not be all-pervasive if, indeed, local or regional governments
exist and are expected to carry out specific responsibilities.

If indeed Native people in small communities desire more authority
for local government, why has the GNWT stalled in devolving powers
to local or regional governments? Why did Yellowknife want to retain
central control of powers that could be municipal responsibilities?
There may be a number of explanations. One, of course, is 'capacity.'[69]
The argument is that local communities do not have the capacity to
shoulder more responsibilities. Indeed, this may be the case in certain communities; there is evidence that with all the advisory committees many community activists are on the go constantly.
Nevertheless, if capacity is to be a reason for turning down devolving

more responsibility to communities, communities might be the best judge of the situation. Let *them* make the decision, not officials in Yellowknife.

A second explanation has been suggested by individuals both in Yellowknife and the communities. These people argue that GNWT officials had to fight tooth and nail to have powers devolved from Ottawa. Consequently, they were not about to turn around and suddenly devolve those powers to local or regional governments. In other words, elected and administrative officials in Yellowknife have been consolidating their recently won authority and are not interested in giving it up to local authorities.

A third argument is that the territorial government feels that the NWT is making progress in taking its rightful place alongside provinces in Canadian federation. The discussion paper, for example, says: 'Relations with the Government of Canada have improved as the GNWT has obtained more provincial-type programs and northerners increase their participation in intergovernmental affairs.'[70] Officials in Yellowknife see this improved position as a strength, and many of these officials see devolution of territorial powers as a mark of weakness.

A final explanation is complex and involves engendering a sense of legitimacy by NWT residents for the GNWT. The territorial government realizes it has a legitimacy problem, particularly within the smaller communities. But many GNWT officials, mainly Executive Council members and upper echelon civil servants, feel that they can overcome this problem if the government can effectively deliver public services. These officials feel that greater involvement by Yellowknife will, in time, lead to people accepting the GNWT as legitimate. In other words, effective government performance, even though it is viewed as imposed, can gain the confidence of residents of the territories. As Katherine Graham put it: 'All this might suggest that the development of local government in the NWT will go on hold until the GNWT assures itself of a legitimate role in the future governance of the NWT.'[71]

The legitimacy argument raises what seems to be an interesting contradiction. Many residents of the territories question the legitimacy of the GNWT, as they did that of the federal government. Their accusation is that territorial officials are making most of the decisions in regard to housing, education, economic development, health care, social services, and transport; that local and regional governments have rarely had the power to influence fundamental conditions in communities. Yet many GNWT officials seemed to be assuming that if they just have a chance to do *more* – perform more services in an effective way – then residents would begin to accept the GNWT as a legitimate government. This assumption ignores the real issue in communities, which is that most public decisionmaking centralized in Yellowknife denies local participation in the process. In short, this is an issue of democracy.

This debate shows that a power struggle is going on in the NWT. Many small community residents want greater authority for local governments. Many GNWT officials, thus far, have been unwilling to alter the existing territorial-local division of powers. They have not understood the value of a significant role for local or regional governments: In a democracy, there is an inherent value in local residents doing what they can for themselves rather than having it done for them by outsiders.

The Carrothers Commission and Drury may have been right in stating that creating viable local governments is an integral part of political development in the NWT. One must remember that recommendations in these reports reflected the strong community bias detected in their travels throughout the region – a community bias that still exists. For example, Paul Quassa, a chief land claim negotiator for the TFN has said: 'We don't want to keep being run by a government that really doesn't know what the aspirations of the Inuit are from this area. And I think in total we want to run our own lives, our day to day living, and we want to have a say in what goes on and what will happen in the future.'[72] And Peter Ernerk, a former MLA from the Keewatin region, says:

> The issue of the Health Board, for instance, in Rankin Inlet, in the Keewatin region. How can the people in the Keewatin region successfully feel that they have the authority to deliver health matters when the chairperson of the Keewatin Health Board is a regional director, directed by the minister in Yellowknife to deliver the services? How can we have such power? How can they think they're actually delivering devolution to the communities? How can they think that they're transferring authority and decision making power from Yellowknife to the communities?[73]

John O'Neil, who has written extensively on the health care issue, has summed up community feelings: 'I think there is a strong perception in the regions that their expectation of local autonomy or regional autonomy and authority in health care, and perhaps other areas, is being undermined by the growth of bureaucracy in Yellowknife, and I think there's a strong sense that Yellowknife isn't developing regional structures such as the health board to the extent that was promised when the negotiations for devolution of health services were entered into.'[74]

The issue of a centralized or decentralized government, of local and regional autonomy, is *the* burning constitutional issue in the NWT. Certainly the priority of strong local governments has been an important part of political development in the rest of Canada. Functional local governments, not always formalized, preceded the organization of provincial or the federal governments. Alexis de Tocqueville, travelling in North America in the 1830s, recognized the importance of local government institutions in the development of a democracy on this continent:

> It is not without intention that I begin this subject with the township. The village or township is the only association which is so perfectly natural that, wherever a number of men are collected, it seems to constitute itself.
>
> The town or tithing, then, exists in all nations, whatever their laws and customs may be: it is man who makes monarchies and establishes republics, but the township seems to come directly from the hand of God. But although the existence of the township is coeval with that of man, its freedom is an infrequent and fragile thing.
>
> Municipal freedom is not the fruit of human efforts; it is rarely created by others, but is, as it were, secretly self-produced in the midst of a semi-barbarous state of society. The constant action of the laws and the national habits, peculiar circumstances, and, above all, time, may consolidate it; but there is certainly no nation on the continent of Europe that has experienced its advantages. Yet municipal institutions constitute the strength of free nations. Town meetings are to liberty what primary schools are to science; they bring it within the people's reach, they teach men how to use and how to enjoy it. A nation may establish a free government, but without municipal institutions it cannot have the spirit of liberty.[75]

Tocqueville saw the supreme importance of local governments in the development of a free society. Local governments can evolve 'naturally' in order to deal with local problems. But this development is not always permitted to happen. In fact, it may be a rare occurrence: 'The immunities of townships, which have been obtained with so much difficulty, are least of all protected against the encroachments of the supreme power. They are unable to struggle, single-handed, against a strong and enterprising government, and they cannot defend themselves with success unless they are identified with the customs of the nation and supported by public opinion.'[76]

Residents in many NWT communities might suggest that Tocqueville's appraisal is as applicable today as it was 150 years ago. The interesting fact is that northern communities have never been able to develop like the rest of North America. The development sequence was reversed. The federal government moved in with a presence – eventually, an overwhelming presence. This was followed by the creation of the GNWT, which came on with a vengeance after 1967. Local governments, then, have never had the authority to deal substantively with local problems. Neither the federal nor territorial governments have been willing to pass the torch of responsibility to local government organizations. Community councils in the territories have never enjoyed the powers available to most local governments in southern Canada.

In light of the importance of strong local government, why does the GNWT not go ahead and devolve responsibilities? Given the size of the territories, is a province-like government needed to make decisions for about 54,000 people? As Ned Franks once asked, 'does a population of fewer than 60,000 really need a bureaucracy of 4,000.'[77] That bureaucracy today consists of over 6,000 people. Fewer people live in the NWT than live in many small cities in Canada. Why is it necessary to create an entire provincial-like apparatus to govern some sixty small communities? Should not the communities do what they can in terms of resolving their problems? Then, when needed, they could band together and form regional organizations to take care of more extensive problems. Finally, for problems that regions could not handle, there would be the territorial apparatus.

Given the circumstances in 1967, the GNWT was the logical vehicle to assume government power from Ottawa and to develop a governing mechanism in the NWT. The problem now, however, is that this vehicle seems to be entrenched and it has been reluctant to give up power to local or regional organizations. In part, the problem rests with elected officials who are reluctant to surrender part of their power and influence to local officials. Also, many administrative officials may be opposed to decentralization. Any move to expand powers at the local and regional levels would seriously detract from responsibilities now exercised by Yellowknife administrative departments. Autonomous regional education or hospital boards are cases in point.

This struggle over power reminds one of a statement by Robert Stanfield, former leader of the federal Progressive Conservative Party. While his quote refers to the federal system, it may well apply to all levels of government: 'While the House of Commons has been losing control, so also has the Government. The ministers just do not have the time to run such a vast show and make such a vast range of decisions. Consequently, more and more is for all practical purposes being decided by and implemented by the bureaucracy.'[78] Territorial politicians and bureaucrats who oppose 'devolution' may be undermining their own position. Their resistance to devolution in the territories may only strengthen the resolve of community residents to find a way to control their own destiny.

The position of the current GNWT (1991-5) on decentralization is just beginning to take shape. Following the October 1991 election, Nellie Cournoyea was chosen government leader. She then assigned ministerial portfolios. One important document seems to have had a significant impact on the new GNWT's initial approach to governing. This is *Strength at Two Levels: Report of the Project to Review the Operations and Structure of Northern Government*,[79] also known as the 'Beatty Report' since the project was chaired by Garry H. Beatty of Manitoba. It may be the most important document to come before the GNWT since its move to Yellowknife twenty-five years ago.

The project was initiated by the Financial Management Board of the previous government (1987-91). It was established to generate recommendations involving two related crises in the NWT. The first was precipitated by the federal government's budgetary restraints. Federal government transfers make up the bulk of GNWT revenues. Ottawa's move to cut financial support to provinces and territories is critical for the NWT because of its limited tax base and because it would be virtually impossible for the GNWT to make up the revenue shortfall. The second crisis the GNWT faces is how to maintain services to residents in the face of declining budgets. Obviously the GNWT must find ways to deliver services more effectively.

In one way the GNWT got its money's worth in the Beatty Report. The thrust of the recommendations was to downsize some of the Yellowknife bureaucracy, enabling local governments to do more. In other words, the idea was to get greater efficiency out of local governments, which exist but are underpowered in terms of responsibilities. Thus, the report, in the name of economy, argues for what Carrothers and Drury argued for in the name of political legitimacy.

DIVISION OF THE NWT

As mentioned in the previous chapter, proposals for division of the NWT go back almost three decades. Initially, non-Native residents in the region thought that division would enable the Western Arctic to achieve early provincehood. Subsequently (latter 1970s), the Inuit maintained their support for division in their Nunavut proposal. Essentially, the idea of division was fostered by the notion that a divided NWT (two or more smaller territories) would enable local citizens to have greater control over public decisions influencing their lives. In 1980, the Legislative Assembly's Special Committee on Unity had a different rationale for division. The travel and discussions by its members 'reinforced anew, and most unequivocally: the Northwest Territories as a geo-political jurisdiction simply does not inspire a natural sense of identity amongst many of its indigenous peoples; its government does not enjoy in the most fundamental sense the uncompromising loyalty and commitment of significant numbers of those who are now subject to it.'[80] There is no reason to believe that these attitudes have changed over the last decade.

By November 1981, the Dene-Métis submitted their claim for Denendeh. With the Dene, Métis, Inuvialuit, and Inuit claims on the table, territorial division became a real possibility. In January 1982, the Special Committee on Constitutional Development organized a constitutional conference. Out of this conference grew the Constitutional Alliance, made up of the Nunavut Constitutional Forum (NCF) and the Western Constitutional Forum (WCF).[81] The purpose of the alliance was 'to realize significant constitutional, political and administrative change within the NWT.'[82]

Events began to move rapidly and division seemed a possibility. In April 1982, a territorial plebiscite was held on the division issue.[83] The results indicated that 56 per cent of NWT voters supported dividing the territories. The more interesting results, perhaps, were by community. Most communities in which non-Natives were a majority opposed division, although there were exceptions. Most Native communities supported division. In the Nunavut region, 79.5 per cent of the voters supported division; small and large communities supporting the yes vote. In the Denendeh region, the vote was split, approximately 50 per cent supporting division. But in the small communities, 60.1 per cent supported division, and eleven of the sixteen predominantly Dene communities supported division. In the predominantly Inuvialuit communities of the Western Arctic (Holman, Paulatuk, Sachs Harbour, and Tuktoyaktuk), two supported division and two opposed.

In November 1982, the federal government stated that it would support division provided there was consensus on the division boundary. By 1985, a tentative agreement had been reached on the boundary – a boundary including the Inuvialuit within the Eastern Arctic claim area. The Inuvialuit then pulled out of the NCF, and the dispute between the Inuit and Inuvialuit led to a breakdown in the agreement. In 1986, negotiations between the NCF (without the Inuvialuit) and the WCF were held; their representatives were Steve Kakfwi for the Dene-Métis and John Amagoalik for the Inuit. This agreement was ratified in 1987 as the Iqaluit Agreement.

The agreement outlined a constitutional base for governments in Nunavut and Denendeh.[84] In the Western Arctic, the Dene-Métis, because of their possible minority status, advocate guaranteed representation in any new assembly created as a result of division. In the Eastern Arctic, Nunavut as a territory would be governed by majority principles. The Inuit know they have a substantial majority in the region and they do not foresee any sudden change in that position. In the Denendeh and Nunavut proposals, strong local and regional governments are emphasized.

The Iqaluit Agreement also broke down, in part because the Dene and Métis wanted the division line moved farther east and wanted a guarantee of Native control of resource management. With the collapse of the Iqaluit Agreement, division seemed a dead issue in the NWT. The territorial government's support for the Constitutional Alliance was not renewed after October 1989. Thus, without the alliance setting the agenda for division, the GNWT assumed a more significant role in constitutional development. Indeed, the GNWT became very active in the process of division. For example, in the legislative assembly, Dennis Patterson, government leader, said the following:

> I would like to touch on division, Mr. Chairman. I think our government recognizes that in the long term, division of the NWT will likely occur. I still believe that division is a fundamental desire of the people of Nunavut. Most people I talk to from Nunavut say it is a question of when, not if. But I believe that in the meantime, political and constitutional development must continue, albeit in ways which do not prejudice the realization of division. We also must recognize that division cannot happen without the resolution of the Dene/Métis and the TFN claims boundaries.[85]

On 19 October 1990, the GNWT took another step toward division by signing an agreement-in-principle with the Tungavik Federation of Nunavut (TFN) for division of the territories.[86] A number of factors, however, would have to precede division: a mutually agreed upon boundary between the Dene-Métis and the Inuit would have to be found, and the federal government would have to legislate the division and financially support the creation of a Nunavut territorial government. The process would require approximately six to seven years.[87]

Several points about the agreement should be noted. The current leadership of the GNWT may or may not support division. But political leaders from the Eastern Arctic (particularly) can hardly ignore their constituents' strong support for division. At the same time, the GNWT's commitment to division does not mean it is a fait accompli. The federal government must legislate division, and, while various federal ministers have said they would support division once a boundary is established, actual passage of the legislation in Parliament may be a different matter.

Agreement on a boundry is a precondition for division of the NWT.[88] In 1991, the federal government asked John Parker to review the boundary dispute and make a recommendation to the minister of Indian Affairs and Northern Development. Parker submitted his recommendation in April 1991, and it was accepted by the minister. It suggested moving the boundary east of the 1989 agreement, expanding the lands in the Dene and Métis claims. Negotiations between the Dene and Métis organizations, the TFN, and the federal government have resulted in a line although not a line on which all individuals in the Western Arctic agree. And Native organizations in Manitoba and Saskatchewan would like more guarantees for traditional land use in Nunavut. The extent of support or opposition for the line will be more definite after the plebiscite, scheduled for May 1992.

An important development in the division issue was the GNWT's establishment of a Commission for Constitutional Development in April 1991. Steve Kakfwi, the minister responsible for Political and Constitutional Development, explained the role of the committee. It would be examining 'political and constitutional development in the western territory and [ensuring] that there be some process set up so that communities and regions can articulate to a commission, with some resources provided to them, their view of what kind of governments they want for the communities, [and] how the regions are going to be involved in such a process.'[89] Jim Bourque, former deputy minister of Renewable Resources, chairs the committee, which is to report to political leaders in the spring of 1992. One of their objectives is to listen to what individuals in the Western Northwest Territories have to say about government in the region and to offer options for continental change. In the Eastern Arctic, the Nunavut Steering Committee was established to work out the transition to Nunavut as a territory. The committee has two representatives from TFN (John Amagoalik and John Merritt) and two representatives from the GNWT (David Simailak and Elizabeth Snider). The federal government is also involved, as it is expected to carry much of the cost for establishing Nunavut.

In any event, division remains a major issue in the NWT. One reason it remains an issue is that many residents, particularly Native residents, feel they can best accomplish their goals with smaller territorial governments linked to more powerful local and regional governments.

LAND CLAIMS

For the Dene-Métis and the Inuit, land claims are a burning issue. The Dene-Métis have lived under the shadow of disputed treaties 8 and 11. For the Inuit, there has never been a treaty with the federal government. Therefore, since the mid-1970s, federal officials and Native people, for different reasons, have said the claims issue must be resolved.[90] Native people want the lands they own or control clarified so that they can get on with their own development with some sense of permanence. The federal government, with one eye to resource development and another eye to the growing legality of Aboriginal claims, would like to establish certainty with regard to land distribution. This would clear the air for even greater resource development. Land claim settlements in the NWT will clarify ownership of lands and management of resources in the region.

All of this led to the signing of an agreement-in-principle between the federal government and both Native groups: the Dene-Métis in the fall of 1988 and the Inuit in the spring of 1990.[91] In both documents, Native people would attain: (1) specified lands (in fee simple) with subsurface resource rights, (2) joint management of renewable resources on additional lands, (3) compensation for prior use of land in the regions, and (4) joint environmental screening of projects. The Dene-Métis, in April 1990, initialled a final agreement, which had to go to its membership for ratification. Native people were required to agree to what they called 'extinguishment' of all aboriginal rights. The Inuit, with some reservations, accepted the terms of this agreement and began working on land selection.[92]

The Dene-Métis, on the other hand, have encountered a problem. At the Dene Assembly in July 1990, the organization split over the extinguishment in the final agreement.[93] The Dene from the upper Mackenzie Valley opposed extinguishing Aboriginal Title, while the lower river bands wanted to get on with resolving the claims. The Delta and Sahtu bands were not necessarily happy with extinguishment but went along with it. The issue also split many Dene and Métis peoples. Many Métis in the southern part of the NWT also favoured the agreement-in-principle as it was written. With no guarantee of having Aboriginal title in the first place, some of the Métis resented the fact that the Dene would hold up the entire process in order to guarantee their own claim.

This issue has resulted in the federal government, in November 1990, rescinding the final agreement with the Dene-Métis collectively and the minister for Indian and Northern Affairs agreeing to settle land claims on a regional basis.[94] Of the five regions, Delta, Sahtu, North Slave, South Slave, and Deh Cho, the Delta and Sahtu regions are going ahead with developing a regional agreement with the federal government. The North Slave people are considering it, while the Deh Cho and South Slave peoples are pursuing a number of options, one of which is to go to the courts for a resolution of the issue of Aboriginal claims.

The Delta region was first off the mark, and by 13 July 1991 had signed an agreement with the federal government.[95] The agreement, for more than 2,000 *Gwich'in* living in Fort McPherson, Arctic Red River, Aklavik, and Inuvik, includes the following provisions:

(1) 6,280 square miles (16,264 square kilometres) of land held in fee simple, without subsurface rights
(2) 2,342 square miles (4,299 square kilometres) of land held in fee simple, with subsurface rights
(3) $75 million paid over fifteen years
(4) Resource royalties: 7.5 per cent of the first $2 million paid to the federal government, 1.5 per cent on additional royalties
(5) 600 square miles (1,000 square kilometres) of federal land in the Peel River Basin of the Yukon
(6) a framework of agreement on self-government

The agreement was taken to the communities, where 94 per cent of the electorate supported it. Participation rates were very high – 91 per cent of the 1,100 eligible voters.[96]

The AIP between the Inuit and the federal government included $580 million over a fifteen year period and 136,291 square miles of land held in fee simple, without subsurface rights; 14,000 square miles of land held in fee simple with subsurface rights; resource royalties of 50 per cent of the first $2 million paid to the federal government and 5 per cent paid on additional royalties; and support in principle by the federal and territorial governments for the establishment of Nunavut land. The land agreement was signed on 5 July 1991, with the regional breakdown in Table 23.[97]

Nunavut will encompass an area slightly larger than half the province of Alberta.

There are interesting views on the breakup of the Dene Nation as a basis for claim settlements. It can be argued, first, that the entire Dene Nation is weakened by the split, and that regional settlements may mean less in terms of overall benefits. This position is based on the assumption that there is strength in numbers. The second

TABLE 23

Quantum of Nunavut land use regions (all areas in square miles)

Region	Surface of region	Per cent of land	Subsurface	Land area of region
North Baffin (7 communities)	33,230	17.3	2,595	192,519
South Baffin (5 communities)	25,500	22.6	1,310	112,675
Sanikiluaq (1 community)	900	75.0	900	1,204
Keewatin (7 communities)	36,890	18.0	4,790	204,943
East Keewatin (7 communities)	14,276	17.5	1,050	81,577
West Kitikmeot (4 communities)	25,495	17.0	3,060	149,971
Totals of Nunavut	136,291	18.3	14,000	742,889

SOURCE: *Nunavut Forum* 1(1991):1

argument is that once Native people in the regions have their designated lands under a land claim agreement, they might be in a good position to negotiate with the federal government for self-government on their lands. The federal government has said they would negotiate self-government with Native people in the territories. Native people might also use this threat to negotiate with Ottawa as a lever with the territorial government in order to obtain greater local and regional powers. In other words, if the GNWT does not devolve greater powers to existing local and regional public governments in the Western Arctic, then Native people in the regions could negotiate self-government with the federal government and, thereby, set up Native governments on their lands obtained through the land claim settlement. Such a move would create enclave governments on Native lands within the NWT. Thus, constitutional development in the territories could become very complex, involving negotiations between the three major players, the Native organizations, the GNWT, and the federal government.

CONCLUSION

Over the last decade, the nature of the GNWT has changed dramatically. Representative government and a form of responsible government have been achieved. The commissioner-in-council government has been transformed into a cabinet government. The NWT Act may not have been changed, but de facto powers now lie with elected members of the Legislative Assembly. Therefore, in one way, this evolution follows the pattern of Alberta and Saskatchewan prior to 1905; greater autonomy is gradually achieved and, in time, perhaps, full provincial status.

While many residents of the NWT applaud the evolution of a province-like government, many Native people remain discontented with the territorial government. Their feelings are expressed clearly in their testimony before committees examining, for example, problems with education and housing and in their continued commitment to division of the territories. Many feel the government in Yellowknife has been too centralized and too insensitive to local problems. Community residents feel that local or regional governments should have greater authority in culturally sensitive policy areas like education, housing, health care, and economic development. These people advocate a more decentralized model of government, in which there is a great deal of local and regional autonomy. The two views on the ways in which the GNWT should continue to evolve is a fundamental constitutional problem in the region today.

For Native people the issue is crucial. Greater government authority at the local or regional levels would give them the opportunity to come to grips with their cultural dilemma – to face their cultural dilemma in the manner in which *they* choose.

CHAPTER SEVEN

Self-Government
and Political Development
in the Northwest Territories

The evolution of a viable governmental system in the NWT is an ongoing process. Current problems in this evolution are: (1) development of a process that residents of the NWT see as a legitimate form of government, and (2) accommodating that process to the parameters of the Canadian constitution. Achieving the latter is not an insurmountable problem. It would appear that the Canadian constitution is sufficiently flexible to accommodate any proposals advanced thus far for constructing a territorial government. Achieving the former, however, may be a problem.

In the NWT there is no unanimity on what form the governmental process should take. In fact, there are fundamentally different views on the type of government system that should be adopted. Over the years, the system has evolved as a centralized form of government. Many residents of the territories now challenge the idea of a centralized territorial government and argue that the system should be more decentralized. Native organizations, the GNWT, and the federal government are involved in trying to reconcile the issue of decentralization. The struggle over this issue has created its own political dynamic in the region.

No doubt the conflict over the nature of the governmental process is a direct result of the NWT context. The fact that Native people are a majority of the population (58 per cent) in this jurisdiction is important. Native people have been politicized and are now an integral part of the political process. They are a force in setting the political agenda for the region. While all Native people are not of one mind, there is a great deal of evidence to suggest that many Native people support the movement toward more authority for local and regional levels of government. There is a reason for their position on this issue. For years they experienced the heavy hand of government, first from

Ottawa and since 1967 from Yellowknife. Many Native people are convinced that a more decentralized process will provide them an opportunity to control more directly the important public decisions that influence their lives. For these people, one view of self-government consists of expanding the powers of local governments under the Municipal Act. These powers would include greater influence and control over public policies such as education, health care, housing, social services, police service, and economic development.

POLITICAL DYNAMICS OF SELF-GOVERNMENT

Self-government is a contentious term. When Native people speak of self-government, non-Natives often misinterpret this position as the creation of a sovereign entity outside the boundaries of the Canadian nation-state. Even though it is contentious, it is a term the federal government has used at least since the Joint Parliamentary Committee hearings in the late 1940s. 'Self-government' has many connotations.[1] It has a particular meaning, given the history of Native people. For example, the Department of Indian Affairs for years controlled most of the administrative decisions for bands. Since the 1950s, bands have been electing councils as legislative bodies. However, the federal government has been slow in giving up its power to band councils. Therefore, for many Native people, self-government is often synonymous with band government. It means empowering band councils with responsibility – at the very least, responsibilities enjoyed by most Canadians under municipal governments. With these powers, Native people would then have the ability to control public decisions affecting the preservation of their culture and economic development on Native lands. In the NWT, self-government is often synonymous with strengthening local and regional governments, and, for the Inuit, it is synonymous with division of the territories.

Native People's Position

The stakes in the decentralization conflict are extremely high for Native people. The problem is that it is not just a self-government, or decentralization, issue. While self-government is a crucial goal, the idea is linked intricately with other goals: land claim settlements, cultural preservation, and economic development. In other words, self-government is the cornerstone of Native policy goals in the region.

The linkage between self-government and land claims, cultural preservation, and economic development needs explaining. In the first place, land is crucial for Native people in the region. Land has been the very reason that peoples in the region have been able to survive over thousands of years. During this time, Native people worked out their own way of life as hunters and fishers. They developed living patterns as well as a religion, a technology, and a governing system which enabled them to survive in one of the harshest environments in the world. The land was the key to this survival, because it was from the land that they derived their food, clothing, and shelter. Thus, for Native people there is a certain sanctity in the land. Nowhere has this been expressed more forcefully than in the Berger hearings. Clarifying land holdings in the NWT, then, is an essential factor in determining their future survival in the region.

The second important goal linked to self-government is cultural preservation. Native people in the region are very aware of differences between their indigenous traditional culture and the dominant Canadian culture. Today, living in these two worlds creates the cultural dilemma facing most Native people. While most Natives are not adverse to taking what they want from the dominant Canadian culture, they would also like to retain many of the traditions and values of their own culture. While the dominant Canadian culture is very seductive in terms of the things it offers, most Native people are firmly opposed to being assimilated into that culture. Many desire to be able to live a bi-cultural existence, with one foot in a traditional culture and one foot in the modern culture. They would like to have the *choice* of living in two worlds. Therefore, preserving part of the traditional culture is a critical objective for Native people, and self-governing powers are an integral part of this presentation.

A third goal is economic development. It is obvious that the standard of living for most Native people is far below the average for most Canadians. This situation must be rectified. Economic development, however, is itself part of the cultural dilemma facing Native people. As they opt for a higher standard of living, it may be more difficult to preserve traditional cultural values. Economic development, then, may clash with the goal of cultural preservation. Most Native people now feel that rectifying economic development will have to come from within their communities. Native people must assume responsibilities for economic development. This means they must have the power locally to influence and control the process of economic development.

If Native people are going to be able to influence how they attain these three goals, then self-government has a comprehensive and virtually self-evident meaning arising from the interdependence of the goals themselves:

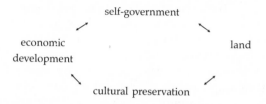

Self-government is a crucial part of linking the goals of land, cultural preservation, and economic development. Land is the anchor for maintaining a traditional way of life. Without land, there would be no base from which to retain a part of their cultural heritage. With land and its resources, Native people may have a fighting chance to improve their economic condition and to keep their environment an attractive place in which their young people will desire to reside. Thus, the connection between self-government and gaining some control of the changes faced by Native people. Native people must have greater powers at the local level of government in order to control the disposition of land, to influence culture, and to effect economic development. This is why self-government is the cornerstone of Native policy and must be considered as part of a package of goals. For Native people self-government is the key to social, economic, and political development in the NWT.

GNWT Position

As noted in the previous chapter, the GNWT has put out mixed messages on the centralization-decentralization issue. For years, the government of the territories advocated devolution of responsibilities to local and regional governments. The executive of the government commissioned a study of regional governments, and, in 1987, its findings were tabled in the *Report on the Regional and Tribal Councils in the Northwest Territories.* The report was an endorsement of decentralization.[2] Essentially, it recommended strengthening the role of regional councils. The government's response to the report was negative. A document tabled on 4 November 1988 recorded the response: 'The final Report of the Review Coordinating Committee did not fulfill our expectations of a comprehensive analysis of regional and tribal councils in the broader context of the evolution of government in the N.W.T.'[3] This document went on to note that there appeared to be a contradiction between recommendations for stronger regional councils and the government's idea of prime public authority at the local level of government.[4] The contradiction might be questioned, given the nature of the local-regional-territorial model of government discussed below.

However, in 1987, the government did pass the Charter Communities Act, proclaimed law on 1 January 1988.[5] This act enabled local communities to create a single community council at the municipal level by combining responsibilities of the band council (a product of the Indian Act) and the local government council (a product of the GNWT's Municipal Act). A single municipal council would represent a single source of authority in communities rather than having, for example, competing band and hamlet councils. The act also dealt with a number of changes (e.g., elections) and reiterated the areas in which councils could enact by-laws.

The Charter Communities Act was a response to a 1982 proposal from Fort Good Hope to strengthen the role of the community council, 'A Draft Proposal For Community Government.'[6] In 1980, the GNWT had approved the operation of Fort Good Hope's Dene Community Council, a single local government council that combined band and local government responsibilities. In the 1982 proposal, the people of Fort Good Hope were requesting greater powers for that council. Changes in local government responsibilities would include:

(a) land use planning (regulation of all types of land use, including the regulation of non-renewable resource development and the siting of buildings, roads, and airstrips);
(b) renewable resource management (including fisheries, wildlife, and forests);
(c) environment;
(d) health services (including the delivery of health services to people in the bush);
(e) education (initially, the primary responsibility in this area will be to co-ordinate the planning and development of a recognized community education authority, as outlined in the plan presented by our community to the Territorial Government's Special Committee on Education in November 1981);
(f) culture and recreation;
(g) housing (including the purchase of housing for community government employees);
(h) site development (including capital expenditures, operations and maintenance and acquisition and transfer of lands, buildings, equipment, and vehicles for community purposes);
(i) expropriation of lands for community purposes;
(j) economic development and employment;
(k) utility franchises;
(l) retail goods;

(m) licensing of businesses and regulation of hours of business;
(n) liveries;
(o) by-laws for the protection of persons and property;
(p) domestic animals;
(q) selection of community holidays;
(r) information services;
(s) site services (including garbage pick-up and disposal, garbage dump site maintenance, road maintenance, water supply, sewage pick-up and disposal, airstrip maintenance, fire protection).

The exercise of these powers would in some areas be shared with the interim Territorial Government or its successor. In other areas, the community government would co-ordinate its exercise of powers over community lands, with the exercise of similar powers over outlying lands by Denendeh-wide authorities.[7]

While the GNWT pushed its idea of prime public authority at the local level of government, it has never granted anything near the Fort Good Hope list of powers. In fact, the territorial government has never been precise in defining, within the idea of prime public authority, what the division of powers might be between the GNWT and local councils.

The powers available to local governments are spelled out in the Charter Communities Act. On the surface, powers of municipalities in the North seem equivalent to those possessed by municipalities in the South. Again, local councils in the NWT can establish by-laws governing: roads, sewage and drainage, garbage and waste, water supply, airports, fire prevention, ambulance service, public health (i.e., the power to regulate property for health reasons), recreation, building control and protection of heritage resources, business licensing, taxis, public transit systems, animals, public nuisances, adult publications, firearms and fireworks, inoperable vehicles, contracts, and the acquisition of property.[8]

These powers are, in fact, included within most municipal charters in the South. People in municipalities in the South also have powers extending beyond the above, for example, powers included in the Fort Good Hope proposal. Such powers include education, housing, health care, social services, planning, economic development, and policing. These powers may not always be a part of the responsibilities of a municipal government delegated by a province, yet they are an integral part of local responsibility for local affairs. Responsibilities for education and hospitals, for example, may fall to an autonomous local board empowered through provincial or territorial legislation. Or social services and housing responsibilities may represent legislative powers delegated from a provincial or territorial government to municipal governments. The same applies to economic development and policing responsibilities: the Department of Economic Development and Tourism and the Department of Justice could delegate responsibilities to local authorities.

Since the elections in October 1991 and the formation of a new Executive Committee in November, it appears the GNWT has shifted its policy on decentralization. As mentioned in Chaper 6, economic factors, as much as anything, explain the shift. John Pollard, the minister of Finance in the new government, states the problem:

> The government of the NWT is in a difficult financial situation. The money we are receiving from Ottawa and from our own taxes and other types of income is not enough to pay for our current levels of spending ... The main reason that the government is in financial trouble is the low growth in the grant from Canada over the last two years because of changes that the federal government imposed on us in the formula financing arrangements in 1988 and 1990. We estimate that the 1988 and 1990 changes in the formula will have cost our government more than $150 million by the end of 1993.[9]

While solutions to the problem include budget cutting, they are more complex. The government leader, Nellie Cournoyea, outlined the initial strategy in a speech to the Legislative Assembly. On the one hand, financial restraint is the order of the day:

> Our budget situation means that tough financial, operational and organizational decisions have to be made right now at both the territorial and community levels. The decisions will not be easy and they will require a great deal of public input, understanding and support. Both government and public expectations will have to decrease. Decisions of cabinet and the Legislature must be based on living within our means.[10]

At the same time, there must be a restructuring of the entire system:

> Mr. Speaker, all of us want to encourage greater community self-sufficiency, with strong community governments making their own decisions on behalf of the people who elected them. We want to see community ownwership of programs and services. We want to see programs and services delivered in a way that reflects the unique conditions of each community, controlled by local people who know the community and who can set their own funding priorities.

The newly organized Ministry of Intergovernmental and Aboriginal Affairs will take the lead role in this area over the coming months. It will be developing approaches and arrangements designed to provide for local control and to set the stage for increased social and economic self-sufficiency at the community level.

Transfers to community governments could include block or multi-year funding. Increased local responsibilities may include responsibility for building houses, building and maintaining local public works, administration of social services, dealing with drug and alcohol problems and education of the young.[11]

These statements do represent a significant change in policy. All the components of the policy are not in place but its cornerstone includes 'community transfer agreements.' Its rationale goes back to the Beatty Report, which linked the transfers of authority to building stronger 'community self-government': 'The challenge now is to efficiently facilitate the transfer of more program authority and resources to those community governments that are demonstrating the interest and are prepared to develop the necessary abilities. This is a key pre-condition for transfer.'[12]

Statements to date do not guarantee a viable policy of decentralization. At this point, entrenched interests will go to work. Many administrators and those who want a strong territorial government will oppose any shift of power from Yellowknife. And Native groups who prefer a more traditional form of self-government may oppose empowering existing local and regional governments. But the seeds of change are planted and a policy shift could result in a more decentralized process in the NWT. The coming months, however, will determine if the GNWT can indeed break a pattern of authority that began in 1967.

Federal Government's Position

Self-government negotiations put the federal government right in the middle of the GNWT-Native conflict over decentralization. Rick Van Loon, senior assistant deputy minister for Northern Affairs, has spoken of the government's position in this controversy. In an interview in 'True to the North' (April 1990) he suggested that Native groups in the NWT see the GNWT

as a temporary government, something that will be 'dealt with' in due course, and so on. At the same time, we are devolving powers to that

allegedly temporary entity. The more powers it has, the more permanent it is. So there is a divergence, if you like, between the views of the
aboriginal groups about the permanence of the government of the Northwest Territories and our devolving powers to it.

I think our challenge, if you like, as the federal government is to watch
this evolution, try to be sufficiently light-handed that we don't throttle
anything that is a workable mechanism, yet keep in mind that these still
are young governments and that perhaps a little more monitoring than
would be appropriate for provincial governments is necessary for a little
while yet. I don't think there's any doubt that the end point of constitutional evolution in the north is effective provincehood, that is, territorial
governments will be as complete in their sovereignty as provincial governments are in theirs or the federal government is in its. But we're some
distance away from that yet and it'll be an interesting ten years of ex-
periencing to see how we get there.[13]

Thus, the federal government, at least according to Van Loon, is not
trying to shape the nature of the constitutional process of the NWT.
When the federal government negotiates self-government with Native people, there is a chance that these people can obtain a great deal
of power in governing their own lands. In DIAND's guidelines for self-
government negotiations, 'essential' and 'optional' subject matters
include:

Essential Subject Matters
Legal Status and Capacity
Structure and Procedures
Membership
Lands and Resources
Financial Arrangements
Application of the *Indian Act*, other laws, and authorities
Implementation Plan

Optional Subject Matters
Infrastructure and Public Works
Education
Social and Welfare Services, including custody and placement of
children
Administration of Justice
Licensing, regulation and operation of business
Taxation for local purposes
Public order, safety and security
Indian and Northern Health services

Wildlife and wildlife habitat
Indian monies
Agriculture
Protection and management of the environment
Succession
Culture
Traffic and transportation
Access to and residence on reserve[14]

These responsibilities are not significantly different from those requested by Fort Good Hope. Hence, if Native organizations negotiate self-government powers with the federal government on lands distributed under claim settlements, will those powers clash with powers devolved by the federal government to the GNWT? And will those powers clash with powers devolved by the GNWT to municipal governments? In other words, would a self-government arrangement between Native organizations and the federal government effect the division of powers between the territorial government and local councils under the existing Municipal Act? These are complex constitutional questions to be addressed by the federal government, the GNWT, and by Native organizations. It would appear that Native people have a number of alternatives for achieving a more decentralized, self-governing system.

PROSPECTS FOR LOCAL AND REGIONAL AUTONOMY

Within the context of the NWT, Native people are making a strong case for self-government via some form of decentralization. Their vision of self-government is not just a division of powers. Rather, self-government is part and parcel of a much larger goal. As three experts writing on self-government have said, Native people 'are convinced that their special status needs to be fortified by self-government for them to achieve their vision of 'the good society ... Self-government is seen by Indians as necessary to preserve their philosophical uniqueness. They seek self-government so that they can develop their own institutions and shape laws to reflect and enhance their traditional cultural values.'[15] Del Riley, a former president of the National Indian Brotherhood, put this view even more emphatically: 'We want basic human rights. Sometimes it is termed "self-determination." Our quest for self-determination includes controlling those institutions that affect our lives.'[16]

These expressions of self-government are made by Native people across the country: but how does this concept of self-government fit within the Canadian constitution? Is this about an additional level of government or an expansion of the powers of municipal governments? Canadians in general might have a great deal of sympathy for this concept of self-government. In fact, the centralization-decentralization issue is not new in Canada. In the Anglo-American world there has always been a struggle for strong local government. 'The system of local government developed in Great Britain and Ireland in the nineteenth century was ... intended to be local self-government; democracy carried down to the smallest community unit practicable.'[17]

In terms of self-government, what Native people are seeking is not a lot more than what many subjects in this country sought prior to Confederation. Indeed, Kenneth Grant Crawford suggests the fight for some degree of autonomy at the local level began in 1793. 'The struggle for local self-government which extended over the next half century was in part explained by a conflict of views and in part by a competition for political power.'[18] He goes on to point out that British officials felt that unrest in the American colonies stemmed from too much 'democracy' at the local level. In order for these governors to preserve the Crown's influence in British North America, restrictions had to be placed on the power of local institutions. Loyalists, on the other hand, were accustomed to a high degree of local self-rule and were not about to surrender this power without a struggle. 'The agitation' until 1849 resulted in municipalities having the right to 'local self-government' with a minimum of parliamentary or executive control.[19]

What many colonists wanted was a more decentralized, autonomous process. What many Native people in the NWT want today is the same: a more decentralized, autonomous process of government, in which local citizens have control over the decisionmaking process which deals with problems at the local level. The list of powers put forward by Fort Good Hope, for example, is certainly not very different from municipal powers existing in all the regions of Canada. The problem is that never have residents in communities in the NWT had the opportunity to control those powers. For four decades, Native people have lived with many important decisions made by administrative officials in Ottawa or in Yellowknife. Native people are now convinced that with their involvement in the political process, this process should undergo change.

Examples of a more decentralized process of government do exist in the NWT, and three of these experiments should be noted. The work of education and hospital boards in the Baffin region are significant. These organizations are a model of effective regional organizations serving a number of communities. The problem is that members of these organizations often claim that the GNWT still holds too much power in Yellowknife, and the government's response to the Regional and Tribal Councils Review Committee report indicates continued reluctance to alter that power relationship.[20] For the Inuit, the hope is that under a 'Nunavut' territorial government, local and regional governments would have greater authority.

A second example exists within the Department of Renewable Resources. This department is responsible for wildlife management in the territories. In carrying out its responsibilities, it has tried to co-ordinate the management of wildlife with local hunters and trappers associations. In 1983, the department put out a 'Strategic Plan' identifying its objectives. Goal number two in the document was to: 'Increase the involvement of Northwest Territory residents in renewable resource management.' More specifically, objectives in the plan included: '(b) Establish a system which provides renewable resource users with the ways and means to participate in the development of Departmental policy, programs and legislation. (c) Devolve certain Departmental programs to regional and community organizations.'[21]

This plan was an attempt to decentralize the activities of the department. From what one hears from individuals in a number of communities, while problems exist, most people seemed to be happy with attempts at 'joint' management.

A third example exists with wildlife management under the Inuvialuit land claim settlement. Part of the implementation agreement included the co-ordinating body, the Western Arctic Claim Implementation Secretariat (WACIS). The WACIS brings together the Inuvialuit and the federal and territorial governments as joint managers of wildlife in the Inuvialuit region. Operationally, the Wildlife Management Advisory Council (Northwest Territories) and the Fisheries Joint Management Committee (FJMC) interact with the Inuvialuit Game Council and its affiliated HTC's from the six communities in the region. The joint management that has existed for approximately six years seems to have worked to the satisfaction of all three parties to the agreement.[22] Something similar to this joint management model is the basis for joint management structures in the Delta regional and TFN agreements.

Thus, there are examples of a more decentralized, participatory process for making public decisions in the NWT. These examples seem to underscore the fact that the decisionmaking process does not necessarily have to be centred in Yellowknife, and that local residents are supportive of the process when powers are decentralized.

Over the past decade, Native people have dominated the Legislative Assembly. For this reason, political observers often assume that the position of the GNWT and that of the Native people is one and the same. During this time, however, only limited powers have been devolved to local governments. In the communities, many Native people feel they are still battling the same kind of centralized decision-making authority that has existed for decades. The problem now is that they are not fighting an Ottawa-based administration: on the contrary, they are fighting a Yellowknife-based administration.

If, indeed, Native people constitute a majority of the voters, why can they not change the nature of the system? Why can they not precipitate a move toward a more decentralized process? In Chapter 6 a number of explanations were considered. Together, these explanations pointed to a power struggle going on between the central administration of the territories and the citizens of outlying communities. A good part of the answer, then, lies in the nature of large, centralized administrations.

It has been recognized for a long time that large administrations, once institutionalized, pose a problem when it comes to change. Max Weber, writing almost a century ago, says this about large administrations: 'They have a common interest in seeing that the mechanism continues its functions and that the societally exercised authority carries on.'[23] Size and changes in the functions of government over the past forty years have reinforced the power of central administrations at the expense of local autonomy. 'No doubt, in the twentieth century, the exigencies of the welfare state have pressed inexorably in upon the body of local self-government, crushing it almost to death.'[24]

This point is reinforced by Henry Jacoby in *The Bureaucratization of the World*. He argues the contradictory nature of administrations and democracy: 'Centralization of social functions and governmental intervention in heretofore uncontrolled domains, together with all other curtailments of privileges entailed in the expansion of bureaucracy, are always seen as the loss of prestige or actual power by both small and large groups of individuals.'[25] Jacoby notes that Weber indicated the paradoxical nature of this administration – while it is inevitable, it is also undesirable: 'It was undesirable because it stood in the way of true democracy and the development of self-responsible, socially active citizens.'[26] According to these theorists, centralized administration denies the realization of democracy and the full potentiality of citizens. In the NWT, many individuals would probably agree with this argument. They argue that they have been denied the opportunity to exercise powers at the local level – self-governing powers that would give them greater control of their lives.

Many analysts are beginning to question the validity of the centralized formula for development. They draw on evidence suggesting that the idea of a decentralized process has a great deal of merit. G. Shabbir Cheema and Dennis A. Rondinelli have put together a series of readings entitled *Decentralization and Development: Policy Implementation in Developing Countries*.[27] While they focus on the problem of decentralization in developing nations, these problems are not unlike those faced by citizens of the NWT: low socio-economic development, bicultural and bilingual situations, and the experience of a colonial process.

The editors suggest that the question of form of government is critical:

> One of the most crucial and recurring debates in the developing world is about the degree of control that central governments can and should have over development planning and administration. Thus, it should not be surprising that as the directions of development strategy have shifted over the past two decades, new questions about the most appropriate forms of planning and administering development policies have arisen in so many developing countries.[28]

They go on to note that, since the 1950s, development activities in most Third World countries are 'centralized in national government ministries and agencies,' and, indeed, that this type of control has been 'compatible with the major theories of economic development that emerged in the late 1940s.'[29]

However, concentrating power, authority, and programs in this way posed a number of problems:

> Central planning was not only complex and difficult to implement, but may also have been inappropriate for promoting equitable growth and self-sufficiency among low-income groups and communities within developing societies. Through central planning, it was charged, an elite group of political leaders, economists, technicians, and administrators attempted to preempt decision making and prescribe for government agencies, private organizations, and local communities courses of action that reflected their own values and priorities.[30]

The editors indicate that there has been a certain disillusionment with the centralized planning process, and, in turn, it has led to the realization that 'development is a complex and uncertain process that cannot be easily planned and controlled from the centre.'[31] As a consequence, people began to see the possibilities in decentralizing the process. Decentralization includes 'devolution' of authority and functions. It also involves creating autonomous 'local units of government' that are independent, and 'over which central authorities exercise little or no direct control.'[32]

At the same time, the writers in the book point to a number of problems with decentralization. David Leonard, for example, says: 'Weaknesses in administrative and technical capacity are a serious impediment to decentralization.'[33] And Cheema and Rondinelli note that inadequate financial resources are a critical factor in 'obstructing ... decentralization policies.'[34] They conclude that: 'Ultimately, decentralization can be effective only when agencies and actors at the regional and local levels have developed the capacities to perform effectively the planning, decision-making, and management functions that are formally granted to them.'[35]

If one applies the same approach to problems in the NWT, the success or failure of 'development' will, in the end, depend on Native people in the communities not on outsiders. Local residents will ultimately have the responsibility of developing the necessary 'capacities' to achieve this goal. Success or failure, then, will depend on their use of resources to forge solutions to their problems, and self-government is a key factor in this process.

What would a decentralized process in the NWT look like? What form would it take? How would a decentralized process be funded? Would it be possible for such a system to generate its own revenue from within?

LOCAL-REGIONAL-TERRITORIAL MODEL OF GOVERNMENT

There seems to be no reason to consider external models for constitutional development in the NWT. The existing framework of the GNWT, or two territorial governments, can be used as the basis of a model of government to serve the interests of citizens of the region. This model of government includes local, regional, and territorial jurisdictions. Gordon Robertson has suggested that territorial governments be labelled 'autonomous' governments, indicating 'the completeness of the self-government to be accorded them within the federal system.'[36] Since 1967, local governments have been an emerging institution within the territorial government. In 1977, a regional government was instituted in the Baffin area. Since that time, regional governments have become an integral part of the governmental process in the territories. Today regional governments in some form exist in nine jurisdictions: three within the Nunavut area, five within the Denendeh area, and one within the Inuvialuit settlement region. Thus, the local-regional-territorial model appears to be operational in the NWT. The issue is establishing power relationships within that framework.

In terms of extending powers of local and regional governments, Native people seem to be very clear on the issue. They made their views known to the Carrothers Commission, to Drury, to various legislative committees, and to organizations inquiring about problems in the region. Most Native people prefer a more decentralized process over which they would have greater control. Moreover, an apparatus with prime authority at the local and regional levels seems to be part of the designs for Denendeh or Nunavut. There will be one or more territories, but within that (or those) territorial structure, local governments must be empowered with the responsibility for roads, health and hospitals, housing, physical planning, public assistance, economic development, policing, and schools. The delivery of these services can, in some cases, be accomplished by local governments or combined local, regional, and territorial governments.

As mentioned previously, one of the best discussions of the relationship between local, regional, and territorial government is found in *Report on Regional and Tribal Councils in the Northwest Territories*, by the Regional and Tribal Councils Review Co-ordinating Committee.[37] The review committee sent questionnaires to all regional and tribal councils, and, as well, meetings were held with most Native organizations and a number of government officials and organizations. The committee found that while the role of regional governments was principally 'advisory,' many of the regional councils 'wanted to take over more authority for running programs of the Government of the NWT within the region'[38] The committee supported this position in their recommendations, one of the reasons the GNWT issued a response to the report.

It should be noted also that while regional governments were interested in more 'program responsibility' in the region, they were not interested in 'law making powers held by the Legislative Assembly.'[39] Nor were these officials interested in taking over 'ministerial responsibility for setting territorial policy and standards.'[40] For those responding to the committee, there was clearly a role for territorial officials to set the standards across the territories, but there was also significant responsibility for decisionmaking at the regional level.

Thus, strong regional and tribal councils can be seen as a way of rationalizing a move to something resembling a 'county' form of government. Counties have a long tradition in Anglo-American local government, and in 1950, for example, this level of jurisdiction was established in Alberta.[41] Usually, county governments are organized around a number of municipalities. A larger geographic region becomes the basis for organizing responsibilities for a number of municipalities in a more economic way, while smaller communities co-ordinate responsibilities such as health care, housing, schools, transportation, and tourism. For example, it would be impractical to try to have a hospital in each community in a region. On the other hand, ten communities in a region might band together and, with territorial government help, support a regional hospital in order to improve health care service for the region. Much of the funding would come from the territorial government, but an autonomous regional board would be responsible for the regional administration and for raising part of its revenue. County governments, with responsibilities for services such as education, health care, roads, social services, and policing would be like the regional governments that have emerged in the NWT (if the latter had the power to accompany the structure).

An important difference between this local-regional-territorial model and county governments in the South, is that most county councillors are elected directly from constituencies throughout the county. County councils, then, are responsible to the electorate. In the NWT, regional councils are made up of municipal officials chosen by local councils, and they represent the local councils. A mayor of a community, for instance, may be chosen by his or her council to represent the council at the regional level. Thus, regional councils are responsible to local government councils. This is an important distinction in the NWT, because it conforms to the GNWT's idea of prime public authority at the local level. Local councils collectively controlling a regional council still retain PPA. Thus, there would seem to be no contradiction between PPA and strong regional governments.

Regional councils as described above are indigenous to the territories. They are chartered by the GNWT and, indeed, get their core funding (and some discretionary funding) from that government. Yet, in theory, their authority rests with local councils. Local councils delegate responsibilities to regional governments within the guidelines of the Municipal Act. If the GNWT devolves more power to local governments, local governments could, if they choose, increase the responsibilities of regional governments. In terms of authority, the model is as follows:

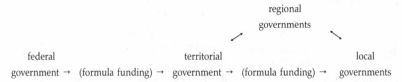

federal government → (formula funding) → territorial government → (formula funding) → local governments

regional governments

The problem today is that the GNWT has had, since 1967, most provincial-type powers devolved from Ottawa. Now many people in the communities feel that some of these powers should be devolved to local authorities (e.g., powers associated with local issues such as health care, housing, or education). The review committee report came down in support of the latter, recommending that, in the devolutionary process, regional governments should be strengthened. The recommendation was for a shift in the balance of power in terms of program delivery.

The problem is not simply one of devolving power to all local governments and, in turn, regional governments. There would have to be flexibility in any legislation. As stated in the report, most communities want to receive more authority and delegate some of that authority to regional organizations. But a few communities, particularly the larger ones, may want no part of regional organizations.[42] In the report, however, it was clear that most communities want some form of regional body to strengthen their hand when it comes to dealing with territorial officials – a means of 'self-defence' against big government.[43] Therefore, additional legislation governing regional organizations would have to be sufficiently flexible to accommodate larger communities which, if they desired, could opt for going it alone rather than being part of a regional organization.

FINANCING LOCAL AND REGIONAL GOVERNMENTS

Financing governments in the NWT is a significant problem because, to date, most territorial revenues have come from the federal government (more than 80 per cent). This is a problem, for autonomy will be limited as long as most public revenue comes from outside the territories. And, of course, as long as economic development in the region remains a problem, one cannot expect to change the local revenue picture.

The review committee report follows a philosophical position similar to that reflected in Drury's report. Essentially, the GNWT should not only devolve powers to local and regional governments but should also sufficiently fund these governments so that they could adequately meet new responsibilities. Some type of per capita grant or formula funding would need to be established by the GNWT in order to support local or regional governments.

Regional funding can be very complicated. In the review committee report, it was clear that there were those who felt most GNWT funds should go directly to regional councils. Others, however, felt the funding should go through local councils and, in turn, be disbursed to regional organizations so that they could carry out responsibilities delegated by the local councils. This is an issue that must be resolved, but, again, any new legislation affecting local and regional govern-

but, again, any new legislation affecting local regional governments might be sufficiently flexible that either position could be covered. A critical factor in either case is accountability. Local and regional government organizations would have to be scrupulous in
accounting for public funds.

Funding for regional and local governments is now heavily dependent upon the GNWT. Until local economies expand, local governments
will remain very dependent. In time, however, local and regional bodies will have to face the fact that if, indeed, they want greater autonomy from the GNWT, they will have to generate more local revenue.
Increasing local revenues no doubt will be the way to get greater discretionary funding.

An argument often heard in Yellowknife regarding increased local
and regional authority is that it would be too expensive. Many of those
who oppose devolving or delegating powers to local or regional bodies suggest it would constitute too much duplication of government
and thus be too costly for the federal and territorial governments to
support. No doubt there is some truth in this argument. But two points
should be noted. First, 'efficiency' in terms of costs is not the only
basis on which governments are constructed. Our federal system is
more expensive than would be a unitary system of government. But
we trade off the higher cost for having a government closer to home
handling problems that are particular to the region and for having
a government over which, supposedly, we have greater control. Also,
a provincial government provides a check on federal authority. Power relationships may be just as much a priority as is financial efficiency.

Second, the cost of extending local and regional authority may not
be as expensive as it seems. As the Beatty Report suggests, governing
institutions are already in place in most communities and regions;
local and regional structures exist, but they lack authority. Therefore,
the problem may not be cost. If these existing governments were further empowered, then there may be no need to create more infrastructure at the local and regional levels. Rather, it would mean that
those organizations already in place would be exercising greater
authority. According to one study commissioned by the Nunavut
Steering Committee, the initial cost of establishing Nunavut as a territory would be $557.8 to $627.7 million, depending on the location of
the capital. Additional costs in annual government budgets would be
$161.3 to $184.5 million.[44]

If, then, the GNWT devolves greater powers to local or regional
governments, greater funding will have to accompany this devolution.
Perhaps settlement of the Energy Accord could be one way of deriv-
ing additional territorial funds for transfers to local and regional coun-

cils, although, as the Alberta government learned, depending on resource revenues can be a precarious way to live. Or the territorial government would have to be willing to cut the size of government in Yellowknife and permit the local communities and the regions to increase their capacity to govern. As Tocqueville, Weber, and Crawford point out, the desire for decentralization has been resisted by central administrations for centuries. Such a course of action, however, would be what many people in the communities desire. In the minds of many residents in the NWT, it would be the way to create a system they could view as legitimate. Central authorities, however, will always point out the high cost of decentralization, and, as long as the NWT remains underdeveloped economically and is dependent on external funding, they will have a point.

CONCLUSION: SELF-GOVERNMENT AND THE CRISIS OF LEGITIMACY

Since 1920, government changes in the NWT have been dramatic. Today the process of government may not be exactly what everyone in the region prefers, but the transformation, particularly since the early 1950s, has been a steady move toward representative and responsible government. During the 1920 to 1950 period, this was not the case. Government in the region did not change much, nor did government policy. Administrators tried hard to sell development in the North, and most contact with Native people was left to the Anglican and Roman Catholic churches, the trading companies, and the RCMP.

The Second World War and its aftermath increased resource exploration, and changes in transportation and communication brought significant change to the NWT and made the North more visible to Canadians. Government policy changes also occurred. State interventionist policies reflected the dominant ideology of the day, and the federal government, over a decade, launched education, health care, housing, and economic development policies. The underlying assumption behind the policies was assimilation. Native people, once a part of the wage economy, would gradually become part of the mainstream of Canadian life.

Government institutions also changed. The GNWT was removed from its departmental moorings in Ottawa, and, in 1967, Yellowknife became the seat of government. The territorial assembly became an elected legislative assembly. The federal government devolved the equivalent of most provincial powers to the GNWT, and the role of the commissioner was assumed by the executive committee, functioning as a cabinet.

By the early 1970s, four Native organizations were operating in the political process, and, after 1975, Native members held a majority in the Legislative Assembly. Today (1992) eighteen of the twenty-four members are Native; they hold six of the eight executive posts and the government leader is a Native.

Indeed, changes in the region have been rapid and pervasive, with a significant impact on the lives of Native people. The clash of cultures is one of the most serious problems in the region. The fact that the two value systems are often incompatible has led to extensive social consequences. This cultural problem brings into focus the fundamentally different view on constitutional development. The view held by most Native people, particularly those in small communities, is that the GNWT should devolve some of its power and strengthen the role of local and regional governments. This position has been evident for years; it is clear in the Berger Inquiry, in the Drury Report, in the Native organizations' proposals for Denendeh and Nunavut, in government evaluations of policies such as education and housing, in the Fort Good Hope proposal for community government, and in the report by the Regional and Tribal Councils Committee. There have been many opportunities for expressions of this argument.

There have been also those who support maintaining a strong centralized role for the territorial government. Few specific statements exist supporting such a position. Materials submitted by the previous government (1987-91) on constitutional development endorsed prime public authority but offered nothing explicit about any change in the division of powers that might accompany the concept. The government's opposition to the Regional and Tribal Councils Committee was obvious. The underlying assumption behind this view is expressed in a statement by Gurston Dacks. In writing about devolution influencing the GNWT he says: 'As the government becomes larger and more powerful, the contrast grows between it and the smallness and the inability of the aboriginal groups to deliver equivalent benefits. As time passes, it becomes less and less credible that aboriginal institutions might be developed which would be as effective as is the government of the NWT.'[45]

Graham White is even more emphatic. He suggests that the relationship between process and legitimacy may be tenuous. However, at another level,

the link is rather more important: an effective government is more likely to be a legitimate government, and governmental effectiveness is very much a function of the form of government, as well as the responsiveness of the principal representative institution and the processes by which governmental decisions are made. To the extent that the Legislative Assembly of the Northwest Territories contributes to effective government by adapting the procedures and operations of the Westminster model to Northern political styles and Northern political needs, the Assembly will promote the overall legitimacy of the existing political system.[46]

A critical point is that size and effectiveness are equated with political legitimacy. The assumption is that as the GNWT does more, and does it efficiently, it will engender in the minds of northerners a sense of political legitimacy. Moreover, in time, the GNWT will be overwhelming and will counter any opportunity for Native people to have significant powers devolved to local and regional governments.

The argument in this book is diametrically opposed to the above. For many residents of the NWT, political legitimacy will come only after devolution or some form of decentralization has occurred within the GNWT. White's position, for example, begs the question about the value of local participation in resolving local problems. The danger in this assumption is that it avoids the issue of how democracy in this hemisphere is linked to a governmental process in which local governments have a broad range of powers. From the evidence marshalled here, it would not appear that the territorial government with its existing power arrangement will become legitimate. With a different power arrangement, many individuals in the NWT might feel they have an opportunity to influence public decisions that directly affect their lives in small communities. Then and only then might they feel that they live under a government to which they consent.

Three related hypotheses can be gleaned from this study:

(1) If the development of a centralized territorial government precedes the development of local and regional governments, it will be extremely difficult for the centralized government to devolve some of its power to local and regional governments.

(2) If centralized bureaucratic agencies make public decisions affecting the essentials of life – for example, education, economic development, housing, health care, policing, and social services – then no matter how elaborate the delivery services, most local residents will resent the decisionmaking process.

(3) If different cultural groups have an opportunity to influence the development of an institutionalized political process, then the nature of that process will reflect the values of those cultural groups.

The first hypothesis is a reflection of the historical experience in the region. Governments in Ottawa, and then Yellowknife, delivered many of the services required by people in NWT communities. These services were necessary if people in the region were to enjoy many of the amenities realized by most Canadians. However, when people in the communities decided that they, rather than administrators from Ottawa or Yellowknife, should be making the public decision affecting the necessities of their lives, the federal and territorial governments were reluctant to change the decisionmaking process. The federal department in Ottawa and the GNWT administration have been very slow in empowering local governments with responsibilities experienced by most Canadians. Denying local residents the opportunity to come to grips with local problems in their own way perpetuates a resentment against the system.

The second hypothesis may be the reflection of human nature. Most individuals have an inherent desire to control their own destiny – at least as far as is possible. The problem in the NWT is that the federal and territorial governments have controlled the delivery of most services – services that local governments would normally control. In other words, no matter how extensive and elaborate the services provided by the senior levels of government, it seems that the people in communities resent not being able to control essential services such as housing. The argument has been made that if the territorial government could just deliver the services efficiently, then, in time, people in the territories would accept that governmental process as being legitimate. From evidence pulled together in this study, this may not be the case. Historically, local residents have cherished the right to deal with local problems. Perhaps local residents will always resent the intrusion of even an efficient centralized system from afar and, in an open society, will question its legitimacy.

The third hypothesis stems from the fact that elected representatives in the GNWT are crafting a system of government that is different from that of any jurisdiction in Canada. It has a 'made in the NWT' stamp on it. It is a consensus form of government without political parties. The legislature has a degree of autonomy that any legislator in the Western world would envy. The legislators elect the eight members of the executive, and, at least on two occasions, have called for a review of ministers after two years. While the government leader assigns portfolios and can change the portfolios of members of the executive, ministers and the government leader are responsible to the legislature. This is a rare case of legislative autonomy, especially in a country where majoritarian politics prevail and legislatures are known to be almost rubber stamps for the executive. This indigenous process reflects in part the influence of an Aboriginal majority in the legislature, particularly since 1979.

The legitimacy question is crucial because it is linked to the cultural dilemma Native people are facing. Native people must make their choices about how to live. If they are to preserve something of their traditional way of life, they must have land and an economic base linked to the land. With such a base, they may be able to preserve a part of their culture. But to do so they must be able to make choices for themselves. In the past, many of these choices were made by trading company employees, missionaries, or government administrators and politicians. If Native people acquire self-governing powers along the lines of the Fort Good Hope proposal in 1982, such a situation will not happen again. With self-governing powers they will have an opportunity to make the decisions that will enable them to develop an economic base on their land and to preserve a semblance of their culture. A more decentralized process will enable individuals in communities to do more for themselves rather than having it done from outside. Self-governing powers are the key to constructing a legitimate political system in the NWT – a system in which there is an accord between political values and structures, and a system to which Native people can consent. Self-governing powers then are a crucial factor in answering the question, whose North?

POSTSCRIPT

After the completion of this manuscript for publication, two important documents were introduced in February 1992 which may influence constitutional development in the NWT. The Commission on Constitutional Development issued its 'Interim Report,' in which there is an extensive discussion about protecting the rights of the diverse groups in the New Western Territory with a new constitution. The Commission also rejected the conventional idea of local, regional, and territorial levels of government. Instead, they advocated the innovative notions of 'district' governments and 'orders' of government, including central and district orders of authority. It is assumed this model of authority would best accommodate the First Nations and non-aboriginal northerners, as well as the different types of communities in the region: 'The District approach would provide more flexibility in allowing some communities like Yellowknife or Norman Wells to remain municipalities or municipal districts. Others, such as the Inuvlaluit communities, may choose to amalgamate into a regional district. A third variation would allow smaller individual First Nations communities, or groupings of them, to create an aboriginal district government' (p. 30).

A second document was tabled by the GNWT and indicates something of the government's design for new authorities in the entire NWT.

Reshaping Northern Government does represent a commitment on the part of the existing government to follow suggestions of the Beatty Report by downsizing the process. Administrative departments will be consolidated and some powers are to be devolved to local governments. The latter will be the subject of a more specific report later.

In effect, the two reports represent different approaches to the problem of decentralization of authority in the NWT. They pose interesting possibilities for people of the region and may add some substance to the political debate on division of the territory – the plebiscite over this division taking place on 4 May 1992.

Notes

1 Excellent critiques of the concepts of political change and political development can be found in Leonard Binder, 'The Natural History of Development Theory,' *Comparative Studies in Society and History* 28(1986):3-33; Stephen Chilton, *Defining Political Development* (Boulder: Lynne Rienner Publishers 1988); Vicky Randall and Robin Theobald, *Political Change and Underdevelopment: A Critical Introduction to Third World Politics* (Durham: Duke University Press 1985); Myron Weiner and Samuel P. Huntington, eds., *Understanding Political Development* (Toronto: Little, Brown and Company 1987); Howard J. Wiarda, 'Toward a Nonethnocentric Theory of Development: Alternative Conceptions From the Third World,' in Howard J. Wiarda, ed., *New Directions in Comparative Politics* (Boulder: Westview Press 1985).

2 Morton Gorden, *Comparative Political Systems: Managing Conflict* (New York: Macmillan 1972), 237.

3 Two examples are C.E. Black, *The Dynamics of Modernization: A Study in Comparative History* (New York: Harper & Row 1966) and Charles Tilly, *From Mobilization to Revolution* (Don Mills, Ont.: Addison-Wesley 1978).

4 One of the best earlier discussions on the problem of culture and political development is in Howard J. Wiarda, 'Toward a Framework for the Study of Political Change in the Iberic-Latin Tradition: The Corporative Model,' *World Politics* 25(1973):206-35. The same theme is found in his later works, such as in note 1.

5 S.N. Eisenstadt, *Modernization: Protest and Change* (Englewood Cliffs, NJ: Prentice-Hall 1966); Samuel P. Huntington, *Political Order in Changing Societies* (New Haven: Yale University Press 1968); and Mancur Olson, Jr., 'Rapid Growth as a Destabilizing Force,' *Journal of Economic History*

3(1963):529-52.

6 Seymour Martin Lipset, *Political Man* (New York: Doubleday and Company 1960), 64.

7 John H. Schaar, *Legitimacy in the Modern State* (New Brunswick, NJ: Transaction Books 1981), 20-1.

8 Herbert J. Spiro, 'Authority, Values, and Policy,' in Carl J. Fredrich, ed., *Authority* (Cambridge: Harvard University Press 1958), 50-3.

9 John Locke, *The Second Treatise of Government* (New York: Library of Liberal Arts [Bobbs-Merrill Co.] 1952), paragraph 171, 98. The idea of linking consent and political legitimacy came from Guy Laforest's 'Letter From the Other Canada,' *Government and Opposition* 25(1990):231-47.

10 Gurston Dacks uses this approach to political development in *A Choice of Futures: Politics in the Canadian North* (Toronto: Methuen 1981), 89-90.

11 *News North*, 7 November 1988, 3.

12 *Nunatsiaq News*, 11 May 1990, 6.

CHAPTER TWO:
GEOGRAPHY, DEMOGRAPHY, ECONOMY, AND CULTURES

1 Excellent geographical descriptions of the North can be found in William C. Wonders, ed., *Canada's Changing North* (Toronto: McClelland and Stewart 1971) and William C. Wonders, ed., *The North* (Toronto: University of Toronto Press 1972).

2 Canada, Department of the Interior, J.F. Morran, 'Local Conditions In the Mackenzie District, 1922' (Ottawa: King's Printer 1923).

3 The best description of Lake McConnell I have heard was given by Derald Smith, Department of Geography, University of Calgary, in a talk at the Arctic Institute of North America, 'The Glacial Lake McConnell System,' 6 February 1990. Smith is working on the significance of this system and his publications will be forthcoming.

4 An authority on this issue is Donat Pharand, *Canada's Arctic Waters in International Law* (Cambridge: Cambridge University Press 1988).

5 Canada, Department of the Interior, Major Ernest J. Chambers, ed., 'The Unexploited West: A Compilation of All of the Authentic Information Available at the Present Time as to the Natural Resources of the Unexploited Regions of Northern Canada' (Ottawa: King's Printer 1914).

6 GNWT, The Honourable Michael A. Ballantyne, Minister of Finance, 1990-1 Budget Address (Yellowknife 1990), 30.

7 See, for example, Robert Page, *Northern Development: The Canadian Dilemma* (Toronto: McClelland and Stewart 1986).

8 GNWT, Department of Renewable Resources, Ed Hull, ed., 'A Way of Life' (Yellowknife: Culture and Communications 1986), 12.

9 GNWT, *Annual Report*, 1988, 57.

10 Discussions of problems with the fur trade and the impact of this trade on Native people can be found in Morris Zaslow, *The Northward Expansion of Canada, 1914-67* (Toronto: McClelland and Stewart 1988), ch. 7; Peter Usher, *The Bankslanders: Economy and Ecology of a Frontier Trapping Community* (3 vols.), (Ottawa: Department of Indian and Northern Affairs 1979); and Arthur J. Ray, *The Canadian Fur Trade In The Industrial Age* (Toronto: University of Toronto Press 1990).

11 An examination of the impact of whaling on the Inuit can be found in W. Gillis Ross, *Whaling and Eskimos, 1860-1915* (Ottawa: National Museum of Canada 1975).

12 GNWT, Department of Renewable Resources, 'A Way of Life,' 19.

13 Canada, *Report of the Royal North-West Mounted Police, 1904* (Ottawa: King's Printer 1905).

14 Canada, 'Local Conditions In the Mackenzie District, 1922,' 9.

15 GNWT, The Honourable Michael A. Ballantyne, Minister of Finance, 1989-90 Budget Address, 29, 30.

16 Canada, Indian and Northern Affairs, 'Northern Mineral Policy,' 1986, 9.

17 GNWT, Department of Economic Development and Tourism, 'The NWT Economy, 1988,' 27.

18 *Globe and Mail*, 17 March 1989, B.1.

19 This point was argued some years ago by K.J. Rea, *The Political Economy of the Canadian North* (Toronto: University of Toronto Press 1968).

20 Two perspectives on the northern economy can be seen in William G. Watson, 'A Southern Perspective on Northern Economic Development,' Michael S. Whittington, Co-ordinator, *The North* (Toronto: University of Toronto Press 1985) and Frances Abele and Peter Usher, 'The Danger to the North,' *Policy Options* 11(1990):4-10.

21 GNWT, Department of Economic Development and Tourism, 'NWT Economic Review and Outlook, 1988,' 10.

22 Ibid.

23 Ibid., 21.

24 GNWT, Bureau of Statistics, *Statistics Quarterly* 11(1989):52.

25 GNWT, Bureau of Statistics, *Personal Income Statistics, Northwest Territories, 1982-4*, 8, 10.

26 GNWT, Bureau of Statistics, *1989 NWT Labor Force Survey*, Report No. 1, 5.

27 Ibid., 12, 14.

28 For 1911-71, GNWT, 'NWT Data Sheets, General Information Sheet,' no date, 4; for 1981 and 1990, GNWT, *Statistics Quarterly* 13(1991):3.

29 Legislative Assembly of the NWT, Special Committee on the Northern Economy, *The Scone Report: Building Our Economic Future* (Yellowknife: GNWT 1989), 11-12.

30 GNWT, *Statistics Quarterly* 11(1989):7.

31 Legislative Assembly of the NWT, Special Committee on the Northern

Economy, Mike Robinson, et al., *Coping With the Cash* (Yellowknife: GNWT 1989), 83-4.

32 GNWT, Bureau of Statistics, *Statistics Quarterly* 9(1987):1.

33 Ewng-Do Cook, 'Ten Amerindian Languages in Canada,' in William O'Grady and Michael Dobrovolsky, eds., *Contemporary Linguistic Analysis* (Toronto: Copp Clark Pitman 1987), 259-70.

34 Keith J. Crowe, *A History of the Original Peoples of Northern Canada* (Montreal: Arctic Institute of North America and McGill-Queen's University Press 1974), 74-8.

35 Inuit migrations are discussed in Keith J. Crowe, *A History of the Original Peoples of Northern Canada* (Montreal: McGill-Queen's University Press 1974).

36 A breakdown of community populations by ethnic group can be found in *Northwest Territories Data Book, 1990/91* (Yellowknife: Outcrop 1990).

37 There are numerous discussions of this problem of cultural change in the North. A few of the more important ones include: Diamond Jenness, *Eskimo Administration: II, Canada*, Arctic Institute of North America, Technical Paper No. 14 (Montreal: Arctic Institute of North America 1964); Keith J. Crowe, *A History of the Original Peoples*; and Nelson H.H. Graburn, *Eskimos without Igloos: Social and Economic Development in Sugluk* (Boston: Little, Brown 1969).

CHAPTER THREE:
FORMULATING PROCESS AND POLICIES

1 Canada, *Statutes*, 38 Victoria, 1875, ch. 49, and 4-5 Edward VII, 1905, ch. 27.

2 Canada, Department of Indian Affairs and Northern Development, *The Historical Development of the Indian Act* (Ottawa: Planning and Research Branch 1975).

3 PAC, R.G. 85, vol. 569, file 77.

4 Department of Indian Affairs, *Annual Report 1920*, Royal Northwest Mounted Police, *Report 1910*, and M.J. and J.L. Robinson, 'Exploration and Settlement of Mackenzie District, NWT,' *Canadian Geographical Journal* 23(1946):46.

5 House of Commons, *Debates*, 1920, 3,280-1, Mr. Meighen.

6 Department of the Interior, *Annual Report*, 1922 (Ottawa: King's Printer 1923) 17.

7 NWT Council Minutes, 2nd Session, 14 June 1922.

8 Department of Northern Affairs and National Resources, *The Northwest Territories Today: A Reference Paper for the Advisory Commission on the Development of Government in the Northwest Territories* (Ottawa: Queen's Printer 1965), 80.

9 PAC, R.G. 85, vol. 572, file 259. Oscar Finnie summarizes this activity in a year-end memorandum dated 31 March 1922.

10 Diamond Jenness, *Eskimo Administration: II, Canada* (Montreal: Arctic Institute of North America 1964), Technical Paper No. 14, 47, 48 and Richard Finnie, *Canada Moves North* (Toronto: Macmillan 1942), ch. 5.

11 Keenleyside's role as commissioner in instituting changes in the North is discussed in Shelagh D. Grant, *Sovereignty or Security: Government Policy in the Canadian North, 1936-1950* (Vancouver: University of British Columbia Press 1988).

12 Department of Mines and Resources, *Annual Report*, 1967 (Ottawa: King's Printer 1948), 74.

13 R.A.J. Phillips, *Canada's North* (New York: St. Martin's Press 1967), 233.

14 NWT Council Minutes, 53rd session, 17 October 1934, 6.

15 *Eskimo Administration*, 63-4.

16 The point was made by Keith Crowe in comments on an earlier draft of this book.

17 Sensitivity to secularizing the educational system was explained to me by Louie C. Audette, an appointed member of the territorial council from 1947 to 1959.

18 NWT Council Minutes, 50th Session, 13 February 1934, appendix.

19 Department of Indian Affairs, *Annual Report*, 1928, 7.

20 *Denendeh: A Dene Celebration* (Yellowknife: The Dene Nation 1984), 17.

21 Report of the RCMP, 1924, 46.

22 Richard Diubaldo, *The Government of Canada and the Inuit, 1900-67* (Ottawa: Indian Affairs and Northern Development 1985), 101.

23 PAC, R.G. 85, vol. 834, file 7,387.

24 G.J. Wherrett, 'Survey of Health Conditions and Medical and Hospital Services in the North West Territories,' *Canadian Journal of Economics and Political Science* 11:49-60.

25 P.G. Nixon has an excellent discussion of this problem in his unpublished paper, 'Early Administrative Development in Fighting Inuit Tuberculosis: Bringing State Institution Back In,' 1987.

26 PAC, R.G. 85, vol. 101, file 353.

27 NWT Council Minutes, 38th Session, 7 December 1932, 5.

28 NWT Council Minutes, 36th Session, 28 September 1932, 4.

29 NWT Council Minutes, 43rd Session, June 1933, appendix.

30 See Peter Clancy, 'Game Policy in the Northwest Territories: The Shaping of Economic Position,' 24, an unpublished paper presented at the annual meeting of the Canadian Political Science Association, Vancouver, BC, 6-8 June 1983.

31 NWT Council Minutes, 6th Session, 28 December 1927, Memorandum from O. Finnie to W.G. Cory, Deputy Minister, 10.

32 Department of Mines and Resources, 'The Northwest Territories: Admin-

istration-Resources-Development,' 1947.

33 NWT Council Minutes, 40th Session, 8 February 1933, appendix.

34 The letter is from the PAC. The specific reference to the source in the archives is unknown.

35 For example, in NWT Council Minutes in the 61st Session, the 65th Session, and the 73rd Session, Roman Catholic Bishop Breynat is lobbying on behalf of Native people.

36 'Game Policy,' 36 and 40.

37 Morris Zaslow, *The Opening of the Canadian North: 1870-1914* (Toronto: McClelland and Stewart 1971), 270.

38 NWT Council Minutes, 6th Session, 28 December 1927, O. Finnie Memorandum, 4.

39 See Morris Zaslow, *The Northward Expansion of Canada, 1914-67* (Toronto: McClelland and Stewart 1988), ch. 8.

40 Shelagh D. Grant, *Sovereignty or Security*, ch. 5.

41 Morris Zaslow, *The Northward Expansion of Canada, 1914-1967*, 226.

42 Ibid., 227.

43 *Sovereignty or Security*, 221-3.

44 Ibid.

45 Ibid., 222-4.

46 Stories of the trials and tribulations of Native people are numerous. Bishop Breynat, OMI, for example, mentioned them at the turn of the century in his book, *The Flying Bishop* (London: Burns and Oates 1955). Conditions in the central Arctic during and after the Second World War are portrayed well by Raymond de Coccola and Paul King, *The Incredible Eskimo: Life Among the Barren Land Eskimo* (Surrey, BC: Hancock House Publishers 1986), and, interestingly, a recent account in *The Globe and Mail* dealt with starvation in the Baker Lake region in 1957-8, 31 December 1988, 1, 2.

47 Some of the problems in administration are discussed in Peter Clancy, 'The Making of Eskimo Policy in Canada, 1952-62: The Life and Times of the Eskimo Affairs Committee,' *Arctic* 40(1987):191-7

48 NWT Council Minutes, Special Session, 2 October 1950, 2.

49 This is the view, for example, of R.A.J. Phillips, *Canada's North*.

50 NWT, Council Minutes, 37th Session, 9 November 1932, 1,

51 Ibid., 2.

52 NWT Council Minutes, 42nd Session, 5 April 1933, 6.

53 *Sovereignty or Security*, 27.

54 Ibid.

55 Ibid.

56 Personal interview with Henry Cook, June 1985.

57 Personal interview with Ben Sivertz, June 1987.

CHAPTER FOUR:
CHANGING POLICIES, NOT THE PROCESS

1 Personal interview with Gordon Robertson, June 1983.
2 Excellent discussions on this new perspective include Allen Moscovitch and Jim Albert, eds., *The Benevolent State: The Growth of Welfare in Canada* (Toronto: Garamond Press 1987); Ronald Manzer, *Public Policies and Political Development in Canada* (Toronto: University of Toronto Press 1985), chs. 1, 2, and 8; Les Pal, 'Federalism, Social Policy, and the Constitution,' in Jacqueline S. Ismael, ed, *Canadian Social Welfare Policy* (Montreal: McGill-Queen's University Press 1985); Michael S. Whittington and Glen Williams, eds., *Canadian Politics in the 1980s*, 2nd ed. (Toronto: Methuen 1984), ch. 1; Keith G. Banting, *The Welfare State and Canadian Federalism*, 2nd ed. (Montreal: McGill-Queen's University Press 1987), ch. 2; Ingrid Bryan, *Economic Policies in Canada*, 2nd ed. (Toronto: Butterworths 1986), introduction; and Leo Panitch, ed., *The Canadian State* (Toronto: University of Toronto Press 1977), ch. 1.
3 One of the best discussions on the northern economy down to the 1960s is in K.J. Rea, *The Political Economy of the Canadian North* (Toronto: University of Toronto Press 1968).
4 House of Commons, *Debates*, 1953, 698.
5 Personal interview with Louis Audette, June 1984.
6 Department of Northern Affairs and National Resources, *Annual Report*, 1954-55, 12.
7 Ibid., 103.
8 Personal interview with Ben Sivertz, June 1987.
9 DNANR, *The Northwest Territories Today: A Reference Paper for the Advisory Commission on the Development of Government in the Northwest Territories* (Ottawa: Queen's Printer 1965), 68.
10 DNANR, *Annual Report*, 1954-5, 103.
11 DNANR, *The Northwest Territories Today*, 68.
12 Government of the Northwest Territories, *Annual Report of the Commissioner*, 1965-6, 40.
13 DNANR, *Annual Report*, 1954-5, 19 and 26.
14 GNWT, *Annual Report of the Commissioner*, 1962-3, 25.
15 DNANR, *The Northwest Territories Today*, 65.
16 Department of Indian Affairs and Northern Development, Treaties and Historical Section Records, File 310-9, vol. 2, memo from E.M. Cotterill, Area Administrator, to Administrator, 29 August 1963.
17 DIAND, Treaties and Historical Section Records, file 310-9, vol. 2, DNANR request to Treasury Board, 9 July 1963, 2.
18 DIAND, Treaties and Historical Section Records, file 210-9, vol. 2, memo to R.A.J. Phillips, Director, Northern Administration Branch, 15 April 1964.

19 DIAND, Treaties and Historical Section Records, file 210-9, vol. 2, memo to R.J.A. Phillips, Director, Northern Administration Branch, to the Deputy Minister, 10 July 1963.

20 DNANR, *Annual Report*, 1964-5, 13.

21 DNANR, *Annual Report*, 1964-5, 13.

22 GNWT, 'Report of the Northwest Territories Council, Task Force on Housing,' 1972, 2.

23 DNANR, *Annual Report*, 1964-5, 30.

24 Ibid., 10.

25 Ibid.

26 Ibid., 17.

27 DRD, Report, 1953, 82.

28 Personal interview with Ben Sivertz, June 1987.

29 Government of the Northwest Territories, *Annual Report of the Commissioner, 1966-7*, 51.

30 DNANR, *Annual Report*, 1964-5, 5.

31 Discussions with Bob Pilot, March 1979.

32 DNANR, *Annual Report*, 1964-5, 26.

33 DNANR, *Annual Report*, 1964-5, 25.

34 DNANR, *The Northwest Territories Today*, 1965, 47, 118, and 16.

35 Interesting background information on the council's ordinances to form local boards is in Edwin Welch, *Archives of the City of Yellowknife*, sources of NWT History, no. 3 (Yellowknife: Northwest Territories Archives 1983), 1-2.

36 Ibid., 3-4.

37 DNANR, *The Northwest Territories Today*, 90, 134.

38 Canada, Advisory Commission on the Development of Government in the Northwest Territories, *Report*, Carrothers Commission (Ottawa 1966), vol. I, 189-90.

39 One of the better brief discussions on division is in Morris Zaslow, *The Northward Expansion of Canada, 1914-1967* (Toronto: McClelland and Stewart 1988), 358-60.

40 Personal Interview with Ben Sivertz, June 1987.

41 The Carrothers Report, vol. I, 152.

42 Ben Sivertz, 'Tuesday Letter Appendix,' 18 October 1966, 1.

43 Ibid., 13 December 1966, 1.

CHAPTER FIVE:
CHANGING THE POLITICAL PROCESS OF THE NWT

1 GNWT, Council of the Northwest Territories, *Debates*, 35th Session, 13 November 1967, 1.

2 GNWT *Statistics Quarterly* 1(1):8.

3 GNWT, *Annual Report*, 1969 and 1979, 20 and 45.

4 A comprehensive discussion of the devolutionary process is found in Gurston Dacks, ed., *Devolution and Constitutional Development in the Canadian North* (Ottawa: Carleton University Press 1990).

5 GNWT, *Annual Report*, 1970, 7.

6 The chapters in *Devolution and Constitutional Development*, by Frances Abele, Peter Clancy, Gurston Dacks, Katherine Graham, John O'Neill, and Geoffrey Weller, provide an excellent discussion of the devolutionary process.

7 An example of instructions can be seen in a telex from Judd Buchanan, Minister of Indian Affairs and Northern Development, to S.M. Hodgson, Commissioner, Northwest Territories, 22 April 1975. While the letters made the changes 'official', in fact often they authorized what had been initiated and sometimes even put into practice by the GNWT.

8 Some of the particulars of this legislative process are discussed in Kevin O'Keefe, 'Northwest Territories: Accommodating the Future,' Gary Levy and Graham White, eds., *Provincial and Territorial Legislatures in Canada* (Toronto: University of Toronto Press 1989).

9 GNWT, *Annual Report*, 1976, 17.

10 After the 1987 election, options considered by the MLA's were discussed in *Native Press*, 13 November 1987, 1, 2.

11 *News North*, 16 November 1987, 2.

12 *Native Press*, and *Globe and Mail*, 13 November 1987, A. 3.

13 GNWT, *Annual Report*, 1978, 42.

14 Canada, 'Constitutional Development in the Northwest Territories,' *Report of the Special Representative*, Drury Report (Ottawa: Supply and Services 1980), 118.

15 'Public Government For The People of the North' (Yellowknife: The Dene Nation and the Métis Association 1981) and 'Building Nunavut: A Discussion Paper Containing Proposals for an Arctic Constitution' (Ottawa: Nunavut Constitutional Forum 1983).

16 There is almost no literature on these advisory committees. One early discussion in their role is in A.R. Zariwey, 'Politics, Administration and Problems of Community Development in the Northwest Territories,' Nils Orvik, ed., *Policies of Northern Development* (Kingston: Queen's University 1973).

17 Peter Clancy discusses these developments in 'Political Devolution and Wildlife Management.'

18 Background information on the BRC can be found in C.M. Drury's files, accumulated while he was special representative of the government, preparing his report, PAC, R.G. 2, vol. 2,714, part 2, and Wilf Bean and Katherine A. Graham, *Regional Government* (Kingston: Institute of Local Government Queen's University 1983).

19 Ibid.
20 Little literature exists on the formation of Native organizations in the NWT. Bits and pieces on their background can be found in Drury's *Report of the Special Representative, Denendeh: A Dene Celebration* (Yellowknife: The Dene Nation 1984); Canada, DIAND, 'The North' (Ottawa 1985), 19-22; and the ITC is covered in Scott Bryce, 'Inuit Tapirisat of Canada: A Pressure Group Organization,' Nils Orvik and Gary Vanderhaden, eds., *Interest Groups in the Northwest Territories* (Kingston: Queen's University 1974).
21 The best discussion on the White Paper, its origins, and aftermath is in Sally Weaver, *Making Canadian Indian Policy: The Hidden Agenda, 1968-70* (Toronto: University of Toronto Press 1981).
22 A thorough discussion of the background to this movement is found in Mel Watkins, ed., *Dene Nation: The Colony Within* (Toronto: University of Toronto Press 1977).
23 Particulars of the case can be found in Bradford W. Morse, ed., *Aboriginal Peoples and the Law: Indian, Métis and Inuit Rights in Canada* (Ottawa: Carleton University Press 1985), 305-14.
24 'Public Government for the People of the North,' (Yellowknife: The Dene Nation and the Métis Association of the NWT 1981).
25 Canada, Indian and Northern Affairs, *The Western Arctic Claim: The Inuvialuit Final Agreement* (Ottawa 1985).
26 'Building Nunavut: A Discussion Paper Containing Proposals for an Arctic Constitution' (Ottawa: Nunavut Constitutional Forum 1983).
27 Canada, 'Northern Frontier, Northern Homeland,' *Report of the Mackenzie Valley Pipeline Inquiry,* vol. 2 (Berger Commission Report), (Ottawa: Supply and Services 1977), xi.
28 This observation was offered by Ewan M.R. Cotterill in an interview, Summer 1984.
29 Ibid. This observation, of course, is from one who worked for the executive of the GNWT and DIAND.
30 Lloyd Barbar's statement to the Standing Committee on Indian Affairs and Northern Development of the House of Commons, 22 March 1973, Canada, Commissioner on Indian Claims, *A Report: Statements and Submissions* (Ottawa: Supply and Services 1977).
31 The impact of the Calder case is discussed extensively in *Aboriginal People and the Law,* ch. 3.
32 Canada, DIAND, *Annual Report,* 1978-9, 40.
33 Michael Asch offers a succinct discussion on Native rights in the NWT, *Home and Native Land: Aboriginal Rights and the Canadian Constitution* (Toronto: Methuen 1984).
34 Interview with Basil Robinson, February 1989.
35 Results of the Berger hearings figure prominently in Robert Page's *Northern Development: The Canadian Dilemma* (Toronto: McClelland and Stewart

1986).

36 Berger Commission Report 8:738.
37 Ibid., vol. 1, 94.
38 Ibid., 100, 107.
39 Ibid., 111, 112.
40 Ibid., 112.
41 Ibid., vol. 26, 2,622.
42 The Drury Report, 145.
43 PAC, R.G. 2, vol. 2,730, file 5,026.
44 Drury Report, 34.
45 Ibid., 39.
46 Ibid., 34.
47 Ibid., 35.
48 Ibid., 42.
49 Ibid., 43.
50 Ibid., 49.
51 Ibid., 53.
52 Ibid., 54.
53 Ibid., 128 and 130.
54 Mark O. Dickerson, 'Commentary: The Drury Report and Political Development in the NWT,' *Arctic* 35(1982):457-64.

CHAPTER SIX:
A MORE AUTONOMOUS GNWT

1 See, for example, Lynda Sorensen, 'Influencing Government Spending: The NWT Backbencher,' Rebecca Aird, ed., *Running the North: The Getting and Spending of Public Finances by Canada's Territorial Governments* (Ottawa: Canadian Arctic Resources Committee 1989), 111-20 and Henry Zoe, 'Committees of the Legislative Assembly,' a presentation for the lecture series on the dynamics of the public service, Management Development Program, Arctic College, Fort Smith, NWT, 10 May 1990.
2 'Committees of the Legislative Assembly,' 3.
3 Northwest Territories Legislative Assembly, Standing Committee on Finance, 'History and Development of the Standing Committee on Finances, 1969-83' (Yellowknife: Department of Information 1983), 7.
4 'Influencing Government Spending,' 118.
5 Interview with John Parker, June 1990.
6 GNWT, *Statistics Quarterly* 12(1990):57.
7 A very forthright assessment of the GNWT administration is offered by C.E.S. Franks, 'Toward Representation of the Aboriginal Population in the Public Service of the Northwest Territories,' Rebecca Aird, ed., *Running the North: The Getting and Spending of Public Finances by Canada's Territorial*

Governments (Ottawa: Canadian Arctic Resources Committee n.d.).

8 GNWT, The Honorable Michael A. Ballantyne, Minister of Finance, 1990-1 Budget Address' (Yellowknife 1990), 44.

9 GNWT, *Statistics Quarterly* 12(1990):109.

10 Jean A. Guertin, 'Formula Financing in Territorial Development,' in *Running the North*, 178.

11 'Budget Address,' 1990, 56.

12 Ibid.

13 Legislative Assembly of the Northwest Territories, Special Committee on the Northern Economy. *The Scone Report: Building our Economic Future* (Yellowknife 1989), 54.

14 See, for example, Colin Irwin, *Lords of the Arctic: Wards of the State* (Ottawa: Health and Welfare Canada 1988).

15 GNWT, Department of Education, 'NWT Education Facts and Figures.'

16 Scone Report, 54.

17 Keith J. Crowe, in *Report on Visit to Keewatin Region, November 22 to December 11, 1967*, 21 December 1967, DIAND file 600-1, vols. 3 and 4.

18 Legislative Assembly of the Northwest Territories, Special Committee on Education, *Learning: Tradition and Change in the Northwest Territories* (Yellowknife 1982), 17.

19 Ibid., 77.

20 Ibid., 11.

21 Ibid., 18, 19.

22 One example is the work of the Department of Education in producing culturally relevant curriculum material. Don Kindt's work in the science curriculum is outstanding.

23 Pearl Benyk, 'Can Northern Schools Make the Grade?' *Up Here*, November/December 1988, 58.

24 Colin Irwin, 'Lords of the Arctic: Wards of the State, A Survey Report,' in *Northern Perspectives* 17(1989).

25 Ibid., 10

26 Ibid., 9.

27 Ibid., 6.

28 Joan Ryan and Michael P. Robinson, 'Implementing Participatory Action Research in the Canadian North: A Case Study of the Gwich' in Language and Cultural Project,' a paper submitted to the International Congress of Ethnology, Lisbon, Portugal, September 1990, 12.

29 Ibid., 13.

30 Northwest Territories Housing Corporation, 'Study on Housing Policy and Program Coordination in the NWT,' 26 April 1990, 22A (Figure 5).

31 Northwest Territories Council, Task Force on Housing, Report, June 1972, 39.

32 Ibid., 4.

33 Northwest Territories Housing Corporation, *Annual Report* 1979, 1.

34 *Man in the North Technical Paper*, a report on a conference-workshop, 'Building in Northern Communities,' Michael Glover, ed. (Calgary: Arctic Institute of North America 1974), 55.

35 Ibid., 53.

36 NWTHC, Report, 1972, 2.

37 Legislative Assembly of the Northwest Territories, Special Committee on Housing, *Final Report*, June 1985, 30.

38 Ibid.

39 Ibid., 32.

40 Ibid., 33, 34.

41 Ibid., 24.

42 Ibid., 107.

43 Legislative Assembly of the Northwest Territories, *Hansard*, Friday, 23 March 1990, 517.

44 NWTHC, 'Study on Housing Policy and Program Coordination in the NWT,' 19.

45 Legislative Assembly of the Northwest Territories, Special Committee on Housing, *Final Report*, 1985, 107.

46 NWTHC, 'Study on Housing Policy and Program Coordination in the NWT,' 46.

47 NWTHC *Annual Report*, 1987-8, 4.

48 *Hansard*, Friday, 23 March 1990, 518-9.

49 A very good assessment of the current economy in the NWT is found in Jack C. Stabler and Eric C. Howe, 'Natives and Northern Development,' *Canadian Public Policy* 16(1990):262-83

50 John Washie, 'Feds Should Change Attitudes,' *Native Press*, 28 September 1990, 11.

51 Scone Report, 13.

52 Ibid., 11.

53 See, for example, Mark O. Dickerson, Michael Pretes, and Michael P. Robinson, 'Sustainable Development in Small Northern Communities: A Micro Perspective,' a paper presented at the First Kluane Conference, Kluane Lake, Yukon, September 1989.

54 *Nunatsiaq News*, 6 July 1990, 5.

55 A good discussion of possibilities is found in Northwest Territories Legislative Assembly, Special Committee on the Northern Economy, Michael Robinson, et al., *Coping with the Cash* (Yellowknife 1989), chs. 2 and 3.

56 Jack Van Camp calculates the potential dividends from claim settlement funds in *Coping With the Cash*, 59-62.

57 Legislative Assembly of the Northwest Territories, *Hansard*, 10 April 1990, 815.

58 GNWT, Department of Economic Development and Tourism, 'Renewable

Resource Development Strategy for the Northwest Territories,' paper prepared by Doris Eggers, 22 November 1989, 2 and 'Building on Strengths: A Community-Based Approach' (Economic Development and Tourism 1990).

59 Doris Eggers, 'Renewable Resource Development Strategy,' 1.

60 Katherine Graham, 'Devolution and Local Government,' Gurston Dacks, ed., *Devolution and Constitutional Development in the Canadian North* (Ottawa: Carleton University Press 1990), 213.

61 Ibid., 205.

62 The GNWT has been using the term 'prime public authority' for a number of years. The first use I recall of the term was in the Drury Report, 53. Drury spoke of the community council being the 'prime public body' in the process of government.

63 GNWT, 'Political and Constitutional Development in the Northwest Territories,' 4.

64 Ibid., 2.

65 Ibid., 5.

66 Ibid., 9.

67 Ibid., 5, 9.

68 Ibid., 10.

69 'Devolution and Local Government,' 313.

70 GNWT, 'Political and Constitutional Development in the Northwest Territories,' 4.

71 'Devolution and Local Government,' 216.

72 Gurston Dacks, 'True To The North,' *Ideas*, Canadian Broadcasting Corporation, 2 and 9 April 1990, 9.

73 Ibid., 12.

74 Ibid.

75 Alexis de Tocqueville, *Democracy In America*, vol. I, (New York: Alfred N. Knopf 1945), 62-3.

76 Ibid., 62.

77 C.E.S. Franks, 'Toward Representation of the Aboriginal Population in the Public Service of the Northwest Territories,' 406.

78 Kenneth Kernaghan and David Siegal, *Public Administration In Canada* (Toronto: Methuen 1987), 267.

79 GNWT, Financial Management Board Secretariat, *Strength at Two Levels: Report of the Project to Review the Operations and Structure of Northern Government* (Yellowknife 1991).

80 GNWT, *Report of the Special Committee on Unity to the 3rd Session of the 9th Assembly*, Frobisher Bay, 22 October 1980, 1.

81 Interesting background material on the alliance is found in 'Partners for the Future: A Selection of Papers Related to Constitutional Development in the Western Northwest Territories' (Yellowknife: Western Constitutional

Forum 1985) *Western Constitutional Forum: Chronology of Events, January 1982-June 1987* (Yellowknife: Western Constitutional Forum 1987).

82 *Report of the Constitutional Alliance*, 24 February 1982, 2; part of an information package of documents issued by James T. Sah-Shee, Chairman, Constitutional Alliance, n.d.

83 Results of the plebiscite are indicated in Frances Abele and Mark O. Dickerson, 'The 1982 Plebiscite on Division of the Northwest Territories: Regional Government and Federal Policy,' *Canadian Public Policy* 11(1985):1-14.

84 'Boundary and Constitutional Agreement for the Implementation of Division of the Northwest Territories Between the Western Constitutional Forum and the Nunavut Constitutional Forum' (Ottawa: Canadian Arctic Resources Committee [CARC] 1987).

85 GNWT, Legislative Assembly of the Northwest Territories, *Hansard*, 6 April 1989, 1,396.

86 *Nunatsiaq News*, 26 October 1990, 1.

87 A thorough discussion of the Nunavut proposal is in John Merritt, Terry Fenge, Randy Ames, and Peter Jull, *Nunavut: Political Choices and Manifest Destiny* (Ottawa: Canadian Arctic Resources Committee 1989).

88 Interesting perspectives on land claims and division can be found in Keith Crowe, 'Claims on the Land,' a two-part article in *Arctic Circle* 1(3, 4), and William C. Wonders, 'The Dene/Inuit Interface in Canada's Western Arctic, NWT,' in Kenneth S. Coates and William R. Morrison, eds., *For Purposes of Dominion: Essays in Honour of Morris Zaslow* (North York: Captus Press 1989).

89 The federal government's intentions were spelled out in *In All Fairness: A Native Claims Policy* (Ottawa: Department of Indian Affairs and Northern Development 1981).

90 DIAND, *Dene/Métis Comprehensive Land Claims Agreement in Principle* (Ottawa 1988), and DIAND, *Agreement in Principle Between the Inuit of the Nunavut Settlement Area and Her Majesty In Right of Canada* (Ottawa 1990).

91 An interesting discussion on Inuit views of the AIP was carried in *Nunavut Forum* 1(3), 14 June 1991 and *Nunatsiaq News*, 14 June 1991.

92 The break between groups in the Western Arctic is discussed in *Native Press*, particularly 20 July 1990, 1 and 5 October 1990, 1.

93 For a brief discussion of the minister's statement on this issue, see *Native Press*, 9 November 1990, 1.

94 *Gwich'in* Tribal Council, Comprehensive Claims Branch (DIAND), Aboriginal Rights and Constitutional Development (GNWT), 'Comprehensive Land Claim Agreement Between Her Majesty the Queen in Right of Canada and the Gwick'in As Represented by the Gwick'in Tribal Council,' 13 July 1991.

95 *News North*, 23 September 1991, 1.

96 *Nunavut Forum* 1(1991):1.

CHAPTER SEVEN:
SELF-GOVERNMENT AND POLITICAL DEVELOPMENT

1 There is an extensive literature developing on Native self-government in Canada. A few of the important sources include 'Aboriginal Self-Government and Constitutional Reform: Setbacks, Opportunities, and Arctic Experiences,' proceeding of a national conference held in Ottawa, 9-10 June 1987 (Ottawa: Canadian Arctic Resources Committee 1988); F. Laurie Barron and James B. Waldram, eds., *1885 and After: Native Society in Transition* (Regina: Canadian Plains Research Centre 1986); Leroy Little Bear, Menno Boldt, J. Anthony Long, eds., *Pathways to Self-Determination: Canadian Indians and the Canadian State* (Toronto: University of Toronto Press 1984); Frank Cassidy and Robert L. Bish, *Indian Government: Its Meaning and Practice* (Halifax: The Institute for Research on Public Policy 1989); David C. Hawkes, *Aboriginal Self-Government: What Does It Mean?* (Kingston: Institute of Intergovernmental Relations, Queen's University 1985); Peter Jull, *Self-Government For Northern Peoples: Canada and the Circumpolar Story*, a report to the government of the Northwest Territories, Aboriginal Rights and Constitutional Development Secretariat (Yellowknife 1985); Simon McInnes and Perry Billingsley, 'Concepts of Responsible Government by Canada's Indians,' paper prepared for the Annual Meeting of the Canadian Political Science Association, Kingston, Ontario, June 1991.
2 GNWT, Regional and Tribal Councils Review Co-ordinating Committee, *Report on Regional Tribal Councils in the Northwest Territories* (Yellowknife: [working draft] 1987).
3 GNWT, 'Government Response to the Report of the Regional and Tribal Councils Review Coordinating Committee,' tabled document no. 57-88 (2), November 1988.
4 Ibid., 1.
5 GNWT, 'Consolidation of Charter Communities Act,' SNWT 1987 (1), C.12, Yellowknife, 1989.
6 Fort Good Hope Dene Community Council, 'A Draft Proposed for Community Government,' 19 January 1982.
7 Ibid., 12, 13.
8 GNWT, 'Consolidation of Charter Communities Act,' 11-23.
9 GNWT, Legislative Assembly of the Northwest Territories, *Hansard*, 9 December 1991, 14.
10 Ibid., 15.
11 Ibid.
12 GNWT, Financial Management Board Secretariat, *Strength at Two Levels: Report of the Project to Review the Operations and Structure of Northern Govern-*

ment (Yellowknife 1991), 46.

13 CBC, 'True to the North,' *Ideas*, 2 and 9 April 1990, 14, 15.

14 DIAND, Policy Directorate, *Self-Government*, 'Self-government on Essential and Optional Subject Matters' (Ottawa 1990), 3.

15 Leroy Little Bear, Menno Boldt, and T. Anthony Long, eds., *Pathways to Self-Determination: Canadian Indians and the Canadian State* (Toronto: University of Toronto Press 1984), xvi.

16 Riley, 'What Canada's Indians Want and the Difficulties of Getting It,' in *Pathways to Self-Determination*, 159-60.

17 Basil Chubb, *The Government and Politics of Ireland* (Oxford: Oxford University Press 1970), 269.

18 Kenneth Grant Crawford, *Canadian Municipal Government* (Toronto: University of Toronto Press 1954), 24.

19 Ibid., 32.

20 These points were expressed to me by Ron Mongeau, executive officer of the Baffin Regional Council, and by Iola Metuq of Pangnirtung, who had participated in local government.

21 GNWT, Department of Renewable Resources, 'Strategic Plan' (Yellowknife 1983).

22 The structure of the Western Arctic Inuvialuit Claim Implementation Organization is described in DIAND, Western Arctic (Inuvialuit) Claim Implementation, *Annual Review, 1988-89* (Ottawa: Supply and Services 1989). Also, the Arctic Institute of North American hosted a 'Workshop' involving participants in the implementation process, and participants outlined the workings of the different organizations and the favourable impressions on the workings of the organizations. And see Peter Clancy, 'Political Devolution and Wildlife Management,' Gurston Dacks, ed., *Devolution and Constitutional Development in the Canadian North* (Ottawa: Carleton University Press 1990).

23 H.H. Gerth and C. Wright Mills, *From Max Weber: Essays in Sociology* (Oxford: Oxford University Press 1958), 228-9.

24 *The Government and Politics of Ireland*, 269.

25 Henry Jacoby, *The Bureaucratization of the World*, trans. Eveline Kanes, (Berkeley: University of California Press 1973), 174.

26 Ibid., 147.

27 G. Shabbir Cheema and Dennis Rondinelli, eds., *Decentralization and Development: Policy Implementation in Developing Countries* (Beverly Hills, Calif.: Sage Publications 1983).

28 Ibid., 7.

29 Ibid., 10.

30 Ibid., 13.

31 Ibid., 14.

32 Ibid., 22.

33 Ibid., 291.

34 Ibid., 304.

35 Ibid., 299.

36 Gordon Robertson, *Northern Provinces: A Mistaken Goal* (Montreal: Institute for Research on Public Policy 1985), 48.

37 GNWT, *Report on Regional Tribal Councils.*

38 Ibid., section 4, 3.

39 Ibid., 4.

40 Ibid., section 8, 8.

41 Jack Masson, *Alberta's Local Governments and Their Politics* (Edmonton: University of Alberta Press 1985), 92-8.

42 GNWT, *Report on Regional Tribal Councils*, section 6, 15.

43 Ibid., 12.

44 The best discussion on possible costs of division is found in Barbara Heindenreich, 'Cost Implications of Division of the Northwest Territories,' Rebecca Aird, ed., *Running the North: The Getting and Spending of Public Finances by Canada's Territorial Governments* (Ottawa: Canadian Arctic Resources Committee, n.d.). The current figures were quoted in *Nunatsiaq News*, 1 November 1991, 1 and *The Press Independent*, 1 November 1991, 1.

45 Gurston Dacks, 'Devolution and Political Development in the Canadian North,' Gurston Dacks, ed., *Devolution and Constitutional Development in the Canadian North* (Ottawa: Carleton University Press 1990), 349-50.

46 Graham White, 'Westminster in the Arctic: The Adaptation of British Parliamentarism in the Northwest Territories,' *Canadian Journal of Political Science* 24(1991):522-33.

Bibliography

BOOKS, ARTICLES, AND REPORTS

Abele, Frances. 1989. *Gathering Strength*. Calgary: Arctic Institute of North America

Abele, Frances and Mark O. Dickerson. 1985. 'The 1982 Plebiscite on Division of the Northwest Territories: Regional Government and Federal Policy.' *Canadian Public Policy* 11(1):1-15

Abele, Frances and E.T. Dosman. 1981. 'Interdepartmental Coordination and Northern Development.' *Canadian Public Adminstration* 24(3):428-51

Abele, Frances and Peter Usher. 1990. 'The Danger to the North.' *Policy Options* 11(1):4-10

Aird, Rebecca, ed. 1989. *Running the North: The Getting and Spending of Public Finances by Canada's Territorial Governments*. Ottawa: Canadian Arctic Resources Committee

Alexander, Colin. 1976. *Angry Society*. Yellowknife: Yellowknife Publishing

Aquilina, Alfred P. 1981. *The Mackenzie: Yesterday and Beyond*. North Vancouver: Hancock House Publishers

Arctic Institute of North America. 1991. *Old Pathways and New Directions: Towards A Sustainable Future*. Proceedings of the First Annual Kluane Lake Conference. Calgary: Arctic Institute of North America

Armstrong, Terence, George Rogers, and Graham Rowley. 1978. *The Circumpolar North: A Political and Economic Geography of the Arctic and Sub-Arctic*. London: Methuen

Asch, Michael. 1989. 'Wildlife: Defining the Animals, the Dene Hunt and the Settlement of Aboriginal Rights Claims.' *Canadian Public Policy* 15(2):205-19

-. 1984. *Home and Native Land: Aboriginal Rights and the Canadian Constitution*. Toronto: Methuen

Barber, Lloyd. 1977. *A Report: Commissioner On Indian Claims, Statements and Submissions*. Ottawa: Supply and Services

Barr, William. 1991. *Back From the Brink: The Road to Muskox Conservation in the Northwest Territories*. Calgary: Arctic Institute of North America

Barron, F. Laurie and James B. Waldram, eds. 1986. *1885 and After: Native Society in Transition*. Regina: Canadian Plains Research Centre

Bean, Wilf and Katherine A. Graham. 1983. *Regional Government*. Yellowknife: The Western Constitutional Forum and Legislative Assembly Special Committee on Constitutional Development

Berger, Thomas R. 1977. *Northern Frontier, Northern Homeland: Report of the Mackenzie Valley Pipeline Inquiry*. 2 vols. Ottawa: Supply and Services

Bregha, Francois. 1979. *Bob Blair's Pipeline: The Business and Politics of Northern Energy Development Projects*. Toronto: James Lorimer

Breynat, Gabriel Joseph Elie. 1955. *The Flying Bishop*. London: Burns and Oates

Brody, Hugh. 1987. *Living Arctic: Hunters of the Canadian North*. Vancouver: Douglas & McIntyre

–. 1975. *The People's Land: Eskimos and Whites in the Eastern Arctic*. Harmondsworth: Penguin

Canadian Arctic Resources Committee. 1988. *Aboriginal Self-Government and Constitutional Reform: Setbacks, Opportunities and Arctic Experiences*. Proceedings of a national conference, Ottawa, 9-20 June 1987. Ottawa: Canadian Arctic Resources Committee

–. 1987. *Boundary and Constitutional Agreement for the Implementation of Division of the Northwest Territories Between The Western Constitutional Forum and the Nunavut Constitutional Forum*. Ottawa: Canadian Arctic Resources Committee

Carrothers, A.W.R. 1966. *Commission on the Development of Government in the Northwest Territories* (Carrothers Commission), 2 vols. Ottawa: Indian Affairs and Northern Development

Cassidy, Frank and Robert L. Bish. 1989. *Indian Government: Its Meaning in Practice*. Ottawa: Institute for Research on Public Policy

Clancy, Peter. 1987. 'The Making of Eskimo Policy in Canada, 1952-62: The Life and Times of the Eskimo Affairs Committee.' *Arctic* 40(3):191-7

Coates, Kenneth. 1985. *Canada's Colonies: A History of the Yukon and the Northwest Territories*. Toronto: James Lorimer

Coates, Kenneth S. and William R. Morrison. 1989. *Interpreting Canada's North: Selected Readings*. Toronto: Copp Clark

–. 1986. *Treaty Eleven 1921*. Ottawa: Department of Indian Affairs and Northern Development

–., eds. 1989. *For Purposes of Dominion: Essays in Honour of Morris Zaslow*. North York: Captus

Condon, Richard G. 1987. *Inuit Youth: Growth and Change in the Canadian Arctic*. New Brunswick, NJ: Rutgers University Press

Copland, A. Dudley. 1985. *Coplalook: Chief Trader, Hudson's Bay Company, 1923-39*. Winnipeg: Watson & Iwyer

–. 1967. *Livingstone of the Arctic*. Lancaster, Ont.: Canadian Century

Crowe, Keith J. 1991. 'Claims on the Land, 2.' *Arctic* 1(4):30-5

–. 1990. 'Claims on the Land.' *Arctic* 1(3):14-23

–. 1974. *A History of the Original Peoples of Northern Canada*. Montreal: McGill-Queen's University Press

Cumming, Peter A. and Neil H. Mickenberg, eds. 1972. *Native Rights in Canada*. 2nd ed. Toronto: General

Dacks, Gurston. 1990. 'True to the North.' *Ideas*. 2 and 9 April. Toronto: Canadian Broadcasting Corporation

–., ed. 1990. *Devolution and Constitutional Development in the Canadian North*. Ottawa: Carleton University Press

–. 1986. 'Politics on the Last Frontier: Consociationalism in the Northwest Territories.' *Canadian Journal of Politicial Science* 19(2):345-61

–. 1981. *A Choice of Futures: Politics in the Canadian North*. Toronto: Methuen

Dacks, Gurston and Kenneth Coates, eds. 1988. *Northern Communities: The Prospects for Empowerment*. Edmonton: Boreal Institute

De Coccola, Raymond and Paul King. 1986. *The Incredible Eskimo*. Surrey, BC: Hancock House

De Poncins, Gontran, in collaboration with Lewis Galantiére. 1941. *Kabloona*. Chicago: Time-Life Books

Dene Nation. 1984. *Denendeh: A Dene Celebration*. Yellowknife: The Dene Nation

Dene Nation and the Métis Association of the NWT. 1981. 'Public Government for the People of the North.' Yellowknife: The Dene Nation and the Métis Association of the NWT

Diubaldo, Richard. 1985. *The Government of Canada and the Inuit, 1900-1967*. Ottawa: Indian Affairs and Northern Development

–. 1981. 'The Absurd Little Mouse: When Eskimos Became Indians.' *Journal of Canadian Studies* 16(2):34-40

–. 1978. *Stefansson and the Canadian Arctic*. Montreal: McGill-Queen's University Press

Dosman, E.J., ed. 1976. *The Arctic In Question*. Toronto: Oxford University Press

–. 1975. *The National Interest: The Politics of Northern Development, 1968-75*. Toronto: McClelland and Stewart

Drury, C.M. 1979. Report of the Special Representative (Drury Report). *Constitutional Development in the Northwest Territories*. Ottawa: Supply and Services

Duffy, R. Quinn. 1988. *The Road to Nunavut: The Progress of the Eastern Arctic Inuit Since the Second World War*. Montreal: McGill-Queen's University Press

Dunn, Martin. 1986. *Access to Survival: A Perspective on Aboriginal Self-Government for the Constituency of the Native Council of Canada*. Kingston: Institute of Intergovernmental Relations, Queen's University

Finnie, Richard. 1942. *Canada Moves North*. Toronto: Macmillan Company of Canada

Fleming, Archibald. 1956. *Archibald of the Arctic*. New York: Appleton-Century-Crafts

Franks, C.E.S. 1987. *Public Administration Questions Relating to Aboriginal Self-Government*. Kingston: Institute of Intergovernment, Queen's University

Freeman, Minnie A. 1978. *Life Among the Qallunaat*. Edmonton: Hurtig

Freuchen, Peter. 1935. *Arctic Adventure*. New York: Farrar and Rinehart

Frideres, James S. 1988. *Native Peoples in Canada*. 3rd ed. Scarborough: Prentice-Hall

Fumoleau, René. 1967. *As Long As This Land Shall Last*. Toronto: McClelland and Stewart

Getty, Ian A.L. and Antoine S. Lussier, eds. 1983. *As Long As the Sun Shines and Water Flows: A Reader in Canadian Native Studies*. Vancouver: University of British Columbia Press

Graburn, Nelson H.H. 1969. *Eskimos Without Igloos: Social and Economic Development in Singluk*. Boston: Little Brown

Grant, Shelagh D. 1989. *Sovereignty or Security? Government Policy in the Canadian North, 1936-1950*. Vancouver: University of British Columbia Press

Griffiths, Franklyn, ed. 1987. *Politics of the Northwest Passage*. Montreal: McGill-Queens University Press

Hall, Sam. 1987. *The Fourth World: The Heritage of the Arctic and Its Destruction*. New York: Vintage

Hamelin, Louis-Edmond, ed. 1984. 'Managing Canada's North: Challenges and Opportunities.' *Public Administration* 27(2):141-252

Hamelin, Louis-Edmond. 1979. *Canadian Nordicity*. Translated by William Barr. Montreal: Harvest House

Hawkes, David C. and Evelyn J. Peters. 1987. *Issues in Entrenching Aboriginal Self-Government*. Kingston: Institute of Intergovernmental Relations, Queen's University

Hawkes, David C. 1985. *Negotiating Aboriginal Self-Government: Developments Surrounding the 1985 First Ministers' Conference*. Kingston: Institute of Intergovernmental Relations, Queen's University

Holmes, Douglas. 1989. *Northerners: Profiles of People in the Northwest Territories*. Toronto: James Lorimer

Irwin, Colin. 1989. 'Future Imperfect: A Controversial Report for Inuit Society Strikes a Nerve in the NWT.' *Northern Perspectives* 17(1):1-12

Jenness, Diamond. 1968. *Eskimo Administration V: Analysis and Reflections*. Montreal: Arctic Institute of North America

–. 1964. *Eskimo Administration II: Canada*. Montreal: Arctic Institute of North America

Judd, David. 1969. 'Canada's Northern Policy: Retrospect and Prospect.' *The Polar Record* 14(92):593-602

–. 1969. 'Seventy-Five Years of Resource Administration In Northern Canada.' *The Polar Record* 14(93):791-806

Jull, Peter. 1991. *The Politics of Northern Frontiers in Australia, Canada and Other 'First World' Countries*. Darwin: North Australia Research Unit, Australian National University

Jull, Peter and Sally Roberts, eds. 1991. *The Challenge of Northern Regions*. Darwin: North Australia Research Unit, Australian National University

Leising, Fr. William A. 1959. *Arctic Wings*. Garden City, NY: Echo Books

Leslie, John and Ron Maguire, eds. 1978. *The Historical Development of the Indian Act*. Ottawa: Treaties and Historical Research Centre, Indian and Northern Affairs

Lingard, C.C. 1946. *Territorial Government in Canada: The Autonomy Question in the Old North-West Territories*. Toronto: University of Toronto Press

Little Bear, Leroy, Menno Boldt, and J. Anthony Long, eds. 1984. *Pathways to Self-Determination: Canadian Indians and the Canadian State*. Toronto: University of Toronto Press

Lotz, Jim. 1970. *Northern Realities*. Toronto: New Press

Lyall, Ernie. 1979. *An Arctic Man: Sixty-Five Years in Canada's North*. Edmonton: Hurtig

Inuit Committee on National Issues. 1987. *Completing Canada: Inuit Approaches to Self-Government*. Kingston: Institute of Intergovernmental Relations, Queen's University

Inuvialuit Regional Council. 1989. 'The Inuvialuit Perspective of the Discussion Paper on Political and Constitution Development in the Northwest Territories.' Inuvik: Inuvialuit Regional Council

McCullough, Karen M. 1989. *The Ruin Islanders: Early Thule Culture Pioneers in the Eastern High Arctic*. Ottawa: Canadian Museum of Civilization

McInnes, Simon and Perry Billingsley. 1991. 'Concepts of Responsible Government by Canada's Indians.' Paper prepared for the Annual Meeting of the Canadian Political Science Association, Kingston, Ontario, June

MacLeod, W. 1977. *Water Management in the Canadian North: The Administration of Inland Waters North of 60°*. Ottawa: Canadian Arctic Resources Committee

Malone, S.M. 1983. *Guaranteed Representation of Aboriginal Peoples In Institutions of Public Government*. Yellowknife: Legislative Assembly Special Committee on Constitutional Development

Merritt, John, Terry Fenge, Randy Ames, and Peter Jull. 1989. *Nunavut: Political Choices and Manifest Destiny*. Ottawa: Canadian Arctic Resources Committee

Metayer, Maurice, ed. and trans. 1966. *I, Nuligak*. Markham, Ont.: Simon & Schuster

Milligan, Shirley and Walter Kupsch, eds. 1986. *Living Explorers of the Canadian Arctic*. Yellowknife: Outcrop

Moody, Joseph P. with W. de Groot van Embden. 1955. *Arctic Doctor*. New

York: Dodd, Mead

Moore, Andrew. 1945. 'Survey of Education in the Mackenzie District.' *Canadian Journal of Economics and Political Science* 11(1):61-82

Morisset, Jean and Rose-Marie Pelletier, eds. 1986. *Ted Trindell: Métis Witness to the North*. Vancouver: Tillacum Library

Morrison, William R. 1985. *Showing the Flag: The Mounted Police and Canadian Sovereignty in the North, 1894-1925*. Vancouver: University of British Columbia Press

-. 1985. *A Survey of the History and Claims of the Native Peoples of Northern Canada*. 2nd ed. Ottawa: Treaties and Historical Research Centre, Indian and Northern Affairs

Morrow, Justice W.G. 1979. 'Adapting the Canadian Justice System to the Needs of the North.' Reprint of a talk by Mr. Justice Morrow in the University of Calgary alumni magazine, CAUM 11(2):3-8

Morse, Bradford W., ed. 1985. *Aboriginal Peoples and the Law: Indian, Métis and Inuit Rights in Canada*. Ottawa: Carleton University Press

Naysmith, Jolin. 1975. *Land Use and Public Policy in Northern Canada*. Ottawa: Department of Indian Affairs and Northern Development

Neatby, L.H. 1958. *In Quest of the Northwest Passage*. New York: Thomas Y. Crowell

Nixon, P.G. 1988. 'Early Administrative Developments in Fighting Tuberculosis Among Canadian Inuit: Bringing State Institutions Back In.' *The Northern Review* 2:67-84

Northwest Territories Data Book 1990-91. 1990. Yellowknife: Outcrop

Nunavut Constitutional Forum. 1983. *Building Nunavut: A Working Document with a Proposal for an Arctic Constitution*. Ottawa: Nunavut Constitutional Forum

O'Keefe, Kevin. 1989. 'Northwest Territories.' In Gary Levy and Graham White, eds., *Provincial and Territorial Legislatures in Canada*. Toronto: University of Toronto Press

Orvik, Nils. 1973. *Policies of Northern Development*. Kingston: Group for International Politics, Department of Political Studies, Queen's University

Orvik, Nils and Alfred Zariwny, eds. 1974. *Interest Groups in the Northwest Territories*. Kingston: Group for International Politics, Department of Political Studies, Queen's University

Page, Robert. 1986. *Northern Development: The Canadian Dilemma*. Toronto: McClelland and Stewart

Peters, Evelyn J. 1987. *Aboriginal Self-Government Arrangements In Canada: An Overview*. Kingston: Institute of Intergovernmental Relations, Queen's University

Pharand, Donat. 1988. *Canada's Arctic Waters in International Law*. Cambridge: Cambridge University Press

-. 1984. *The Northwest Passage*. Dordrecht, Netherlands: Nijhoff

Phillips, R.A.J. 1967. *Canada's North*. New York: St. Martin's

Pryde, Duncan. 1972. *Nunaga: Ten Years Among the Eskimos*. London: Eland Books

Ponting, J. Rick. 1988. *Profiles of Public Opinion on Canadian Natives and Native Issues*. Calgary: Research Unit for Public Policy Studies, University of Calgary

Ponting, J. Rick and Roger Gibbins. 1980. *Out of Irrelevance: A Socio-Political Introduction to Indian Affairs in Canada*. Scarborough: Butterworth

Rasmussen, Knud. 1921. *Across Arctic America*. New York: Greenwood Press

Ray, Arthur J. 1990. *The Canadian Fur Trade in the Industrial Age*. Toronto: University of Toronto Press

Rea, K.J. 1968. *The Political Economy of the Canadian North*. Toronto: University of Toronto Press

Robertson, Gordon. 1987. 'Innovations North of Sixty.' *Policy Options* 8(4):

–. 1985. *Northern Provinces: A Mistaken Goal*. Montreal: Institute for Research on Public Policy

Robinson, M.J. and J.L. 1946. 'Exploration and Settlement of the Mackenzie District, NWT.' *Canadian Geographic Journal* 33(1):43-9

Robinson, Mike, et al. 1989. *Coping with the Cash*. Yellowknife: Legislative Assembly Special Committee on the Northern Economy

Schledermann, Peter. 1990. *Crossroads to Greenland: 3000 Years of Pre-History in the Eastern Arctic*. Calgary: Arctic institute of North America

Schwartz, Bryan. 1986. *First Principles, Second Thoughts: Aboriginal Peoples, Constitutional Reform and Canadian Statecraft*. Montreal: Institute for Research on Public Policy

Sissions, Jack N. 1968. *Judge of the Far North*. Toronto: McClelland and Stewart

Stabler, Jack C. and Eric C. Home. 1990. 'Native Participation in Northern Development: The Impending Crisis in the NWT.' *Canadian Public Policy* 16(3):262-83

Tennant, Paul. 1990. *Aboriginal Peoples and Politics*. Vancouver: University of British Columbia Press

Thomas, Lewis Herbert. 1978. *The Struggle for Responsible Government in the Northwest Territories*. 2nd ed. Toronto: University of Toronto Press

Tungavik Federation of Nunavut. 1991. 'A Report on Land Claims.' *Nunavut* 10(2):1-27

Usher, Peter J. 1989. *Towards A Strategy for Supporting the Domestic Economy of the Northwest Territories*. Yellowknife: Legislative Assembly's Special Committee on the Northern Economy

–. 1971. *Fur Trade Posts of the Northwest Territories, 1870-1970*. Ottawa: Department of Indian Affairs and Northern Development

–. 1970. *The Bankslandes: Economy and Ecology of a Frontier Trapping Community*. 3 vols. Ottawa: Department of Indian Affairs and Northern Development

Watkins, Mel, ed. 1977. *Dene Nation: The Colony Within*. Toronto: University of Toronto Press

Weaver, Sally M. 1981. *Making of Canadian Indian Policy: The Hidden Agenda 1981.* Toronto: University of Toronto Press

Western Constitutional Forum. 1984. *The WCF Constitutional Workbook: A Guide to Laws, Institutions, Powers and Finances.* Yellowknife: Western Constitutional Forum

–. 1985. *Partners for the Future: A Selection of Papers Related to Constitutional Development in the Western Northwest Territories.* Yellowknife: Western Constitutional Forum

–. 1987. *Western Constitutional Forum: Chronology of Events, 1982-1987.* Yellowknife: Western Constitutional Forum

Wherrett, G.J. 1945. 'Survey of Health Conditions and Medical and Hospital Services in the North West Territories.' *Canadian Journal of Economics and Political Science* 11(1):49-60

White, Graham. 1991. 'Westminster in the Arctic: The Adaptation of British Parliamentarism in the Northwest Territories.' *Canadian Journal of Political Science* 24(3):499-523

Whittington, Michael S. (co-ordinator). 1985. *The North.* Toronto: University of Toronto Press

–. 1986. *Native Economic Development Corporations: Political and Economic Change in Canada's North.* Ottawa: Canadian Arctic Resources Committee

Wonders, William C. 1972. *The North.* Toronto: University of Toronto Press

–., ed. 1971. *Canada's Changing North.* Toronto: McClelland and Stewart

Young, T. Kue. 1988. *Health Care and Cultural Change: The Indian Experience in the Central Subarctic.* Toronto: University of Toronto Press

Zariwny, A.R. 1977. *Development of Local Government in the Northwest Territories.* Kingston: Centre for International Relations, Queen's University

Zaslow, Morris. 1988. *The Northward Expansion of Canada, 1914-1967.* Toronto: McClelland and Stewart

–., ed. 1981. *A Century of Canada'a Arctic Islands.* Ottawa: Royal Society of Canada

–. 1971. *The Opening of the Canadian North: 1870-1914.* Toronto: McClelland and Stewart

GOVERNMENT DOCUMENTS

Canada. Department of Indian Affairs and Northern Development. 1990. *Self-Government on Essential and Optional Matters.* Ottawa: Policy, Self-Government Sector

–. Department of Indian Affairs and Northern Development. 1966-90. *Annual Report.* Ottawa: Supply and Services

–. Department of Indian Affairs and Northern Development. 1989. 'The Canadian Aboriginal Economic Development Strategy.' Ottawa: Supply and Services

–. Department of Indian Affairs and Northern Development. 1988. 'A Northern Political and Economic Framework.' Ottawa: Supply and Services

–. Department of Indian Affairs and Northern Development. 1987. 'Comprehensive Land Claims Policy.' Ottawa: Supply and Services

–. National Health and Welfare. 1987. *Report on Health Conditions in the Northwest Territories.* Ottawa: Supply and Services

–. Department of Indian Affairs and Northern Development. 1985. *Living Treaties: Lasting Agreements. Report of the Task Force to Review Comprehensive Claims Policy.* Ottawa: Indian Affairs and Northern Development

–. House of Commons, Report of the Special Committee. 1983. *Indian Self-Government in Canada.* Ottawa: Supply and Services

–. Department of Indian Affairs and Northern Development. 1982. *Outstanding Business: A Native Claims Policy.* Ottawa: Supply and Services

–. Department of Northern Affairs and National Resources. 1965. *The Northwest Territories Today: A Reference Paper for the Advisory Commission on the Development of Environment in the Northwest Territories.* Ottawa: Northern Affairs and National Resources

GNWT. Department of Finance. 1991. *1991-92 Budget Address.* Yellowknife: Culture and Communications

–. Department of Finance. 1991. *1991-92 Main Estimates.* Yellowknife: Culture and Communications

–. Bureau of Statistics. 1991. *Statistics Quarterly.* Yellowknife: Culture and Communications

–. Executive Council. 1991. 'A Position Paper On Political and Constitutional Development.' Yellowknife: Tabled Document No. 22-91-(1), 25 February 1991

–. Department of Economic Development and Tourism. 1990. *Building On Strengths: A Community Based Approach.* Yellowknife: Culture and Communications

–. 1990. *Proposal for the Finalization and Implementation of the Northern Accord.* Yellowknife: Culture and Communications

–. Northwest Territories Housing Corporation. 1990. *Study On Housing Policy and Program Coordination in the NWT.* Yellowknife: NWT Housing Corporation

–. Legislative Assembly. 1989. *Seize the Day: A Report to the Legislative Assembly on Political and Constitutional Development in the Northwest Territories.* Yellowknife: Executive Council

–. Municipal and Community Affairs. 1989. 'A Discussion Paper on Financing Municipal Government.' Yellowknife: Municipal and Community Affairs

–. Legislative Assembly of the Northwest Territories. 1989. *The SCONE Report: Building Our Economic Future.* Yellowknife: Special Committee on the Northern Economy

–. Bureau of Statistics. 1989. *1989 NWT Labor Force Survey.* Three Reports. Yellowknife: Culture and Communications

–. Executive Council. 1988. 'A Discussion Paper on Political and Constitutional

Development in the Northwest Territories.' Yellowknife: Tabled Document
No. 76-89(1), 15 March 1989

–. Legislative Assembly. 1988. *Workshop on the Northern Economy: Survey of Presentations*. Yellowknife: Special Committee on the Northern Economy

–. 1988. 'Direction for the 1990s.' Yellowknife: Culture and Communications

–. 1988. 'NWT Economic Review and Outlook.' Yellowknife: Culture and Communications

–. 1987. *Report on Regional and Tribal Councils in the Northwest Territories*. Yellowknife: Regional and Tribal Councils Review Co-ordinating Committee.

–. Devolution Office. 1987. 'Planning for Devolution: Principles, Process and Guidelines.' Yellowknife: Devolution Office

–. Legislative Assembly. 1987. *Final Report of the Special Committee on Housing*. Yellowknife: Legislative Assembly Special Committee on Housing

–. Legislative Assembly. 1986. *Third Report: Special Committee on Rules, Procedures and Privilege*. Yellowknife: Special Committee on Rules, Procedures, and Privilege

–. Department of Local Government. 1983. 'Design For Devolution: A Public Discussion Paper on Proposed Local Government Legislation.' Yellowknife: Department of Local Government

–. Legislative Assembly. 1982. *Learning: Tradition & Change In the Northwest Territories*. Yellowknife: Legislative Assembly Special Committee on Education

–. Department of Local Government. 1980. *Community Planning and Development in Canada's Northwest Territories*. Yellowknife: Town Planning and Lands Division, Department of Local Government

–. Legislative Assembly. 1979. *Position of the Legislative Assembly on Constitutional Development*. Yellowknife: Legislative Assembly

–. Council of the Northwest Territories. 1972. *Task Force on Housing: Report*. Yellowknife: Council of the Northwest Territories

LAND CLAIM AGREEMENTS

Canada, Department of Indian Affairs and Northern Development. 1984. *The Western Arctic Claim: The Inuvialuit Final Agreement*. Ottawa: Indian and Northern Affairs

Canada, Department of Indian Affairs and Northern Development. 1988. *Comprehensive Land Claim Agreement in Principle Between Canada and the Dene Nation and the Métis Association of the Northwest Territories*. Ottawa: Indian and Northern Affairs. (This agreement was withdrawn in the fall of 1990, the federal government agreeing to negotiate with these people on a region by region basis.)

Canada, Department of Indian Affairs and Northern Development. 1990. *Agreement-In-Principle Between the Inuit of the Nunavut Settlement Area and*

Her Majesty in Right of Canada. Ottawa: Indian and Northern Affairs
Canada, Department of Indian Affairs and Northern Development. 1991.
*Comprehensive Land Claim Agreement Between Her Majesty The Queen In Right
of Canada and the Gwich'in As Represented By the Gwich'in Tribal Council.*
Ottawa: Indian and Northern Affairs

Index

Set in CG Palacio by CompuType, Vancouver, BC
Printed on acid-free paper ∞
Printed and bound in Canada by Friesen Printers,
Altona, Manitoba

Copy-editors: Joanne Richardson and Paul Norton
Indexer: Laura Houle